Back to Basics

by
Judson Cornwall, Th.D

Sharon Publications Ltd
49 Coxtie Green Road
Pilgrims Hatch
Brentwood
Essex
England
CM14 5PS

Dedicated to
Dr Sam Sasser and his wife Flo :
two ministers of the grace of God who
have consistently contended for the
basics.

Contents

Preface

Seated on the platform of a church in which I had often shared ministry during the heights of the Charismatic renewal, and had dedicated the building the congregation was worshiping in, the pastor leaned over and whispered in my ear, "Can you identify anyone, Judson?"

After scanning the auditorium, I admitted to recognizing less than a dozen persons.

"It's a whole new congregation and most of them are young people," the pastor responded. "They have not seen a visitation of God. Few of them have any Bible knowledge. Please reach back into your memory and preach to them what you shared with the congregation we had twenty years ago. They need to know the same things."

I have been unable to shake her words. As I have shared them with other pastors, they have agreed that we have a new generation of persons in our churches. Many of them have no fundamental knowledge of the basic principles of God and His Word. They do what we do, but they lack a reason for doing it.

Early this year, my spirit began to burn with the need for a book that dealt with simple basics. *Back to Basics* is the fruit of that passion.

I have not tried to write a doctrine book. They are available. I have sought to write for men and women who may not have sufficient theological knowledge to be comfortable reading a formal book on church doctrine. I believe that even children can learn the basics, especially the children of God.

I admit that this work is not exhaustive. I have, with counsel from others, arbitrarily chosen 17 themes, but, except for the size book it would create, I could easily have touched 27 or 37 subjects.

Since I began this book, I have been amazed at how many pastors and traveling speakers are declaring that God is telling them, "Get back to basics." Perhaps God's Spirit wants to build a strong foundation for what He is about to do in the earth. Maybe the cry of David is resounding in our generation: "O LORD God of Abraham, Isaac, and of Israel ... prepare their heart unto thee" (1 Chronicles 29:18).

Judson Cornwall
Phoenix,
Arizona

Chapter 1

The Basics of the Scriptures

It has become increasingly popular to criticize, rationalize, censure, and ignore the Bible. Most of our educational institutions have ruled the Bible out of their curriculums. So called "higher criticism" in some of our pulpits has so belittled the Scriptures that God's Word is no longer the heart of most sermons. The press and television daily attack its principles of morality, righteousness, love and equality of man, and parents have set it aside as the guide to child rearing.

Accordingly, children have bypassed the Bible as a guide for their moral development and a standard for their behavior. We are paying a tremendous price in crime as the result. From the highest echelon of public service to the lowliest laborer Americans have, in the main, set the Bible aside for other things.

In spite of this wholesale rejection of the Bible, nothing in human experience is more blessed or beneficial than the Word of God. Everything we know came into existence when: "God said let there be ..." (Genesis 1:3). Even man, whom God shaped from the dust of the earth, became a "living soul" (Genesis 2:7) when God breathed the breath of life (an unspoken sigh) into Adam's nostrils.

In the poetic prologue to his gospel, the Apostle John couples the living word with the spoken and written word. He wrote: "In the beginning was the Word, and the Word was with God, and the Word was God. The same was in the beginning with God. All things were made by him; and without him was not any thing made that was made. In him was life; and the life was the light of men" (John 1:1-4).

In the Garden of Eden, Adam and Eve had fellowship with the voice of God (Genesis 3:8). God was their instructor, their companion, and their friend. The direct communication they had with God gave them a living touch of heaven here on earth. Their knowledge of God and life came out of this intimate and personal relationship with the spoken word of God.

Adam and Eve's sin separated them from this direct communication with God, although they still had access to God through the blood sacrifice God instituted. While these offerings kept a contact with God, Adam and Eve must have longed for the "good old days" when they walked and talked with God directly, but, as far as the Bible records, God never restored it to them.

God did, however, continue to speak to persons like Enoch, Noah, and Moses, to name a few. God not only spoke *to* these persons; He spoke *through* them. Enoch became a preacher of righteousness, (Jude 1:14), and Noah proclaimed God's message while he was building the ark.

God had not withdrawn Himself from men and women, but they had departed from the fellowship of His Word. Perhaps God did not stop talking, but people ceased to listen. Disobedience consistently closes our ears to the voice of God. Still, from time to time God broke through this barrier of disobedience and communicated directly with persons as when He called Abraham out of Ur of the Chaldees. Repeatedly God directed Abraham with a voice that was unmistakably the voice of God.

Similarly, Joseph seemed to hear the voice of God distinctly. Sometimes it was in dreams, sometimes in visions, and other times it seemed to be direct communication. Because he believed this was divine communication, he dared to act on it and became a deliverer for Egypt during a seven year famine.

The most outstanding individual to whom God spoke directly is Moses. God Himself said that He spoke to Moses, "Mouth to mouth" (Numbers 12:8). Moses not only heard God speak, he courageously proclaimed these words to others, as when he told Pharaoh of Egypt that Jehovah demanded ho

10

release God's people from slavery to serve Him in the wilderness, and, subsequently, in the Promised Land.

At Mt. Sinai, God gave the laws that would govern the culture of the Hebrews for thousands of years. Moses not only heard God clearly and reported it accurately, he did what none before him had ever done. He followed God's example of carving the ten commandments in stone. Moses wrote what God had spoken. For the first time, God passed His word from one generation to another without the danger oral tradition had posed. It was no longer grandpa's memory of what God had said. It was a written record of God's Word. The Bible had its beginnings in the writings of Moses, but many inspired writers would follow.

Moses, of course, did not know that he was writing the beginning books of the Bible, nor could he have known the difficulties others would suffer in bringing the Bible into being. Some subsequent writers were imprisoned, beaten, banished, and murdered. Usually persons to whom the prophets spoke rejected their messages.

Canonizing these sixty-six books together into an accepted whole was the work of many conventions, or *diets*, where the clergy of the day debated over which books would be accepted as inspired and which would be rejected as uninspired. In a most supernatural way, the Holy Spirit guarded and guided this process.

Once this canon was established, monks and dedicated scholars devoted their entire lives to hand-copying these Scriptures. Complete copies were very rare and almost unobtainable by individuals.

When Wycliffe dared to translate the Bible from Latin into English (1380 AD), the church excommunicated him. His Bible was designed not for scholars but for the common people. Someone has said, "It was plain, vigorous, homely, and yet with all its homeliness full of a solemn grace and dignity that made men feel that they were reading no ordinary book."

It required copyists ten months to prepare Wycliffe's Bible, but following his death, Gutenberg invented printing with movable type. About the year 1450, Gutenberg's printing press wa at work in Mentz, Germany. Its first completed book was the Bible.

Printing made the Bible available for the common people. Tyndale's version of the Bible was an English translation from the original languages. Tyndale had to print the Bible secretly in Germany and smuggle copies into England. Officials confiscated copies of the Bible and publicly burned them, and those who read the translation often paid with their lives. Tyndale himself was imprisoned, treated shamefully, and in 1536 was strangled at the stake and his body burned for the crime of translating and printing the Bible in the language of the people.

It is unlikely that any other book has been so consistently berated, banned, burned, and banished, but the harder religious and civil governments have tried to destroy the Bible, the more widely it has spread around the world. Today we have translated and published the Bible in almost every language and dialect in the world.

Wherever this book of God has gone it has had an amazing impact on society. The Bible became the basis for the English and subsequent American code of law. Where persons have embraced the Bible their standard of living escalated, the place of women in society rose significantly, and education was made available to the masses. Even a casual comparison of the nations who have rejected God's Word with those that openly responded to the Bible will convince a person of the power of the Bible to affect society for good and godliness.

It was the Bible that produced the reformation which brought society out of the dark ages. It was the preaching of the Bible that produced such a revival in England that the United Kingdom escaped the revolution that devastated France. It was the principles of the Bible that brought the early pilgrims to America, and that Book guided the formation of the constitution of the United States.

The Bible has a profound influence on society wherever it is read. Little wonder, then, that the greedy, the immoral, the power hungry, and the selfish persons of this world have so resisted the invasion of God's Word.

The Bible's Source

The uniqueness of the Bible is not its unified message of redemption nor its timelessness. The great distinction of the Bible is its source. This magnificent book is the Word of God in written form. The Apostle Peter tells us, "For the prophecy came not in old time by the will of man: but holy men of God spake as they were moved by the Holy Ghost" (2 Peter 1:21).

God moved through persons of His choosing to make known the message Jehovah wanted to share with us. The Holy Spirit not only communicated God's voice, but He guarded the vocabulary these persons used in writing this down. The Bible did not come into existence through Spirit dictation or automatic writing. The Holy Spirit communicated divine thoughts and governed, through inner guidance, the way these inspired persons wrote them.

The character and nature of the writer remained undisturbed, but the message he wrote was exact to God's communication. Jeremiah and John sound very different, but each man was moved by the Holy Spirit to accurately write the message God wanted to send. God breathed His message into each writer.

It is essential for Christians to know and believe that the Bible is the inspired Word of God. We need to hear from God, for He created men and women with a need to communicate with Him. Our lives are empty and unfulfilled without it. God did not create Adam with an ability to rule himself. He created him, and us, to be ruled; not to be rulers. The happiest person on earth is the God-governed man or woman. He or she has learned to submit to a higher principle of guidance than self-discipline or self-determination.

Moving beyond self-will into the divine will requires knowing the nature and meaning of that divine will. We cannot find it in ourselves, for the Bible tells us, "The heart is deceitful

above all things, and desperately wicked: who can know it?"
(Jeremiah 17:9). Rather than leave it up to each individual to
learn the will and ways of God, Jehovah mercifully wrote His
desires for our lives in the book we call the Bible.

Someone has wisely said, "The Bible is the manufacturer's
instruction manual for people." Perhaps we could add, "If all
else fails, read the instructions." But why wait until we meet
failure? God's book offers God's instructions for God's creation.
It reveals His holy nature, our depraved nature, and how we
can have that divine nature alive in us now. This God-inspired
Book, when quickened by God's inspiring Spirit, becomes "A
lamp unto my feet, and a light unto my path" (Psalm 119:105).
David said:

> *The law of the LORD is perfect, converting the soul:*
> *the testimony of the LORD is sure, making wise the*
> *simple. The statutes of the LORD are right, rejoicing*
> *the heart: the commandment of the LORD is pure,*
> *enlightening the eyes. The fear of the LORD is clean,*
> *enduring for ever: the judgments of the LORD are true*
> *and righteous altogether. More to be desired are they*
> *than gold, yea, than much fine gold: sweeter also than*
> *honey and the honeycomb. Moreover by them is thy*
> *servant warned: and in keeping of them there is great*
> *reward.*
>
> *(Psalm 19:7-11)*

The Bible's Structure

Since the Bible is the Word of God we would expect it to be
amazing — and it is. The Bible is a compilation of sixty-six
books written by forty or more persons over a span of several
thousand years. Because of this time span most of these writers never met one another and did not even know about the
written works of the others. Still, they maintained a Spirit-
inspired theme of God's self-revelation and His plan of
redemption.

These sixty-six books of the Bible have two main divisions called testaments (or covenants). We have the Old Testament and the New Testament. Both divisions have five subdivisions. They are:

OLD TESTAMENT
Pentateuch (Books of the Law): Genesis to Deuteronomy
Books of History: Joshua to Esther Hebrew
Poetry: Job to Song of Solomon & Lamentations
Major Prophets: Isaiah to Daniel
Minor Prophets Hosea to Malachi

NEW TESTAMENT
The Gospels — Biographical: Matthew to John
Historical: Acts
Pauline Epistles — Doctrinal: Romans to Philemon
General Epistles — Practical: Hebrews to Jude
Prophetical: Revelation

For those interested in statistics let me give you a further breakdown of the Bible. The King James Version contains:

3,538,493 letters
773,693 words
31,373 verses
1,189 chapters
66 books

While it can be argued that the Old Testament is a covenant God made with His special family — the Jews — whereas the New Testament is a covenant Christ made with His church, this is a dangerous over-simplification that tends to give us two Bibles. God gave us one Bible with two divisions. The Old Testament looks forward to Christ's cross, while the New Testament looks back to its finished work. An old quotation puts it, "The New is in the Old contained, and the Old is in the New explained."

While it is true that the Old Testament is a story of God's special family, the New Testament tells us that by faith *we* can participate in the great covenant promises God gave to Israel. Paul taught that God has grafted believing Gentiles into His great family (see Romans 11:17), and he further stated that, "Now all these things happened unto them for ensamples: and they are written for our admonition, upon whom the ends of the world are come" (1 Corinthians 10:11).

If we yield to the temptation to set the Old Testament aside and exclusively embrace the New Testament, we will have a very limited revelation of God, for God progressively revealed His person, His power, and His purposes in the Old Testament. It is there that we learn about His nature through the revelation of His compound names, such as *Jehovah-Jireh*, "The Lord will provide", or *Jehovah-Nissi*, "The Lord our banner."

Some say that the Old Testament is law, but the New Testament is grace. While it is true that God gave a strict code of behavior to mold the Hebrew family into a structured nation, the Old Testament abounds with demonstrations of God's grace. It shows in God's protective sign on murderous Cain. Further, Genesis specifically declares, "Noah found grace in the eyes of the LORD" Genesis 6:8). Later, God's mercy to Israel and Judah was abundant. He warned and chastened His family, but He demonstrated amazing grace in all of it.

We need to remember that the New Testament is not all grace. It has much law in it. Jesus consistently upheld major points of the Old Testament law, and He often made them even more stringent. He moved the point of guilt from the deed to the desire of the heart. Paul, a great teacher of grace, made the churches he founded very aware of the Law of God.

The division of Old and New Testament is not so we can contrast one with the other. Each is the Word of God to our lives for, "All scripture is given by inspiration of God, and is profitable for doctrine, for reproof, for correction, for instruction in righteousness: That the man of God may be perfect, throughly furnished unto all good works" (2 Timothy 3:16-17). Rather than compete with each other, the two testaments of the Bible complete each other. We need both Testaments to have an enlarged concept of God and a complete picture of redemption.

Although the Bible spans all times in its application, it actually records but a brief period of the history of the world. After giving us the story of creation, the Bible zeros in on a special family that became a special nation. Most of the Old Testament is concerned with the period from the call of Abraham to the return of the exiles from Babylon.

The Bible is a revelation of God's availability to sinful persons. It touches many other subjects, but redemption is its major theme. God's Word obviously is not a record of human history, for entire dynasties and races of people come and go with no Scriptural mention. The Bible records only such history as affects Israel or God's self-revelation. When it touches history it is accurate, but it is not a history book. Equally, it has proven to be accurate when it mentions science, but it is not a scientific text book.

With few exceptions, the Bible doesn't bother to try to explain *how* God did what He did. This divine book is not written as a do-it-yourself text book. God is far greater than our finite minds can comprehend. Even if He tried to explain His works, we wouldn't understand the explanation. God declared through Isaiah: "For my thoughts are not your thoughts, neither are your ways my ways, saith the LORD. For as the heavens are higher than the earth, so are my ways higher than your ways, and my thoughts than your thoughts" (Isaiah 55:8-9).

Paul expressed this another way: "But as it is written, Eye hath not seen, nor ear heard, neither have entered into the heart of man, the things which God hath prepared for them that love him" (1 Corinthians 2:9). God's Book is not mere information; it is inspiration and revelation. It is God's provision to let us see into the coming kingdom of God and to know something of God's divine nature.

17

Searching the Bible

The first step to meeting God in His Word is, obviously, to read the Bible. How can we know what God has said if we've never read His book?

A pastor invited me to lunch and proceeded to ply me with argumentive questions about one of my recent books. I had clearly written the answers to these questions in the book. When I asked him if he had read the book, he admitted that he had read "a few pages." I told him that I was unwilling to discuss the book any further until he had read it. Is it possible that God feels similarly?

Over the years of ministering to preachers and pastors, it has shocked me to discover the number of them who admit that they have never read the Bible through. How unfair to pick and choose bits and pieces of this masterpiece to proclaim a personal philosophy. God did not write His Word to give us "texts." He wrote His book to bring us to Jesus who can give us life.

Reading the Bible from cover to cover is not the difficult task that some may suppose. Huffman and Shantz in *Mastering the English Bible* say that the average reader (reading at 250 words per minute) can read the Old Testament through in 48 hours and the New Testament in only 15 hours. David A. Hastie declares that the entire Bible can be read in only 50 hours.

During the last fifteen years that I pastored, I set up a Bible reading program for my congregation. We had assigned reading portions for the week, and we asked for a weekly report that we posted on a large bulletin board. We ceremoniously presented a special certificate to those persons who completed reading the Bible through.

This consecutive reading of the Bible gave my congregation a much broader view of the Scriptures, and it greatly enlarged their concepts of God. It made preaching easier for me and more meaningful for them since I confined my Sunday preaching to the passages read during the week.

Most persons could read the Bible through by turning their TVs off for one program each evening and substituting Bible reading in its place. Extremely busy persons could play cassettes of Bible reading while driving to and from work, or while doing repetitive work that requires little mental concentration.

There are many published guides to reading the Bible through in a year. If none is available, divide the days in the year (365) into the number of chapters in the entire Bible (1,189) and you'll discover that you will need to read less than three chapters a day to complete this project.

It is usually worthwhile to have a colored pen or pencil close at hand, for as you read, the Holy Spirit will quicken a verse or so to you. Underline or highlight this. When you read it later, it will likely come alive to you again. Also, don't hesitate to write notes in the margin of your Bible. Often a gemstone of truth flees your mind as you continue to read further. Write down that "apple of gold" (Proverbs 25:11) right where you picked it. It will renew its preciousness every time you reread the passage.

Some new converts have hesitated in marking their Bibles because its title is *Holy Bible*. But it is the message and the Person it points to that are holy. The book itself is but paper, ink, and leather or plastic. As one of my minister friends likes to say, "If your Bible is too holy to be marked, give it away and purchase one that *can* be marked."

Studying the Bible

The Bible needs to be more than read. It needs to be studied. There are rich treasures of divine truth to be mined by the person with effective tools and personal diligence.

Some primary tools for Bible study are a Bible concordance, a Bible dictionary, paper, and pen. A study Bible and additional translations of the Bible are valuable tools, as are Bible commentaries.

Even without one of these tools, however, any true believer can become a student of the Bible. Remember that the true author of the Bible (the Holy Spirit) lives within each believer. Who better understands what is written than the One who wrote it?

Start your Bible study by breathing a prayer for the guidance and illumination of God's Spirit. Jesus said that when the Holy Spirit came, "He will guide you into all truth: for he shall not speak of himself; but whatsoever he shall hear, that shall he speak: and he will shew you things to come" (John 16:13).

The Bible is a big book. Don't try to master its 66 books all at once. Pick a book, preferably one of the smaller New Testament books, and read it through multiple times.

Then write on paper the principal points in the book and form an outline. Let this outline of the book grow as you continue to read and meditate on the book. Then find another believer and share what you have discovered in the book. If you've missed the heart of the book, he or she may be able to help you see it. If you've mined real treasure, it will help them to hear you tell it. In either case the vocalization of what you've learned will crystallize your thinking and greatly increase the impression this truth makes on your heart and mind.

Of course, you don't have to do all your Bible studying alone. Find a Bible study group and get involved in it. Practice taking notes when your pastor preaches. Invest in some books written by persons who have found life in the Word and have learned to communicate it in simple terms.

Sometimes you may want to do a word study in the Bible. Use your concordance to trace this word throughout the Scriptures. See if you can find a pattern of teaching in these verses. Does one verse contain additional material that affects your understanding of this word? Does the Old Testament use the word differently than does the New Testament?

In doing word studies, it is often helpful to know the meaning of the original Hebrew or Greek word. Strong's Concordance makes this easy to find through its number system for all major words in the Bible.

Other times you may choose to do a topical study in your Bible, and you'll compare the different verses that touch this topic. For instance, to study the verses with their context for the subject *redemption*, is to open your eyes to a broader perspective of our salvation. You will better understand the work of Christ on Calvary's cross after such a study.

It is not so important what style of Bible study you use. What *is* important is that you discipline yourself to study God's book. It will never be wasted time.

Swallowing the Bible

Two men in the Bible were commanded to eat God's written word. In the Old Testament, Ezekiel records the incident: "And he said unto me, Son of man, cause thy belly to eat, and fill thy bowels with this roll that I give thee. Then did I eat it; and it was in my mouth as honey for sweetness" (Ezekiel 3:3).

In the New Testament it was John on the Isle of Patmos, observing what he later wrote as the book of Revelation, who obeyed this command. He wrote: "I took the little book out of the angel's hand, and ate it up; and it was in my mouth sweet as honey: and as soon as I had eaten it, my belly was bitter" (Revelation 10:10).

While I fear that eating the literal Bible could cause severe indigestion, it is still true that the best binding for the Bible is the human skin. We need to get the word beyond our minds and into the mainstream of our lives.

God's Word becomes extremely practical when we "swallow" it; when we get it activated in the digestive processes of our hearts and minds. The psalmist said: "Thy word have I hid in mine heart, that I might not sin against thee" (Psalm 119:11). He saw the Bible as a preventive instrument to sin, not merely a pardoning agent for sin.

Another of Israel's inspired poets said, "The entrance of thy words giveth light; it giveth understanding unto the simple"

(Psalm 119:130). It is not the mere reading of the Bible that brings illumination. It is when that Word gains entrance to our inner spiritual nature that the light goes on in our spirits. We are like a light bulb that cannot give light until electricity energizes it.

As seen in England and America today, the Bible is often:

Purchased, but seldom pursued ...
Sold, but seldom studied ...
Owned, but seldom obeyed ...
Preserved, but not practiced ...
Beloved, but not believed ...
Revered, but not read ...
Collected, but not checked ...
Catalogued, but not consulted ...
Translated, but not touched ...
Enshrined, but greatly neglected ...
Quoted, but also questioned.

We who have ministered in Russia and have seen thousands of people pleading for a copy of the Bible, wonder why people in the Western world with its myriad of Bible translations and millions of copies available in almost every color of the rainbow, neglect what others treasure so highly. Has familiarity bred contempt?

If merely searching the Scripture brings light, then the Jews in Christ's day should have brilliantly illuminated their geographic area of our globe. But to these scribes and religious teachers Jesus said: "[Ye] search the scriptures; for in them ye think ye have eternal life: and they are they which testify of me. And ye will not come to me, that ye might have life" (John 5:39-40).

The purpose of God's written Word is not merely to inform the reader. The Bible seeks to introduce men and women to Jesus. He and He alone can save us from our sins and secure our standing before God as justified, sanctified, and glorified.

We could read the Bible all day and study it all night and never come to the life of God. The life that is available to us right now, God has vested in His Son Jesus. John put it, "This is the record, that God hath given to us eternal life, and this life is in his Son. He that hath the Son hath life; and he that hath not the Son of God hath not life" (1 John 5:11-12).

Having introduced the basics of the Bible, let me introduce you to the basics of salvation, for the testimony of the angels to Joseph before the birth of Jesus was, "Thou shalt call his name JESUS: for he shall save his people from their sins" (Matthew 1:21).

that now God has bestad in The Son Jesus. John xii. 8. "This is the reason, that the faith goeth with the multitude, and that life is in his Son. He that hath the Son hath life and he that hath not the Son he hath not life" (I John v. I. 12).

...draws attention at the basis of the Bible to one introduced upon in the parts of a quiet time for the testimony of the angels to Joseph before the birth: "Thou shalt call His name JESUS for he shall save his people from their sins" (Matthew i. 21).

Chapter 2

The Basics of Salvation

The first statement in the Bible is: "In the beginning God ..."
When looking at the fundamentals of a Christian life and ministry we, too, must begin at the beginning. The Christian life cannot be lived until Christ transforms a sinner into a saint (in the making). He does this with His life; not with doctrine. Salvation is a process that restores us to the relationship God had established with Adam and Eve in the garden before sin intervened.

It is obvious, of course, that sin still separates us from God. The prophet was inspired to write: "Your iniquities have separated between you and your God, and your sins have hid his face from you, that he will not hear" (Isaiah 59:2). Since heaven is viewed as God's dwelling place, we cannot share His home and be separated from Him at the same time. Only those who have embraced God's salvation will ever enter into heaven.

But what is "salvation?" What do preachers mean when they speak of being "born again?" Is this the same as "being redeemed?" At the birth of Jesus a heavenly host of angels proclaimed, "For unto you is born this day in the city of David a Saviour, which is Christ the Lord" (Luke 2:11). This is heaven's definition. Salvation is wrapped up in the person of Jesus Christ.

These magnificent heavenly beings did not preach the sinfulness of men and women. They rightly assumed that earth's inhabitants are aware of their fallen state. Life itself teaches that sin is genetic; righteousness is not. David admitted,

"Behold, I was shapen in iniquity, and in sin did my mother conceive me" (Psalm 51:5), while Paul placed the origin of sin in Adam when he wrote: "Wherefore, as by one man sin entered into the world, and death by sin; and so death passed upon all men, for that all have sinned" (Romans 5:12). He also said: "For all have sinned, and come short of the glory of God" (Romans 3:23).

Even the human conscience argues against human sinlessness. Every honest person knows he or she has sinned — and *dis*honest persons know it, but won't admit it. We have preferred to go our own way from infancy. Children inherently prefer the "no no" to the approved. No wonder, then, that God declares: "All we like sheep have gone astray; we have turned every one to his own way; *and the LORD hath laid on him the iniquity of us all*" (Isaiah 53:6).

We have all jumped the fence, but it is that last phrase that gives us a ray of hope. God has laid on Jesus all our iniquities — our disobediences. He has provided a way out of our self-willed sinfulness. Jehovah chose to release part of His essential nature to be born of Mary in Bethlehem. This child matured into perfect manhood, and at his baptism in the river Jordan "There came a voice out of the cloud, saying, *'This is my beloved Son: hear him'*" (Luke 9:35). This God/man became the substitute for all of us when He took our sins in His own body at Calvary and died the death God had prescribed in His law for sinners. The cross cancels the penalty those laws imposed.

As, by faith, we enter into this substitutionary work of Christ we may speak of it as "salvation" in light of escaping the death penalty. Like the condemned criminal who receives a pardon one hour before his scheduled execution, we can say that we've "been saved at the last moment".

We often refer to this experience of salvation as being "born again" when we remember that Jesus told Nicodemus, "Marvel not that I said unto thee, Ye must be born again" (John 3:7). He offered this leader of the Jews an opportunity to have a new beginning. Paul caught this theme of Jesus and wrote: "If any man be in Christ, he is a new creature: old things are passed away; behold, all things are become new" (2 Corinthians 5:17). Salvation is the only way we can actually start over again. We are far more than merely forgiven our sins; "all things become new". We are given another chance at life, but this time without the controlling power of sin.

Sometimes we speak of this experience as *redemption*, as when bondsmen are released from slavery. God's work in Christ on Calvary has redeemed us from every control of sin. We read, "Blessed be the Lord God of Israel; for he hath visited and redeemed his people" (Luke 1:68). The ransom has been paid. Sin, satan, and selfishness no longer control our lives. We are free to serve the Lord and to enjoy life, but, of course, this means that we will have to learn to live as free men and women. Responsibilities we never experienced as slaves are now ours. God's redemption restores our free will and right of choice. What we will become as "Christians" does not rest on God's caprice; it rests upon our choices. The grace of salvation works from within to without, but it never violates the will of the person being saved.

The Person of Salvation

God's "so great salvation" (Hebrews 2:3) and Jesus Christ are inseparable. Peter declared to the rulers of Israel: "Neither is there salvation in any other: for there is none other name under heaven given among men, whereby we must be saved" (Acts 4:12). The entire New Testament relentlessly ties salvation to Jesus, for God's bountiful and merciful dealings with Israel proved that no person, however instructed in the Law of God, can save himself or herself. Paul declared, "We have believed in Jesus Christ, that we might be justified by the faith of Christ, and not by the works of the law: for by the works of the law shall no flesh be justified" (Galatians 2:16).

Gabriel, God's mighty angel, told Joseph, "And she shall bring forth a son, and thou shalt call his name JESUS: for he shall save his people from their sins" (Matthew 1:21). The very name *Jesus* means *Savior*. Salvation, then, is far more than a doctrine or even an experience. It is a relationship with a Person named Jesus.

Jesus is the Savior. He is the Redeemer. Only through Him can anyone be "born again". Jesus not only told Nicodemus that he had to be born again to see the kingdom of God (see John 3:3,5), but He answered this leader's "How?" by saying, "That which is born of the flesh is flesh; and that which is born of the Spirit is spirit" (John 3:6). The new birth is exclusively a work of Christ's Spirit. Christ died to pay our penalty for sin, but He rose and ascended back to the throne of God to bring us into a life that is as new as the birth of an infant into this world. Codified religion plays no part in this great miracle.

To realize that salvation is wrapped up in the person of Jesus is to understand that neither mental assent nor emotional ecstasy produce a salvation experience. None of us is able to save himself or herself. We can only accept what Christ has provided by dying for us.

The word *salvation* occurs 164 times in 158 verses of our Bible. The men who wrote our Psalms loved to use the word. They spoke of the "God of my salvation", "His salvation", "Thy salvation", and the "salvation of God". These singers of divine doctrine consistently ascribed salvation to the Almighty. The prophets also spoke of God's salvation, and the theme of the New Testament is: "God hath not appointed us to wrath, but to obtain salvation by our Lord Jesus Christ" (1 Thessalonians 5:9).

Consistently religion seeks to find a bloodless redemption, but God has no backup plan for delivering men from sin. His redemption in Christ Jesus works. Why would He need another plan? He told us, "By grace are ye saved through faith; and that not of yourselves: it is the gift of God" (Ephesians 2:8). Allowing God to do the whole work of saving us without our help is more than many persons can accept. We don't want salvation by grace plus nothing. We prefer to obtain it by grace plus works, but there is no further work to be done. On the cross Jesus cried: "It is finished" (John 19:30). As our hymnals put it, "Jesus paid it all. All to Him I owe".

Redemption is a work of divine mercy accomplished by the incarnation, obedience, death, and resurrection of Christ, which involves the total Godhead and envelops the entire life of the redeemed. No work of God is more complete than His work of redemption, for it has judicial, ethical, physical, intellectual, and moral aspects to it, and Jesus is the Provision for each of them.

The *judicial side* of redemption satisfies the law of God. The law says, "The soul that sinneth, it shall die" (Ezekiel 18:4,20), and Jesus became that dying soul, for Paul wrote, "Christ hath redeemed us from the curse of the law, being made a curse for us" (Galatians 3:13). Whatever claims God's law had against us have been totally satisfied in the work of Jesus at Calvary.

But redemption is far more than an act that satisfies God, for in its *ethical side*, Christ has redeemed us from all unrighteousness as His own possession, purifying us unto good works (see Titus 2:14). Jesus has overcome the world's temptation that leads us into evil, and He has also completely broken the power of the prince of this world — the devil. Not only is God's law satisfied; our lives are purified. God is seen as *just* while we are *justified*. All this is the work of Jesus Christ our Lord.

As to the *physical aspect* of our redemption, Jesus has released our total persons — spirits, souls, and bodies — from the power of sin. By the same substitutionary work at Calvary that satisfied God's demands, Jesus bought our souls and spirits back from darkness and provided healing for our bodies. Furthermore, when Jesus returns, He will raise the dead; insuring them against further pain or death, and give them glorified bodies similar to the one He received when He rose from the dead. Jesus is not only the prototype of divine health and resurrection power, He is the producer of it.

Similarly, the redemption that Jesus offers to men and women acts upon their intellectual nature; delivering them from darkness unto light, and Jesus, Himself, is that Light. Sin has clouded the minds of persons, but when Jesus removes that sin, our human intellect is released from bondage and enabled to develop without the hindrances of the satanic kingdom.

Redemption does not *restrict* man's reasoning faculty; it *releases* it.

Jesus has also redeemed our *moral nature* in delivering our wills from the bondage of sin and enduing them with the power to choose and execute works of righteousness. He is both our pattern of morality and our source of it. No matter what facet of salvation we may observe, Jesus is the cause and completer of it, for the New Testament promises us: "But now is Christ risen from the dead, and become the firstfruits of them that slept" (1 Corinthians 15:20), and, "If the Spirit of him that raised up Jesus from the dead dwell in you, he that raised up Christ from the dead shall also quicken your mortal bodies by his Spirit that dwelleth in you" (Romans 8:11). We are also assured, "As he is, so are we in this world" (1 John 4:17). Our hope of redemption rests in the person of Jesus. Nothing more; nothing less!

The Promise of Salvation

Nothing in the Bible rests on greater assurances than our salvation. God affirms, explains, and applies His promise of redemption from Genesis through Revelation. This consistent theme is often called the scarlet cord of the Bible, for the blood of Jesus binds the sixty-six books of the Bible into an integral whole. This thread of blood meets in the horizontal arms of Christ's cross. Christ's pierced right hand holds the cord that reaches back to Genesis, while the bleeding left hand holds the cord that runs through the book of Revelation.

We have divided our Bible into two divisions: Old and New Testaments. These testaments were covenants God made with His people — covenants to save His people from their sins and to restore them to fellowship with Himself. We further divide these Testaments into five divisions each. All ten divisions of the Bible speak of God's promise to save His people.

The *Books of the Law* record Moses' song where he sang, "The LORD is my strength and song, and he is become my salvation: he is my God, and I will prepare him an habitation" (Exodus 15:2).

The *Historic Books* say: "And say ye, Save us, O God of our salvation, and gather us together, and deliver us from the heathen, that we may give thanks to thy holy name, and glory in thy praise" (1 Chronicles 16:35).

The *Poetic Books* also extol the salvation of the Lord. The Holy Spirit often spoke more through their lips than they realized. For instance, David sang: "The LORD shall help them, and deliver them: he shall deliver them from the wicked, and save them, because they trust in him" (Psalms 37:40). Perhaps he was looking at a threatening invasion of Philistines, we don't know, but it is also a prophetic declaration of God's purpose to save His people.

The *Major Prophets* declare: "Behold, the LORD'S hand is not shortened, that it cannot save; neither his ear heavy, that it cannot hear" (Isaiah 59:1), and, "For I am with thee, saith the LORD, to save thee" (Jeremiah 30:11).

The *Minor Prophets* speak of God's great joy in providing us salvation. Zephaniah shouted: "The LORD thy God in the midst of thee is mighty; he will save, he will rejoice over thee with joy; he will rest in his love, he will joy over thee with singing" (Zephaniah 3:17).

In the *Gospels* of the New Testament, Jesus promised: "The Son of man is come to save that which was lost" (Matthew 18:11), and, "For the Son of man is not come to destroy men's lives, but to save them" (Luke 9:56).

The *Historic Book of Acts* says, "Be it known therefore unto you, that the salvation of God is sent unto the Gentiles, and that they will hear it" (Acts 28:28).

In the *Pauline Epistles*, the Apostle wrote: "For after that in the wisdom of God the world by wisdom knew not God, it pleased God by the foolishness of preaching to save them that believe" (1 Corinthians 1:21), while in the *General Epistles*, James said, "Receive with meekness the engrafted word, which is able to save your souls" (James 1:21), and Peter and Jude wrote: "And account that the longsuffering of our Lord is salvation; even as our beloved brother Paul also according to the wisdom given unto him hath written unto you" (2 Peter 3:15); "I gave all diligence to write unto you of the common salvation" (Jude 1:3).

The only *Book of Prophecy* in the New Testament rejoices that: "Now is come salvation, and strength, and the kingdom of our God, and the power of his Christ" (Revelation 12:10). All ten divisions extend promises of salvation.

The persons in the Old Testament looked forward in faith to the fulfillment of God's promise to save His people. They saw the cross in types and shadows. In that same faith, we New Testament saints look backward to the cross of Jesus. We see it in reality. Both groups viewed God's redemption through the binoculars of faith and promise.

Life has taught us that a promise is only as good as the person making that promise. Since these promises come from the heart and hand of God, they are immutable and incorruptible. The Old Testament promises, "God is not a man, that he should lie; neither the son of man, that he should repent: hath he said, and shall he not do it? or hath he spoken, and shall he not make it good?" (Numbers 23:19). In the New Testament, Jesus assures us, "I am the way, the truth, and the life: no man cometh unto the Father, but by me" (John 14:6).

God by nature cannot lie, and Jesus by nature is the truth — "For all the promises of God in him are yea, and in him Amen, unto the glory of God by us" (2 Corinthians 1:20). You can safely stake your life on God's promises to save you from sin. Millions of persons before you have done this, and they have testified that God is true to His word. Jesus promised, "Him that cometh to me I will in no wise cast out" (John 6:37).

Pictures of Salvation

Our salvation is so important to God that He not only consistently promises it in every book of the Bible, He demonstrates that salvation with visual aids, types, shadows, and human experience. From Cain and Abel of Genesis to the bleeding Lamb of Revelation there are hundreds of redemptive pictures to help us understand God's "so great salvation".

Since the heart of our salvation is the substitutionary death of Jesus, the Old Testament provisions, practices, and prophecies graphically point to the coming cross. The Gospels piercingly picture the cruel cross, while the Epistles powerfully explain the completed work of the cross.

It is the book of Revelation that exalts the Christ of the cross. From the coats of skins God made in Eden (see Genesis 3:21) to Zechariah's "fountain opened to the inhabitants of Jerusalem for sin and for uncleanness" (Zechariah 13:1), the Old Testament abounds with types and shadows that foretell the coming sacrifice by Jesus. For instance, Noah offered a blood sacrifice to God as a thank offering when he stepped out of the ark. It instinctively pictured Jesus who has delivered us from destruction and has become our thank offering or peace offering unto God.

Similarly, when Abraham prepared to offer his son Isaac as a requested sacrifice on Mt. Moriah, God acknowledged his obedience, spared Isaac, and provided a substitute ram. Jesus is that substitute for each of us who, like Isaac, were under God's sentence of death. Jesus took our place at Calvary and died the death we deserved.

The passover lamb offered in Egypt before the departure of the Hebrews was a graphic illustration of Jesus. This lamb was chosen, separated, slain, and its blood sprinkled on the door posts of the house of those who were to be spared the slaughter of their first born. There could be no more vivid picture of the personal salvation Jesus purchased for us at the price of His own blood.

At the bitter [poisonous] waters of Marah, God told Moses to cut down and cast a tree into the waters. Immediately the waters were made safe and sweet. This prefigured both the crucifixion of Christ and the power of His cross to remove the poison from our lives — the bitterness. God's salvation sweetens the redeemed.

33

Parallel to this are all the many animal sacrifices required by the law. These sacrifices were God's guaranteed means of approach. Sin that had separated persons from God was covered at the Brazen Altar where these animals were slain. Once the sin was atoned, fellowship with God was restored. Whether lamb, goat, bullock, or turtledove, all were types of Jesus who would be offered once and for all instead of daily. He, God's Lamb, would become our guaranteed route to approach God.

When in the wilderness God sent a plague of fiery serpents to punish the Hebrews for their consistent murmuring, He responded to their pleas for healing by instructing Moses to make a bronze replica of one of the serpents and erect it on a pole. Moses told the people that if they would look to the bronze serpent, they would live. In his gospel, John declared this to be a type of Christ, for he wrote: "As Moses lifted up the serpent in the wilderness, even so must the Son of man be lifted up: That whosoever believeth in him should not perish, but have eternal life" (John 3:14-15). The secret to personal salvation from sin is still, "Look and live".

In his twenty-second Psalm, David graphically portrays the crucifixion of Jesus. Jesus quoted its first verse from the cross: "My God, my God, why hast thou forsaken me?" (Psalm 22:1; Matthew 27:46). The whole Psalm describes both the torment Jesus suffered and the jeering of those who watched it. What makes this all the more interesting is that crucifixion was a Roman invention. Neither David nor Isaiah could have known about this form of death. What they saw came by revelation of the Holy Spirit. God pictured His plan hundreds of years before it was implemented.

Similarly, the prophetic insight of Isaiah caused him to describe the brutality, suffering, and shame of Christ's crucifixion in his memorable fifty-third chapter. He ends his picture by saying: "Yet it pleased the LORD to bruise him; he hath put him to grief: when thou shalt make his soul an offering for sin ... He shall see of the travail of his soul, and shall be satisfied: by his knowledge shall my righteous servant justify many; for he shall bear their iniquities" (Isaiah 53:10-11).

We might say that the scarlet cord of the blood of Jesus gets larger and more radiant the closer it gets to Calvary. The pastels of the first pictures give way to the vivid colors of the prophets. The song that begins in triple pianissimo, crescendos to triple forte at its conclusion. Everything in the Old Testament pointed to a coming redeemer who would offer His life as a satisfaction to the problem of sin. God showed exactly what He would do, and He did exactly what He pictured. He always does.

The Purpose of Salvation

The purposes of God's salvation are many and varied, but may I suggest that there are *three* major objectives in God's redemption. His strategy was:

1. To release us from sin
2. To restore us to life
3. To reinstate us to fellowship

God's plan to *release us from sin* involved the work of the cross and the action of the blood of Jesus. Calvary answers the problem of sin, the penalty of sin, the power of sin, and the presence of sin. Christ's cross completely answers God's problem with sin, society's problem of sin, and our individual problems with this heinous force the Bible calls sin.

God's salvation completely satisfied His laws. Since Calvary, He declares us to be not guilty. He wrote: "Their sins and iniquities will I remember no more" (Hebrews 10:17). Legally we are "unsinned". The theological word for this is *justification*. By action of His will, God cannot recall our cleansed sins. The applied blood has blotted out heaven's record of our sins as completely as a newly formatted computer disk is erased of its former data. Paul explained it: "You, being dead in your sins and the uncircumcision of your flesh, hath he quickened together with him, having forgiven you all trespasses; Blotting out the handwriting of ordinances that was against us, which was contrary to us, and took it out of the way, nailing it to his cross" (Colossians 2:13-14).

All charges have been dropped and the court records have been destroyed. In God's sight we are sinless because God nailed every record of our sins to Christ's cross. This includes satan's records. Neither heaven nor hell has legal proof of our forgiven sins.

Far more than merely releasing us from the penalty of sin, God wanted to release us from sin's power in order to *restore* us to victorious living. Far too many persons who have embraced God's forgiveness have failed to embrace His provision of restoration to life. They live in a self-imposed guilt for sins of the past. Being forgiven does not blank out our memory of sins committed. Sometimes these remembrances induce deep feelings of guilt or trigger renewed desires to sin. Either way, sin exerts a negative power over their lives.

Although gloriously forgiven, each of us continues to live in an earthly body that has lusts and desires that almost naturally respond to the enticements of sin. Old cravings remain after our cleansing. Our enemy makes the most of those cravings. He knows how to entice each of us.

In a very real sense, we might say that there is a residual power in sin. Even after we have been cleansed from its power, we wrestle with the way it has taught us to live. We were "servants of sin" (Romans 6:17), and we developed a lifestyle in that service. The longer we served as sin's slave, the more difficult it is to break the servile attitude.

God delivered the Israelites from Egyptian slavery overnight, but it took an additional forty years to get the slavery syndrome out of the people. Similarly, God removes us from sin in a single confrontation with Christ's cross, but it often takes further work of that cross to totally remove the effects of sin from our hearts. This same salvation that removed the penalty of our sins has removed the power and presence of that sin from our lives, for the blood of Jesus deals with more than the negative power of sin. It offers us the positive power of Christ's sinless life.

Jesus willingly died the death we deserved at Calvary, and He also shared His life that we did not deserve. We are not merely cleansed from sin; we are empowered with divine life. Paul testified: "I am crucified with Christ: nevertheless I live; yet not I, but Christ liveth in me: and the life which I now live in the flesh I live by the faith of the Son of God, who loved me, and gave himself for me" (Galatians 2:20).

Just as Christ's death led to resurrection in a higher form of life, so the penitent sinner who identifies completely with Christ's cross and dies with Him subsequently identifies with Christ's new life by allowing Christ to live in him. The New Testament says so simply: "For ye are dead, and your life is hid with Christ in God" (Colossians 3:3).

The best answer to sin is not mere cleansing from its stain, but immunity to its presence. When we allow the sinless life of Christ to dominate our natures, we will enjoy the truth that, "Sin shall not have dominion over you" (Romans 6:14). This Christ, who died vicariously for us, lives as the "Savior of the World" who "saves His people from their sins". God's salvation restores us to the sinless life Adam enjoyed before the fall.

A third purpose of salvation is our *reinstatement* to fellowship with God. The theological word for this is *reconciliation*. We must remember that the Bible never speaks of God being reconciled to man. God has never been at enmity with man. Nothing has changed in Him since the original creation. Sin separates *us* from *God*. It never separates *God* from *us*, for we are assured: "When we were enemies, we were reconciled to God by the death of his Son, much more, being reconciled, we shall be saved by his life" (Romans 5:10).

The work of God's reconciliation is to bring us out of our rebellion, pardon our sins so we have a legal right to approach Him, and to cleanse us from our sins so we can stand in His holy presence. It is our wills, minds, and lives that need to be changed. Our self-wills need to become submitted wills. Our wicked minds need to be purified by the blood of Jesus, and our lives that lived in rebellion to God's Word need to be lived harmonious to God's commands. We need a drastic change, but we are incapable of change without outside help. That is why God sent Jesus as our outside helper. The record declares: "Wherefore in all things it behoved him to be made like unto his brethren, that he might be a merciful and faithful high priest in things pertaining to God, to make reconciliation for the sins of the people" (Hebrews 2:17).

The work of a reconciler is to bring peace, not to impose laws and regulations. He seeks to understand both sides of the problem and to produce a harmonious restoration of relationship. Christ's work as a reconciler began in His incarnation. He became like us to understand us better and to enable us to relate to Himself more openly. That is why the Spirit reminds us that we have a great high priest who can "be touched with the feelings of our infirmities" (Hebrews 4:15).

Jesus has been here. He has wrestled with sin and temptation. He knows the weaknesses of our flesh. He also knows how to be victorious in all things, and through His victory we can enter into the presence of God as redeemed, reconciled, and restored persons. We need not bow our heads in shame, for we are encouraged to lift our hands and shout praises unto our God. The New Testament assures us: "You, that were sometime alienated and enemies in your mind by wicked works, yet now hath he reconciled in the body of his flesh through death, to present you holy and unblameable and unreproveable in his sight" (Colossians 1:21-22). This verse summarizes the four basic steps in Christ's conciliatory work.

1. The need comes out of people's alienation from God.
2. The nature of God's work is restoration back to God.
3. The means God uses is the blood of Jesus Christ.
4. The net result is unreproveable acceptance by God.

Reinstatement to fellowship with God required the work of the entire Godhead; it was not left for Jesus to do on His own. The New Testament declares that: "God was in Christ, reconciling the world unto himself, not imputing their trespasses unto them; and hath committed unto us the word of reconciliation" (2 Corinthians 5:19).

Jesus has dared to commit the word or message of available reconciliation, but He and He alone could provide that reconciliation. He has brought back redeemed persons into an intimate relationship with Himself.

The Prerequisites of Salvation

While there is absolutely nothing we need or can do to prove our salvation, there are at least three things we *must* do to become a participant in God's salvation.

1. We must confess
2. We must repent
3. We must believe

Only a person who has no understanding of the action of a court could misunderstand what God means when He calls for us to confess. Confession is saying "I am guilty." This is absolutely essential to salvation. Until we admit that we have sinned, we will never enter into salvation. It is foolish to pretend that we have not sinned, for the Bible declares: "All have sinned, and come short of the glory of God" (Romans 3:23). Since all the facts have been presented, we might as well admit that we have done it and throw ourselves upon the mercy of heaven's court.

Confession is more than merely admitting that we have done wrong. It is a personal affirmation that we are deserving of the judgment of the law. It is admitting that we have sinned before God in violating His Word. It is saying to God: "I plead guilty, Your Honor."

Subsequent to confession must come *repentance*. These two words are not interchangeable. The Greek word our New Testament translates as *repent* literally means a 180 degree turn. It is like the command "about face", or "to the rear march". When a person headed north repents, he finds himself headed south. It is a complete change in the direction of life. We not only repent from sin, we also repent from dead religious works we thought would bring us salvation. The New Testament speaks of, "The foundation of repentance from dead works, and of faith toward God" (Hebrews 6:1). We turn from works to faith in God's work.

While confession is an expression of past deeds, repentance is a life adjustment that affects future action. Often confession flows out of our emotions, but repentance is a deliberate act of our wills. How often God pleaded through His prophets for Israel to "turn from your wicked ways" and "turn to God". It is still the pleading of the Holy Spirit.

In reporting his call to divine service, Paul told King Agrippa, "I was not disobedient unto the heavenly vision: but shewed first unto them of Damascus, and at Jerusalem, and throughout all the coasts of Judaea, and then to the Gentiles, *that they should repent and turn to God*, and do works meet for repentance" (Acts 26:19-20, emphasis added). Repentance is turning to God.

The third step in embracing salvation is to *believe*. Paul put it so simply in saying, "If thou shalt confess with thy mouth the Lord Jesus, and shalt believe in thine heart that God hath raised him from the dead, thou shalt be saved" (Romans 10:9). It is not difficult to believe that we have sinned, nor is it too difficult to believe that we must turn from our wicked ways to serve the living God, but it is sometimes difficult to believe that God's provision of salvation actually works.

None of us needs to try to produce faith. The Bible declares: "God hath dealt to every man the measure of faith" (Romans 12:3). We need not produce it; we need but release it. Without faith we would not dare sit in a chair, drive a car, or eat in a restaurant. Our lives are filled with minor exercises of faith. Receiving saving grace is little more than doing toward God what we do in our daily lives: trust the work of another. Perhaps we should make an acrostic of the word *faith* as a reminder:

Functionally
Acknowledging
I
Trust
Him

The New Testament clearly teaches that once we have confessed and repented, nothing more is expected of us than the exercise of our faith. Paul wrote: "Therefore being justified by faith, we have peace with God through our Lord Jesus Christ: By whom also we have access by faith into this grace wherein we stand, and rejoice in hope of the glory of God" (Romans 5:1-2). He also reminded us, "For by grace are ye saved through faith; and that not of yourselves: it is the gift of God" (Ephesians 2:8).

The key to maintaining saving faith is to consistently pay attention to what God has said about our salvation rather than to our emotions or memory circuits. We have an enemy who loves to remind us of past failures, and our own defiled consciences tell us that we are not worthy to be saved. Both tell us the truth about our past lives, but the Bible tells us the truth about our present standing before God. We *must* believe what God says over what our inner voice tells us.

Faith is strengthened, undergirded, and renewed when we read what God has said. Daily Bible reading is a must to maintain our sense of victory. When we do not hear the voice of God in His Book, we tend to believe the voice that we *do* hear.

Daily communication with God in prayer is another valuable way of maintaining faith, for when He speaks to our hearts, how could we help but believe what He says? He does not speak words of condemnation to His children. He speaks words of grace and guidance. The beautiful eighth chapter of Romans begins by affirming: "There is therefore now no condemnation to them which are in Christ Jesus, who walk not after the flesh, but after the Spirit" (Romans 8:1). Receive this pledge. Believe this promise. Your heart may condemn you, but God is greater than your heart.

The Apostle John knew how easily our hearts condemn us. He wrote: "For if our heart condemn us, God is greater than our heart, and knoweth all things. Beloved, if our heart condemn us not, then have we confidence toward God" (1 John 3:20-21).

41

These basics of salvation do not cover every facet of Christ's program of salvation, but they tell us everything (and more) that we need to know to desire it and obtain it. Remember the basic facts of salvation:

1. You need to be saved.
2. Jesus is the Savior.
3. This salvation is complete and waiting.
4. God has promised this salvation to you.
5. God has pictured this salvation for you.
6. God asks but three things of you: Confess, Repent, Believe.
7. All you need do is act on what you now know.

As an outward act of your confession of faith, I suggest that you fill out the declaration below and sign it. We all need a definite action to affirm our faith. I further suggest that you phone a friend and tell him or her that you have accepted Jesus as your Lord and Savior. I also urge you to associate with fellow believers in a church that believes the Bible and embraces the atoning work of Calvary.

Affirmation of Salvation

Today I have confessed (acknowledged) before God that I am a sinner deserving His judgment. I repent — turn from — my sinful ways and turn to God's righteousness as taught in the Bible.

I believe that Jesus is the Christ, the Son of the Living God, and I want to serve Him with all my heart and soul.

I release faith that God has heard my prayer and has honored His pledge to save me. I accept His salvation as a gift of His grace, and I rejoice in this great provision.

I will no longer think of myself, nor refer to myself, as a sinner. I am now a child of God who lives in the love of God. I will joyfully confess to others that my life has changed and my future is now secure in Christ Jesus.

Signed: *K Saunders* / *Peter Saunders*   Date: 11/8/95 19/2/95

Chapter 3

The Basics of Christian Culture

The more widely I travel the world in my teaching ministry, the more I become aware of how culture — behavior typical of a group or class of persons — strongly molds individuals. You may transfer an Italian from Italy to America, but he will basically speak, behave, and react as an Italian. The same thing can be said of any race of people. There are characteristics and attitudes that seem part of the generic strain. We may have all come from Adam and Eve, but we are not alike.

These cultural differences can build nearly insurmountable barriers between races, or it can induce such animosity and hatred as to foster genocidal wars between cultures. We are experiencing several such wars at the present time.

When I speak of "Christian culture" I am not suggesting that the cross of Christ produces uniformity among Christians. This is not only untrue; it is undesirable.

When God called a family and made a nation out of it, He allowed great diversity. No two tribes were alike, but they learned, under God, how to function as a unit.

Even during their wanderings in the wilderness, they maintained their distinctive differences. God provided for each tribe to camp and travel as units without mixing as a unit. In time of war, they went to battle as tribes. Even when they entered the land of promise, God allowed two and one half tribes to remain on the far side of Jordan for their inheritance.

In the past two decades there has come a cry for unity in the Christian camp, and that cry can be interpreted as a call to uniformity. I don't expect to see this before Jesus returns. We don't need complete uniformity, but we do need conformity to the life of Christ. He introduces us to an entirely different culture than the one into which we were born.

A Chosen Generation

God told Israel, "Thou art an holy people unto the LORD thy God: the LORD thy God hath chosen thee to be a special people unto himself, above all people that are upon the face of the earth" (Deuteronomy 7:6), and Paul told the Christians, "According as he hath chosen us in him before the foundation of the world, that we should be holy and without blame before him in love" (Ephesians 1:4). This divine choice is not in any way coupled with the goodness or value of the chosen ones. God told Israel, "The LORD did not set his love upon you, nor choose you, because ye were more in number than any people; for ye were the fewest of all people" (Deuteronomy 7:7), and Jesus told His disciples: "Ye have not chosen me, but I have chosen you, and ordained you" (John 15:16).

The call to holiness is just that — a call. God initiates that call; He invites us to respond to His call. The generation of Hebrews that followed the call out of Egypt was unwilling to follow it into the Promised Land, so God extended the call to the next generation. God will have a holy people unto Himself. Whether that includes us is a matter of our personal choice.

The work of Christ at Calvary introduced us to a culture that was foreign to us. Much of it is diametrically opposed to our former way of life. The language, the standards, and the attitudes of true Christians are difficult to copy or comply with.

Persons who have moved to a different nation have found great difficulty learning the language and culture of their adopted land, but the citizens are extremely comfortable in all of it. They were born into that culture — and we must be too. Jesus told Nicodemus:

> *Verily, verily, I say unto thee, Except a man be born again, he cannot see the kingdom of God. Nicodemus*

> *saith unto him, How can a man be born when he is old?*
> *Can he enter the second time into his mother's womb,*
> *and be born? Jesus answered, Verily, verily, I say unto*
> *thee, Except a man be born of water and of the Spirit,*
> *he cannot enter into the kingdom of God. That which is*
> *born of the flesh is flesh; and that which is born of the*
> *Spirit is spirit. Marvel not that I said unto thee, Ye must*
> *be born again.*
>
> *(John 3:3-7).*

While the coming of Jesus into our lives does not make us all think and talk alike, He *does* seek to produce an entirely different life in us and a distinct lifestyle for us. Paul testified to the initial struggle this produced in him when he wrote:

> *For I know that in me (that is, in my flesh,) dwelleth no*
> *good thing: for to will is present with me; but how to*
> *perform that which is good I find not. For the good that*
> *I would I do not: but the evil which I would not, that I*
> *do ... O wretched man that I am! who shall deliver me*
> *from the body of this death? I thank God through Jesus*
> *Christ our Lord. So then with the mind I myself serve*
> *the law of God; but with the flesh the law of sin*
>
> *(Romans 7:18-19; 24-25).*

Paul was merely expressing the conflict the children of Israel must have experienced after they left Egypt and met God at Mt. Sinai. The commandments and instructions God gave the Hebrews cut across the grain of the laws of Egypt. Even the rules of sanitation that God gave were different from what they had observed in Egypt.

These slaves were having to learn to live as freed men and women. Personal accountability and initiative were demanded of them. God called them to an entirely different way of life. He established moral codes far higher than these Hebrews had observed for over 400 years. The laws concerning ownership of property, rights of inheritance, and human rights were equally new to them.

God was introducing a new culture to His fledgling nation. In a unique way, they were the children of Jehovah. God said, "And ye shall be holy unto me: for I the LORD am holy, and have severed you from other people, that ye should be mine" (Leviticus 20:26). These Hebrews walked into a peculiar culture to be a demonstration of Jehovah to the surrounding nations. Their lifestyles would become a testimony of the true and living God wherever they went. Moses told the second generation that was poised ready to enter the promised land:

> *Behold, I have taught you statutes and judgments, even as the LORD my God commanded me, that ye should do so in the land whither ye go to possess it. Keep therefore and do them; for this is your wisdom and your understanding in the sight of the nations, which shall hear all these statutes, and say, Surely this great nation is a wise and understanding people. For what nation is there so great, who hath God so nigh unto them, as the LORD our God is in all things that we call upon him for? And what nation is there so great, that hath statutes and judgments so righteous as all this law, which I set before you this day?*
>
> *(Deuteronomy 4:5-8)*

Just as God chose Israel to demonstrate His righteousness to the nations of the world, He has chosen the Christians of this day for a similar purpose. Before His ascension Jesus said, "Ye shall be witnesses unto me both in Jerusalem, and in all Judaea, and in Samaria, and unto the uttermost part of the earth" (Acts 1:8). The emphasis is on the demonstration — *"be witnesses"* — far more than on the declaration. Changed lives are God's most effective testimonial.

Peter told the Christians, "Ye are a chosen generation, a royal priesthood, an holy nation, a peculiar people; that ye should shew forth the praises of him who hath called you out of darkness into his marvelous light" (1 Peter 2:9). There can be no doubt that the call Israel abandoned has been extended by

God to the New Testament believers — individually and collectively as the Church.

Much as God introduced a new culture to His nation of Israel, He now announces the availability of a divine culture to today's Christians. Jesus told His Father in His high priestly prayer that His disciples "Are not of the world, even as I am not of the world" (John 17:16). Jesus came to introduce a divine dynasty of different people. We have not yet been translated, but we have been transformed (see Romans 12:1-2).

The gospel of Jesus does not attempt to take the Irish out of an Irishman, but it does lift him or her into a higher and superior culture without violating his or her national characteristics.

God told the Hebrews, "Ye shall be holy men unto me" (Exodus 22:31), and Peter ask the New Testament believers, "Seeing then that all these things shall be dissolved, what manner of persons ought ye to be in all holy conversation and godliness" (2 Peter 3:11). God chose us to be holy, for only holy persons can manifest the holiness of Father God.

A Royal Priesthood

Three times in the Bible, God declares us to be a priesthood unto Himself. The first time is in the future tense: "Ye shall be unto me a kingdom of priests, and an holy nation" (Exodus 19:6). The second time is in the present tense: "But ye are a chosen generation, a royal priesthood, an holy nation, a peculiar people" (1 Peter 2:9). The third time is in the past tense: "[Jesus] hath made us kings and priests unto God and his Father; to him be glory and dominion for ever and ever. Amen" (Revelation 1:6). God has determined that His "chosen generation" be priests unto Himself in the past, present, and future.

The function of the priest was to minister unto God and speak for the people. In Israel's case, the people rejected the priesthood of the believer and God chose the tribe of Levi to be their substitutes. Aaron and the Levites were especially holy unto the Lord, that is, they were separated unto the Lord in a special way.

From the moment God made this choice, the life of Aaron (the high priest) and the lives of the Levites (Levitical priests) were never the same. Moses moved them from the general camp site and had them pitch their tents around the Tabernacle. They not only lived separated from the other tribes, they dressed differently, ate differently, and were under different rules for marriage.

Should it be any different for New Testament priests? The New Testament calls us a "royal priesthood". The book of Revelation puts it "kings and priests". We hold the distinction of being a kingdom of priests who also function as kings. We are not like others; God has set us apart unto His service. We minister unto God for people, and we minister God unto those people.

We, as Israel's Levites, are set apart and made a distinct culture to perform our duties better. While many Old Testament regulations do not apply to believer priests, the principle of difference does pertain. Kings and priests live in a different culture from those they serve. We must learn to live in a culture of holiness.

Priests and kings are set apart; "sanctified" to their way of life. About midway in His great High Priestly prayer, Jesus pled with the Father, "Sanctify them through thy truth: thy word is truth" (John 17:17). Jesus specifically asked the Father to sanctify us in the same manner the Father had sanctified Him. (John 17:19). Surely our holiness must be the will of the Father if Jesus prayed for its impartation to us, for He never prayed out of the will of God.

The theme of our Savior's great prayer of intercession was for our sanctification. "Sanctify them," He pleaded. He had already assured the Father that, "They are not of the world, even as I am not of the world" (John 17:16), so His prayer was not for redemption or regeneration. He was asking the Father to complete something that had only begun during His ministry with the disciples — "Sanctify them."

Since the first meaning of "sanctification" is "to set apart unto" it seems that Christ was petitioning the Father to set apart or dedicate the believers to divine service. Certainly that would be the meaning Christ had a little later in His prayer when He prayed, "for their sakes I sanctify myself, that they also might be sanctified through the truth" (John 17:19), for Jesus was unblemished by sin, and His actions were unspotted, therefore He would never use "sanctify" concerning Himself if He meant purification.

The prayer means, "Father, consecrate them to thine own self; let them be temples for thine indwelling, instruments for thy use." Aaron and his sons are said to have been sanctified (Leviticus 8:30). Later a certain tent was sanctified to the service of God, and it became a sanctuary. Everything used in that tabernacle from the altar to the ark, from the bowls to the snuff dishes, was declared sanctified (Numbers 7:1). Because of this sanctification, none of these things could be used for any purpose other than the service of the Lord God. The fire, the bread, the oil, and the incense were all called holy and were reserved for sacred uses under penalty of death for violation. These sanctified things were reserved for holy purposes, and any other use of them was strictly forbidden.

This is one part of the meaning of our Lord's prayer. He wants each of us to be consecrated unto the Lord, reserved and ordained for divine purposes. We do not belong to the world; it has no right or claim on our life anymore. We do not belong to the devil, as his authority over us was broken the moment we were given unto God. We do not even belong to ourselves to live under the dictates of a selfish will and stubborn pride. We are bought with a price, and we belong totally to the one who paid the price. We belong to Jesus, and He presents us to His Father, and begs Him to accept us and sanctify us to His own purposes.

We cannot hire ourselves out to inferior objects, mercenary aims, or selfish ambitions, for we are now under solemn contract to God. We are a kingdom of priests. We are kings and priests. We have lifted up our hand unto the Lord, and we cannot draw back. But who would want to draw back from such a covenant with God? It is both delightful and profitable to us, for although we belong to Him exclusively it puts the complete responsibility for our lives in His hand. If there is a conflict, the battle is the Lord's. If there is a privation, the provision is the Lord's. If there is physical illness, the physician is the Lord, for the same covenant that makes us His makes Him ours. It is the will of Jesus that the Father sanctify us to the service of God, thereby letting us know, and all the world know, that we are God's, because we belong to Christ, and in so doing we have entered into a divine culture.

Jesus did not come to violate the existing culture of His day, but He did offer a behavior standard that was much higher than the normal standard at that time. To a nation of short-tempered people, Jesus said, "I say unto you, That ye resist not evil: but whosoever shall smite thee on thy right cheek, turn to him the other also" (Matthew 5:39).

In Christ's day, Roman law allowed a soldier to command any citizen to carry a burden for the soldier for one mile. Jesus said, "Whosoever shall compel thee to go a mile, go with him twain" (Matthew 5:41). It is from this commandment that we get the saying, "Go the extra mile".

Even concerning forgiveness, Jesus went far beyond the accepted interpretation of the Law of Moses. When Peter asked if he should expand his level of forgiveness to seven times a day "Jesus saith unto him, I say not unto thee, Until seven times: but, Until seventy times seven" (Matthew 18:22).

Jesus consistently lifted the culture of His followers far above the culture of their day. He taught that the motivations of the heart were more important than the manifestations of the body. He argued that since thoughts precede action, we need to control our desires rather than try to restrict our deeds.

Christ came to establish a new nation of believers, and His teachings gave foundation to a new way of living. His Sermon on the Mount is fundamentally the constitution of the divine kingdom on earth. Jesus came to do far more than "Save his people from their sins" (Matthew 1:21). He came to form a new kingdom that would bring heaven to earth, God to men and women, and those men and women to God.

Jesus' sacrifice on the cross brought His divine life into our lives in a transforming measure. He testified, "Yet a little while, and the world seeth me no more; but ye see me: because I live, ye shall live also" (John 14:19). This is not in the future tense looking toward a coming resurrection. It is present tense. It is not a promise for the sweet bye-and-bye. His holy life is available to us in the nasty here-and-now.

A Holy Nation

Peter believed that we have become a "holy nation". Other translators call this "a dedicated nation" (New English Bible), and "a consecrated nation" (Twentieth Century New Testament). This demands a different lifestyle. Paul told the church at Rome, "As ye have yielded your members servants to uncleanness and to iniquity unto iniquity; even so now yield your members servants to righteousness unto holiness" (Romans 6:19), and, "Being made free from sin, and become servants to God, ye have your fruit unto holiness, and the end everlasting life" (Romans 6:22).

There are cultures on this earth that condone stealing, adultery, fornication, drunkenness, and other vices of the flesh. Often they continue in such practices after giving their lives to Christ Jesus. They have merely added Jesus to their culture, but the Bible says that Jesus came to initiate His own culture.

Both the Old and the New Testaments speak clearly and frequently about sexual mores. The Holy Spirit said, "Know ye not that the unrighteous shall not inherit the kingdom of God? Be not deceived: neither fornicators, nor idolaters, nor adulterers, nor effeminate, nor abusers of themselves with mankind, nor thieves, nor covetous, nor drunkards, nor revilers, nor extortioners, shall inherit the kingdom of God" (1 Corinthians

6:9-10). In our permissive society this is an unwelcome message, but it is God's Word to Christian believers.

That form of lifestyle belonged to our old culture. The Christian culture Christ introduced has none of that in it. After writing this list, Paul observantly added: "And such were some of you: but ye are washed, but ye are sanctified, but ye are justified in the name of the Lord Jesus, and by the Spirit of our God" (1 Corinthians 6:11). The cross of Jesus changes our culture, and our obedience changes our nature.

Our obedience brings us to holiness. Peter speaks of the "sanctification of the Spirit *unto* obedience" (1 Peter 1:2, emphasis added), as though the inner workings of the Spirit actually create a "yes" attitude in our hearts. While God will not violate our free moral agency to force us to do His will, He does commission His Holy Spirit to gently urge, cajole, entice, educate, and warn us. He does not violate our wills, but He often makes us willing to obey, for He knows better than we do that obedience is an early step to holiness.

Among the greatest hindrances to holiness is disobedience to the Word and known will of God. All the processes of sanctification stop during times of rebellion. God does not strike us with a heavenly thunderbolt, He just gently withdraws and lets us do our own thing. Frequently, as the misery of having our own way becomes unbearable, we repent of the sin of disobedience and find His grace to be overwhelming. Usually these areas of stubbornness have to do with outward happiness and success. We have to learn that by the surrender of outward happiness and outward success a man may attain inner success. The spirit of the cross is still the path to the highest righteousness.

When Jesus prayed to the Father, petitioning Him to sanctify the believers, He said, "Sanctify them *through thy truth*" (John 17:17, emphasis added). God has joined sanctification and truth together. It has become popular, in some circles, to say that Christianity is a life; not a creed. But Christianity is a life that grows out of truth. Jesus Christ is the way and the truth as well as the life, and He is not properly received unless we accept Him in that threefold character. The Bible, which is God's recorded, written truth, is both a channel for reception of sanctification and a manual for the expression of that holiness. The Scripture alone is absolute, essential, decisive, authoritative, undiluted, eternal, and everlasting truth. Truth given to us in the Word of God will sanctify all believers to the end of time: God will use it for that purpose.

Two factors must accompany this written truth for it to be effectual. First, it must be quickened in our hearts by the Holy Spirit, and second, it must be obeyed in our lives. The laws of God are the directions on the package of life. To disobey means confusion; to obey means fulfillment.

God's command must become our commission, for since God is infinite and eternal, there is no other source of righteousness, justice, law, or holiness. We will either submit to Him and go His way or we must forever do without His nature, His graces, or His presence.

We are a "holy nation" in God's sight. Does the world see the outworking of this divine provision?

A Peculiar People

The Greek word that is translated *peculiar* in Peter's call to holiness (1 Peter 2:9) does not mean odd or eccentric. It means *to possess*. Other Bibles translate it: "A people claimed by God for His own" (New English Bible), "God's own people" (Twentieth Century New Testament), or "a purchased people" (Montgomery).

In my years of Bible reading, I have not yet found a chapter that sounds the command to live the Christian culture better than the second chapter of the book of Titus. In this pastoral epistle, Paul urged Titus to exhort the saints to exemplify sanctification of life and holiness of character through obedience to the Word of God. Paul had already set similar standards of righteousness for the bishops and deacons in the letters to Timothy, but now Paul urged similar standards upon each church member. Lest there be any misunderstanding as to whom he meant, Paul divided the instructions among the aged men, the aged women, the young women, the young men, and the servants. No one was exempt, for Paul assumed that if they were really saints, it should show! "But as for you," Paul wrote, "speak up for the right living that goes along with true Christianity" (Titus 2:1, The Living Bible).

The Aged Men (Titus 2:2)

In stating his plea for demonstrated holiness through obedience to the truth, Paul began with the older men and women of the church. Actually he was merely implementing an earlier observation, "Ye became followers of us, and of the Lord ... so that ye were ensamples to all that believe ..." (1 Thessalonians 1:6,7). Paul saw the church as a large family where the older children automatically become the example for the younger ones. I know, for I was the oldest in our family and was often told that I had to behave as an example to my brothers and sister. Mother has admitted that many of my spankings spared the younger children the need of a spanking, for they learned by the power of my example. Certainly the mature Christians should set the example for holiness of attitude and righteousness of action for the younger ones of the congregation. What we see is always far more powerful than what we hear.

Paul required six things of these older brethren: be sober, be grave, be temperate, be sound in faith, sound in charity, and sound in patience. The Living Bible translates this verse, "Teach the older men to be serious and unruffled; they must be sensible, knowing and believing the truth and doing everything with love and patience" (Titus 2:2). The first three requirements concern their demeanor or bearing, and the final three concern their deportment or conduct.

A true saint who has matured both in years and in his relationship with God will have a demeanor that is serious, sensible, sober, dignified, and discreet. He should outgrow youthful frivolity without losing his zest for life. He should become serious without losing joy, and he should have a distinct dignity without pathetic pride. Having tasted of heavenly things should affect his behavior amidst earthly things.

The final three commands deal with the deportment of the aged men. Their faith should be unmovable, their love unhinderable, and their patience inexhaustible. When they move toward God, their faith and love should be "soundly established" (Knox translation), and when they move toward men and women, their love and patience should be mature and healthy. They are to be the patriarchs of the faith and patterns to the believer.

The Aged Women (Titus 2:3)

"The aged women likewise ..." places the same responsibility for manifesting holiness in demeanor and deportment on the matured women as upon the aged men. Their command is developed a little differently. Paul said, "That they be in behavior as becometh holiness", or, "in deportment as becometh sacred persons" (The Emphasized New Testament), or "to let their deportment testify to holiness" (Conybeare). Lamsa translates it, "to behave as becomes the worship of God". There can be no doubt that Paul is declaring that the actions of the matured saints should reflect the presence of God in their lives.

I observe that two things are prohibited to these women and two things are required from them. First, they were not to be false accusers, or slanderers and scandalmongers as other translators have put it. The Living Bible, simply says, "They must not go around speaking evil of others." How easy it is to fall into this trap, especially when the responsibilities of the home have lightened with the children gone and with time weighing heavily on their hands. Besides this, the younger generation does things so differently than the way they were done in grandma's day. The godly woman will not stoop to gossip, scandal, or critical talk. She should be so full of good news ("gospel" *means* "good news") that she won't have time to discuss bad news, much less scandalize her neighbors.

The godly woman (or man) should not be a talebearer. She should get no "kick" out of sharing the failures of other Christians, nor should she enjoy vicarious sinning by discussing the sin of another person. When her mind is clean, her lips will be pure. What a by-product of the Christian culture!

Secondly, these older women, if they are to manifest holiness, are also prohibited from heavy drinking. They should know that habit is a species of slavery, and Christ has set us free from slavery. They should not need chemical depressants or stimulants, for they do not wrestle with guilt, nor are they plagued with worry and anxiety. These were nailed to Christ's cross long ago. They have "meat to eat" that the world knows nothing of, so why should they stoop to the world's shabby chemical substitutes? They have learned that holiness is basically a relationship with God, and they know that it was excessive wine that cost Noah the intimate relationship with God.

These aged, godly women are urged to teach "good things". "Teachers of goodness", the Living Bible says. "Teachers of that which is good ... teachers of virtue ... teachers of what is right ... of what is noble" other translators say. This, of course, does not imply that all of them should enter the ministry, but rather, "teaching others by their good ensample", as Knox translates it.

The fourth verse especially directs them to be teachers of the young women. How I have watched this work in the churches I have pastored. The simple example of my wife among the women of the congregation began a process of change that probably could not have been effected from the pulpit. They learned much by observing her attitude. It is even more noticeable now when she travels with me throughout the world. Pastors urge me to bring her with me because of the influence she exerts upon the women of the congregation. She would be the first to declare that she is not a teacher, but her life speaks so loudly that she really does not need to say anything.

A godly mother is still the best antidote to sin in the home, and worshiping Marys, praying Hannahs, and godly Annas are visual training programs that the church can offer its young people. People who won't read the Bible will read "living epistles". No wonder, then, that the aged women are commanded to "be in behavior as becometh holiness".

Young Women (Titus 2:4,5)

Paul next addressed his attention to the young women of the church. He first taught these young women to "be sober", which simply means to be sensible or show discretion. The Living Bible calls it "to live quietly". Perhaps Paul sought to deal with the dissatisfaction and discontent of the young mind with its accompanying ambition and hustle. These young saints need to learn and to manifest that gain is not godliness, "but godliness with contentment is great gain" (see 1 Timothy 6:5,6). Undue emphasis upon possessions and positions tends to ungodliness. How sad to see that this is the shallow emphasis of so much of today's ministry that suggests that our relationship to God will be reflected in our bank account and earthly inventories. After getting a glimpse of heaven, what is there on earth worth striving after?

After these younger women learn something about divine wisdom, they are told to learn how to love their husbands and children. It is futile to assume that all women know how to be loving and affectionate wives and mothers. The Bible knows differently. God's Word says that this is a learned response and then commands it of the women, not because the husband and children are especially worthy of the love, but because manifest love is inseparably linked to divine holiness. She who is holy will be loving. Paul's injunction was merely to direct that love into divinely appointed channels, just as he had done for the men in Ephesians 5. Jesus stated, "By this shall all men know that ye are my disciples, if ye have love one to another" (John 13:35). This is more than shaking hands with the preacher and hugging the church members; it is loving the family unit at home so fervently and purely as to draw attention to the Christ who lives within us. This is more than a choice we make; it is a commanded demonstration of holiness. It is part of our Christian heritage.

The following five commands Paul gave to the young women are all concerned with their behavior in the environment of the home. "Be discreet ... be chaste ... be good ... be keepers at home ... and be obedient to their own husbands." When my sister Iverna and I pastored together, we used to impress this upon the women, and occasionally we enforced it. If a husband complained to me that his wife was spending so much time at the church (we had daily prayer services) that his house was not being well kept, we used to call the woman out of the prayer meeting and send her home, telling her that godliness was not only in praying and reading the Bible. True holiness will manifest itself in proper management of the home, morals, money, temperament, and spiritual hunger. Holiness is not merely a spiritual feeling; it is a practical life that affects everything we do.

Paul ended his injunctions to the young women by saying that these commands must be obeyed, "that the word of God be not blasphemed" (Titus 2:5). If the testimony given Sunday is not backed up by the manner of life on Monday it is blasphemous. How seldom do we hear it preached that insubordination in the home is blasphemy in the eyes of God, for it is a refusal to allow the "spirit of holiness" to flow through us in the area of life that is the most important — the home.

Young Men (Titus 2:6-8)

Having spoken at length to the young women, Paul now turned his attention to the young men. "Be sober minded," Paul said. Weymouth translates that, "In the same way exhort the young men to be self-restrained", while Moffatt says, "Tell the young men also to be masters of themselves at all points." Paul did not ask the women to be in control and the men to be "at liberty". He urged a demonstration of holiness that makes self-control a high priority. The young men must be masters of themselves in their sexuality, their ambitions, their frustrations, their spirituality, their finances, and so forth.

Furthermore, these young men in general, and Titus in particular, were urged to be "a pattern of good works". Having urged the young men "to behave carefully, taking life seriously", The Living Bible says, "and here you yourself must be an example to them of good deeds of every kind". Paul did not believe that a man had to be old to manifest a godlikeness. He had instructed young Timothy, "Let no man despise thy youth; but be thou an example of the believers, in word, in conversation, in charity, in spirit, in faith, in purity" (1 Timothy 4:12). I have heard many young men say that no one will listen to them teach the Word because they are so young. Actually it isn't age people look for, it is spiritual maturity and ability to teach. If the young person will demonstrate godliness in his lifestyle, with consistency, people will be willing to listen to what is said.

The Living Bible concludes Paul's charge to these young men by saying, "Let everything you do reflect your love of the truth and the fact that you are in dead earnest about it. Your conversation should be so sensible and logical that anyone who wants to argue will be ashamed of himself because there won't be anything to criticize in anything you say!" (Titus 1:7-8). Even the way the mind is disciplined is a demonstration of holiness, and the Word commands it. We need to learn to use that "mind of Christ" God has shared with us (See 1 Corinthians 2:16). Too often we talk of feelings without being able to back it up with facts. True holiness will demonstrate itself more concretely than that.

Servants (Titus 2:9,10)

Paul completed his commands to live in the Christian culture by speaking to the servants in the church. The Living Bible puts Paul's practical teaching in these words: "Urge slaves to obey their masters and to try their best to satisfy them. They must not talk back, nor steal, but must show themselves to be entirely trustworthy. In this way they will make people want to believe in our Savior and God" (Titus 1:9-10).

If this was required of people who were little more than property, and could be bought and sold like beasts, should it not be even more true of employees who are free to work where they like? I used to teach the men of my congregation that it is a demonstration of holiness to be the best worker on the job; to arrive a little early and to be willing to stay a little late if the work load required it. I urged them to be sparing in their taking of "breaks", and to always be sure that they made the boss more money than they cost him. These men set such a good example that their employers often phoned the church office asking if we had anyone else looking for work. If godliness doesn't work on the job, it isn't true godlikeness; it is a religious substitute used only in church.

So this chapter declares that holiness should be demonstrated in our attitudes, deportment, actions, love lives, and in our use of drugs and drink. The way the house is kept, the way the job is worked, and the way we prepare ourselves to "be ready always to give an answer to every man that asketh you a reason of the hope that is in you with meekness and fear" (1 Peter 3:15) all reveal the depth of our sanctification. Clean morals, contentment with such things as we have, a serious approach to life, and a demonstrated pattern of good works do more to illustrate holiness than a thousand sermons. The honesty of our speech, the soundness of our faith, especially in times of testing, and the fervency of our love, toward both God and the brethren, are gauges God uses to reveal the effectiveness of our walk with him.

But these things are not commanded of the bishops and the deacons; this chapter is written to the layman. This is not the "super" life that qualifies us for high office; this is the normal life of a sanctified Christian. This is not even the optional life of the "deeper" saint; it is the *only* life the Bible describes for a follower of Christ.

We have already discovered that this life cannot be produced by us; it must be presented to us. Accordingly, Paul added, "For the grace of God that bringeth salvation hath appeared to all men" (Titus 2:11). Grace to live in a Christian culture in the midst of a worldly culture has been imparted, and for those who have responded in faith it has been imputed. The life is a divine life; it is godlikeness; it is holiness. It is not something to look forward to, but something to be received right here and now. Life has come! That life will change us. It has come to instruct us, to discipline us, to school us, and to train us how to live godly. Paul says that this life-grace of God will teach us how to do two things: (1) to "deny ungodliness and worldly lusts" and (2) to "live soberly, righteously, and godly, in this present world" (Titus 2:12).

Does this seem too difficult? God knows that we are not capable of really living the Christian life, so He has given His Holy Spirit to live that life in us.

Chapter 4

The Basics of the Holy Spirit

It is fair to say that no one can successfully live the Christian life. Only Christ can live it in us, and He does this through His Spirit. Even Jesus needed the presence of the Holy Spirit during His days on earth.

With the foresight peculiar to prophets, Isaiah saw the coming of Christ and the anointing of the Holy Spirit on His life and through His ministry. He wrote: "The spirit of the LORD shall rest upon him, the spirit of wisdom and understanding, the spirit of counsel and might, the spirit of knowledge and of the fear of the LORD; And shall make him of quick understanding in the fear of the LORD: and he shall not judge after the sight of his eyes, neither reprove after the hearing of his ears" (Isaiah 11:2-3). That Jesus lived and ministered in an unlimited anointing of the Holy Spirit is self-evident. Jesus said of Himself, "For he whom God hath sent speaketh the words of God: for God giveth not the Spirit by measure [unto him]" (John 3:34).

Jesus told His disciples, "Verily, verily, I say unto you, He that believeth on me, the works that I do shall he do also; and greater works than these shall he do; because I go unto my Father" (John 14:12). Just before His ascension, Jesus added: "And, behold, I send the promise of my Father upon you: but tarry ye in the city of Jerusalem, until ye be endued with power from on high" (Luke 24:49). Jesus expected His followers to be endued with the same Holy Spirit that had anointed Him. He promised to send Him; He fulfilled that promise on the day of Pentecost. That indwelling Spirit lives a holy life of wisdom, power, and fellowship with God in each believer.

The Actuality of the Holy Spirit

It is probably fair to say that all Christians believe in the Holy Spirit. What has been such a surprise to me is how many of them fail to see Him as a person. They view Him as an influence or executive force of the Godhead. He is far more than this. The Bible teaches us that the Holy Spirit is one of the three persons of the Godhead. He is divine in the absolute sense, for He has divine attributes ascribed to Him. The Bible calls Him eternal (Hebrews 9:14), omnipresent (Psalm 139:7-10), omnipotent (Luke 1:35), and omniscient (1 Corinthians 2:10-11). God's Word ascribes divine works to Him. It also credits Him with a part in creation (Genesis 1:2; Job 33:4), regeneration (John 3:5-8), and resurrection (Romans 8:11).

He is far more than merely a godly influence, for He exercises the attributes of personality. He has a mind (Romans 8:27), a will (1 Corinthians 12:11), and He has feelings (Ephesians 4:30). Harmonious with these evidences of personality, He reveals (2 Peter 1:21), He teaches (John 14:26), He witnesses (Galatians 4:6), He intercedes (Romans 8:26), He speaks (Revelation 2:7), He commands (Acts 16:6-7), He testifies (John 15:26), He may be grieved (Ephesians 4:30), He may be lied to (Acts 5:3), and He may be blasphemed (Matthew 12:31- 32).

The Holy Spirit is a personality separated and distinct from God, for He proceeds from God, is sent from God, and is God's gift to persons. At the creation of the earth we read: "And the Spirit of God moved upon the face of the waters. And God said, Let there be light: and there was light" (Genesis 1:3). Their work was cooperative, complete, and consecutive, but obviously, two persons were at work. Similarly at the baptism of Jesus we see the Son in the water, the Spirit descending as a dove, and the Father speaking from Heaven. The Holy Spirit was acting harmoniously with God, yet not as the Father, but as the Spirit upon the Son. Yet the Spirit is not independent of God. He always represents the one God. Just how the Holy Spirit can be one with God and yet distinct from God is part of the mystery of the Trinity.

Perhaps you may grasp a better understanding of the person of the Holy Spirit if I list some names given to Him throughout the Bible. He is most frequently called the Holy Spirit. He is also called the Spirit of Christ (Romans 8:9), the Comforter (John 14:16), the Holy Spirit of Promise (Ephesians 1:13), the Spirit of Truth (John 14:17), the Spirit of Grace (Hebrews 10:29), the Spirit of Life (Romans 8:2), and the Spirit of Adoption (Romans 8:15). These names reveal some of His offices and functions for the believer.

There are also names and titles ascribed to Him that speak of His position, such as: the Spirit of God (Matthew 3:16), the Holy Spirit of God (Ephesians 4:30), the Spirit of the Lord (2 Corinthians 3:17), the Spirit of the Father (Matthew 10:20, the Spirit of Jesus Christ (Philippians 1:19), the Spirit of the Son (Galatians 4:6), the eternal Spirit (Hebrews 9:14), the Free Spirit (2 Corinthians 3:17), the Good Spirit (Nehemiah 9:20), My Spirit (Acts 2:17-18), Thy Spirit (1 John 4:13), and His Spirit (1 Corinthians 2:10).

He is obviously the executive of the Godhead. God is the legislature. Christ is the judicial system, for all God's laws are judged in the blood of Christ. It is the Holy Spirit who functions in the office of the executive who puts the laws into operation and penalizes violators and blesses those who obey.

There are other titles given to the Holy Spirit that more specifically speak of His character and work. He is called the Spirit of: Adoption (Romans 8:15), Burning (Isaiah 4:4), Counsel (Isaiah 11:2), Faith (2 Corinthians 4:13), Fear of the Lord (Isaiah 11:2), Glory (1 Peter 4:14), Grace (Hebrews 10:29), Holiness (Romans 1:4), Judgment (Isaiah 28:6), Knowledge (Isaiah 11:2), Life (Romans 8:2), Love (2 Timothy 1:7), Might (Isaiah 11:2), Promise (Ephesians 1:13), Prophecy (Revelation 19:10), Revelation (Ephesians 1:17), Supplication (Zechariah 12:10), Truth (John 14:17), Understanding (Isaiah 11:2), and

Wisdom (Ephesians 1:17). The Holy Spirit is also called: the Voice of the Almighty (Ezekiel 1:24), the Breath of the Almighty (Job 33:4), the Power of the Highest (Luke 1:35), and an Unction from the Holy One (1 John 2:20). These names, titles, and descriptive phrases speak of a person distinct from, but an integral part of, God the Father and God the Son.

We learn more about the Holy Spirit as a person by observing the various symbols the Bible uses to illustrate His functions. He is called a Fire (Matthew 3:11) illustrating His purging, purifying work in the believer, and the fiery boldness and zeal He imparts to them. It also may speak of the warmth and illumination of a fire.

The Spirit is symbolized as a wind (John 3:8; Acts 2:2) that illustrates His mysterious, independent, penetration, and life-giving operation. Jesus spoke of the Spirit as water, an indispensable element of physical life. Water purifies, refreshes, quenches thirst, cleans, and renders sterility.

Paul spoke of the Holy Spirit as a seal in Ephesians 1:13 and 2 Timothy 2:19. A seal conveys the thought of ownership and security.

Repeatedly the Spirit is illustrated in the symbol of oil, for in Bible times, oil spoke of usefulness, fruitfulness, beauty, life, and transformation. It was commonly used for food, light, lubrication, healing, and the soothing of the skin. Spiritually, the Holy Spirit does all these to our lives.

Finally, the Holy Spirit is symbolized as a dove, for this is the form He took when He descended upon Jesus at His water baptism (see Matthew 3:16). The dove symbolizes gentleness, tenderness, loveliness, innocence, mildness, peace, and purity.

The Holy Spirit is a real person as genuine as, but different from, the Lord Jesus Christ. He does not duplicate Jesus; He came to glorify Christ. His work is always harmonious with the work of Jesus. He was very active with the earthly ministry of Jesus from being the instrument of His conception, the confirming witness at His baptism, the source of anointing for His ministry, His guardian at the crucifixion, the means of His resurrection, and the power of Christ's ascension. Jesus and the Holy Spirit always worked hand in hand. They still do!

The Activity of the Holy Spirit to the World

Does any of us completely know the full work of the Holy Spirit to the world of people? We know He was an active agent in the creation of the earth and therefore must remain an active instrument of God in maintaining the operation of our planet. Similarly, He is involved in the lives of men and women for whom this world was created. He preserves, protects, and provides for persons far more than we will ever understand.

In summarizing the ministry of the Holy Spirit to mankind in general, Jesus said: "And when he is come, he will reprove the world of sin, and of righteousness, and of judgment: Of sin, because they believe not on me; Of righteousness, because I go to my Father, and ye see me no more; Of judgment, because the prince of this world is judged" (John 16:8-11).

Jesus declared that the Spirit will act as Christ's prosecuting attorney. The Greek word translated here as reprove can also be translated to convict or convince. The Holy Spirit came to convict or to bring home truths otherwise doubted or discarded. He also presses charges made against conduct in life. Somehow in our self-justification, we fail to know what sin, righteousness, and judgment really are, so we need to be convinced of these facts.

Jesus taught that the Holy Spirit would specifically convince or convict persons of "sin, righteousness, and judgment". Jesus did not leave to our imaginations what He meant by this, for He said, "Of sin, because they believe not on me" (John 16:9). The basic work of the Holy Spirit is to deal with the unbelief in the human heart. Sin has so closed us off from the spirit world that we inherently disbelieve in Christ. It takes the special ministry of the Holy Spirit to instill faith in our hearts.

67

Unbelief is the mother sin. Someone has wisely said of unbelief: "Where it continues, all other sins are retained; when it departs, all other sins are removed." A mere change in mental philosophy will not remove unbelief. It takes an illumination of the Holy Spirit.

The second ministry of the Spirit to men and women is a conviction of the righteousness of Christ. Jesus said it was necessary for the Holy Spirit to convince us of righteousness, "Because I go to my Father, and ye see me no more" (John 16:10). While Jesus was on earth, He became God's standard of righteousness, but when He ascended to heaven that standard was removed from the earth. If we judge righteousness by looking at one another, we will live very unrighteously. The Holy Spirit works in our consciences to remind us of the standard of living God has designed for His people. Paul put it this way: "Their conscience also bearing witness, and their thoughts the mean while accusing or else excusing one another" (Romans 2:15).

The third special ministry of the Holy Spirit is to convince men of "Of judgment, because the prince of this world is judged" (John 16:11). The persons in the world, and, tragically, many Christians, live lives terrorized by the devil. They declare him to be the god of this world and they flee, fear, or fight him. Jesus sent His Holy Spirit to inform all of us that when He cried from the cross, "It is finished" (John 19:30), Satan's judgment was complete. The war is over! Satan is eternally defeated by Jesus. The Holy Spirit wants us to stop having a devil who is too big and a God who is too small. It is the work of the Spirit to convince us that it is God who is sovereign; not the devil.

A fourth work of the Holy Spirit to persons in general is regeneration. When a person responds positively to the convicting work of the Spirit, He is ready to be "born again" or regenerated. In the original creative work of God, His hands formed a body from the dust of the earth. This body was surrounded with beauties of nature, but it could not respond. It was lifeless. God breathed the spirit of life into his nostrils and man became a living soul.

Unfortunately sin deformed, defiled, and disgraced this marvelous work of God. This living soul became dormant and dead to the spirit world that surrounded it. Although God is never far from any of us, we live and act as if the realm of the divine did not exist. But when the Holy Spirit who quickened the body of Adam quickens the soul of a man or woman, he or she awakens to the spiritual world around them and begins to live the spiritual life. Anyone who has witnessed the reactions and subsequent life of a real convert knows that regeneration is not merely a doctrine. It is a practical reality. It is an entrance into a new life. The Holy Spirit is God's agent in effecting this new birth. Paul puts it, "Therefore if any man be in Christ, he is a new creature: old things are passed away; behold, all things are become new" (2 Corinthians 5:17).

The Activity of the Holy Spirit to a Believer

It may take most of eternity to discover all that the Holy Spirit does in the life of one who allows himself or herself to be made into this new creature. Perhaps we can summarize some of this by speaking of the Spirit indwelling, sanctifying, and empowering the believer.

At the point of a person's conversion, Jesus appoints the Holy Spirit to be a personal comforter. Jesus said: "I will pray the Father, and he shall give you another Comforter, that he may abide with you for ever" (John 14:16). The word another places the Holy Spirit in comparison with Jesus. Jesus said He would send "one like Me". The Greek word for Comforter (paraclete) means "one called alongside to help". It suggests the work of a representative or a lawyer.

Jesus assigned the Holy Spirit as a personal lawyer or representative to each believer. When the enemy brings charges against us, we need not respond on our own. Jesus told His disciples, "But when they shall lead you, and deliver you up, take no thought beforehand what ye shall speak, neither do ye premeditate: but whatsoever shall be given you in that hour, that speak ye: for it is not ye that speak, but the Holy Ghost" (Mark 13:11).

We don't even know how to approach God properly, but our personal representative does. We read: "Likewise the Spirit also helpeth our infirmities: for we know not what we should pray for as we ought: but the Spirit itself maketh intercession for us with groanings which cannot be uttered" (Romans 8:26). Paul also reminds us, "He that searcheth the hearts knoweth what is the mind of the Spirit, because he maketh intercession for the saints according to the will of God" (Romans 8:27).

Another thing that happens immediately after our conversion is that the Holy Spirit makes His home in the believer. Jesus said of the Spirit: "Even the Spirit of truth; whom the world cannot receive, because it seeth him not, neither knoweth him: but ye know him; for he dwelleth with you, and shall be in you" (John 14:17). He who has been with us as a guide, protector, and intercessor is to be in us.

During the three plus years that Jesus was with His disciples, He met their needs as a companion who walked with them. Just before His death and subsequent resurrection and ascension into heaven, Jesus promised that the Holy Spirit, who was to do for and with them what Jesus had done, would not merely be with them; He would be in them.

We generally refer to this ministry of the Spirit as indwelling. Although God is always present, "For in him we live, and move, and have our being" (Acts 17:28), it is the special ministry of the Holy Spirit to indwell the hearts of men and women who have been saved.

Sin caused the Spirit to depart from men and women, leaving them in spiritual darkness. In relation to understanding, the unconverted cannot know the things of the Spirit (1 Corinthians 2:14). As touching the will, persons cannot be subject to the law of God (Romans 8:7). When it comes to worship, none can call Jesus LORD (1 Corinthians 12:3). As to daily practice, one in whom the Spirit does not dwell cannot please God (Romans 8:8). Concerning character, these cannot bear spiritual fruit (John 15:4), and persons void of the indwelling Spirit cannot have faith to receive the spirit of truth (John 14:17).

The indwelling of the Holy Spirit is the mark of a New Testament Christian. It is not what a person professes that makes him or her a Christian. It is what he or she possesses that makes the difference. Conversion without the indwelling of the Holy Spirit is impossible, for regeneration by the Holy Spirit involves a union with God and Christ that the Bible calls an indwelling. No one can live the Christian life but Christ, and He lives it in the believer through the Holy Spirit.

Still a third necessary work of the Spirit in the life of believers is sanctification. In regeneration, the Holy Spirit effects a radical change in the soul by imparting a new principle of life. This does not imply that the child of God is immediately perfect. Far from it! He is "born again", but he is a baby who must learn to live a new life.

In each new convert there remains inherited and acquired weaknesses and tendencies to sin. There is still the world, the flesh, and the devil to overcome. The Spirit works in a progressive manner to overcome these faults. It is by gradual degrees that the soul is renewed into the image of Christ. Faith must be strengthened through many tests. Love must be fortified to survive hardship and temptation. Allurements to sin must be overcome, and tendencies and habits must be corrected. None of this can be done by mere action of the believer's will. The Holy Spirit works from within the life to effect changes that will be seen throughout that life.

If the Spirit did a single work and then departed, all converts would fall back into their old ways. Fortunately, the Spirit does not depart; He indwells. From this position within the believer, He continues to work divine means of growth. Peter put it, "As newborn babes, desire the sincere milk of the word, that ye may grow thereby" (1 Peter 2:2).

This work of cleansing and consecration is called sanctification or "setting apart". The Bible says: "God hath from the beginning chosen you to salvation through sanctification of the

71

Spirit and belief of the truth" (2 Thessalonians 2:13). Salvation and sanctification work together like a hand in a glove.

Peter says we are the "Elect according to the foreknowledge of God the Father, through sanctification of the Spirit, unto obedience and sprinkling of the blood of Jesus Christ" (1 Peter 1:2). Our salvation may have been made available from before the foundations of the world, but our sanctification must be worked in us daily in our here-and-now. Paul wrote: "For this is the will of God, even your sanctification, that ye should abstain from fornication: That every one of you should know how to possess his vessel in sanctification and honour" (1 Thessalonians 4:3,4). By faith and repentance we turn to God and are regenerated. Then we are dependent upon the Holy Spirit to teach, urge, enable, and motivate us to godly living — sanctification.

The Baptism of the Holy Spirit

In preaching to the multitudes, John the Baptist said: "I indeed baptize you with water; but one mightier than I cometh, the latchet of whose shoes I am not worthy to unloose: he shall baptize you with the Holy Ghost and with fire" (Luke 3:16). Christ's forerunner made a parallel between what he was doing in baptizing converts in water and what Jesus would do in baptizing them in the Holy Spirit. It is much more than symbolic, for what John did was very literal — it was experiential. Similarly, the baptism Jesus offers is equally something we sense, see, and experience.

Because of John's use of the word baptize, this experience of the enabling of the Holy Spirit is usually called "the baptism of the Holy Spirit". It is after salvation. It is not being baptized into Christ, but it is Christ baptizing us in the Spirit.

Peter's statement on the day of Pentecost was: "Repent, and be baptized every one of you in the name of Jesus Christ for the remission of sins, and ye shall receive the gift of the Holy Ghost. For the promise is unto you, and to your children, and to all that are afar off, even as many as the Lord our God shall call" (Acts 2:38-39). Just before His ascension, Jesus told His disciples: "And, behold, I send the promise of my Father upon you: but tarry ye in the city of Jerusalem, until ye be endued with power from on high" (Luke 24:49). Then on the day of Pentecost, "Suddenly there came a sound from heaven as of a rushing mighty wind, and it filled all the house where they were sitting. And there appeared unto them cloven tongues like as of fire, and it sat upon each of them. And they were all filled with the Holy Ghost, and began to speak with other tongues, as the Spirit gave them utterance" (Acts 2:2-4).

Fundamentally, this baptism of the Holy Spirit is an energizing of the life of the person who is indwelt by the Spirit. Working from His abiding presence within the believer, the Holy Spirit begins a divine energizing of a person's will, thoughts, spirit, and personality. Even the human body submits to the direction of the Holy Spirit. So complete is the presence of the Spirit in the believer that He speaks — with our facilities and cooperation — a language we have never learned: "And they were all filled with the Holy Ghost, and began to speak with other tongues, as the Spirit gave them utterance" (Acts 2:4).

Throughout the book of Acts, whenever persons were baptized in the Holy Spirit, there was a physical, visible evidence of the coming of the Spirit. Wherever this evidence is described, it usually mentions that they spoke with other tongues. James reminds us, "Even so the tongue is a little member, and boasteth great things. Behold, how great a matter a little fire kindleth!" (James 3:5). The Holy Spirit takes the most unruly member of our life and controls it so completely that it can speak a language the mind does not comprehend.

The main feature of being baptized in the Holy Spirit is power for service. Whenever we read of the Spirit "coming upon", "resting upon", "falling upon", or "filling" people, it consistently refers to power for service. It does not refer to the saving work of the Spirit. Remember that the promise of the infilling of the Spirit was given to persons who were already in intimate relationship with Christ. They had already been sent out to preach. They were assured, "Rejoice, because your names are written in heaven" (Luke 10:20). Their moral condition was described by Christ as, "Now ye are clean through the word which I have spoken unto you" (John 15:3). Their relationship to Christ was illustrated by Jesus as, "I am the vine, ye are the branches" (John 15:5). It seems evident, then, that a person may be a disciple of Jesus and yet lack the special endowment of power spoken of in Acts 1:8. More is available!

There is, of course, but one Holy Spirit, but there are many operations of that Spirit. We see this illustrated in electricity. The same electricity that illuminates our houses, operates refrigerators, cooks a meal, becomes heat, and powers our computers, is also the source of energy for hundreds of other accessories. Similarly, the same Holy Spirit regenerates, sanctifies, energizes, illuminates the Word, and imparts special gifts to believers.

Some persons are confused about how to be baptized in the Holy Spirit. I can give you at least five guidelines from the Scriptures. First, repent and turn from sin and iniquity, for the baptism of the Holy Spirit belongs to Christians only. The Spirit of God will not empower a vessel He does not indwell. Sin in the life of a Christian hinders this work of the Spirit. The psalmist reminds us, "If I regard iniquity in my heart, the Lord will not hear me" (Psalm 66:18).

A second step to being baptized in the Spirit is obedience to the Word of God. Jesus Himself coupled obedience with the coming of the Spirit when He said: "If ye love me, keep my commandments. And I will pray the Father, and he shall give you another Comforter, that he may abide with you for ever" (John 14:15-16). We could hardly expect God to entrust the energizing of the Holy Spirit to disobedient sons.

A third action that opens a believer to be baptized in the Spirit is the exercise of faith in God's promises. Jesus repeatedly promised to send the Holy Spirit. We simply need to believe His promise and act on it. The Holy Spirit is a gift of

Christ. We need but reach out in faith to receive it from His hand.

A fourth action that will assist a person in being filled with the Holy Spirit is prayer, for prayer conditions our lives for the Spirit's coming. While prayer does not change God, prayer certainly does change us. One facet of prayer is simply asking for a promised thing. Jesus taught, "Whatsoever ye shall ask in my name, that will I do, that the Father may be glorified in the Son" (John 14:13). Remember that the 120 who were the first to be baptized in the Spirit had been praying in the Upper Room for ten days before the Spirit descended upon them! Although the Holy Spirit has been promised, we are still expected to ask for it. James reminds us, "Ye have not, because ye ask not" (James 4:2).

Still a fifth route to being filled with the Spirit is to have hands laid on you. We read: "Then laid they their hands on them, and they received the Holy Ghost" (Acts 8:17). Consistently through the book of Acts, when the apostles laid hands on believers, they were filled with the Spirit. In modern experience it is often when the minister lays hands on persons while praying for them that the Spirit comes into them in a fresh new way. It is the action of impartation.

The Activity of the Holy Spirit in a Believer

Long before the Holy Spirit seeks to do a work through a believer, He begins to do a work in him or her. He is not too anxious to flow the charasmata (gifts) of God through a believer until the character of God has begun to form in him or her. This inherent nature of Christ that has been made available to believers is often called "The fruit of the Spirit".

Jesus introduced this idea of bearing fruit in His teaching of the vine and the branches. He said: "I am the vine, ye are the branches: He that abideth in me, and I in him, the same bringeth forth much fruit: for without me ye can do nothing" (John 15:5). He is the vine and the believers who have an abiding relationship with Him are the branches. He reminded His disciples that the life was in the vine and its root structure, but that this life bore fruit on the branches. The fruit, then, was not the fruit of the branch, but the fruit of the vine. We bear the nature of Jesus, not our human nature blessed by the Spirit.

Later in the New Testament, we are introduced to this fruit of the Spirit with the words: "The fruit of the Spirit is love, joy, peace, longsuffering, gentleness, goodness, faith, meekness, temperance: against such there is no law" (Galatians 5:22-23). Since Jesus had already introduced the concept of grapes being the fruit that comes from Christ through the believer, we need to accept this passage in Galatians as one fruit with nine different manifestations, just as a bunch of grapes has many separate grapes on the stem.

It is easy to see this fruit described as three triads. The first three "grapes" ripen toward God — love, joy, peace. The fruit of love is simply a result of intimate contact with God whose very nature is love. It is God's love flowing out through us to others. The "grape" of joy is love rejoicing. This grace of God is descriptive of God's kingdom, for the Word tells us, "For the kingdom of God is not meat and drink; but righteousness, and peace, and joy in the Holy Ghost" (Romans 14:17). The third "grape" is peace, another characteristic of God's kingdom that is the result of having experienced the love and joy of God.

These first three fruits come into the life of a believer fully ripened. They characterize our initial responses to God. We respond to God in love, joy, and peace. These are the initial products of the Spirit that others see in our lives, and often, after tasting of our fruit, they are enticed to come to Christ to be able to bear these fruit in their own lives.

The second cluster of fruit to be seen in the person in whom the Holy Spirit indwells, ripens toward his peers. "Longsuffering, gentleness, and goodness" are not directed toward God or ourselves as much as they ripen for the benefit of others. Longsuffering has been defined as patient endurance of injuries inflicted by others. Gentleness has been called love in public. It is a kindly spirit in the midst of harshness. Goodness is love in action. While the other two fruits in this cluster are passive, this grace is very active. It not only forebears, it acts.

The third cluster of fruit is much slower to ripen, for it grows close to the vine and is often shielded from the sun. It is a fruit that ripens to ourselves. It is described as: "Faith, meekness, and temperance". The fruit of faith speaks of fidelity. It is faithfulness in things to ourselves — things that others may never know about. It probably extends from marital fidelity to faithfulness in prayer and Bible reading. It moves these beyond the practice of disciple to the reception of the divine nature.

Similarly, the fruit of meekness ripens in the life of a believer who continues to abide in the vine. Meekness is never to be equated with weakness. It is a gentle answer to a rough question. The Bible's use of the word generally refers to teachableness. It is submission to the will of God. Moses was described as "Very meek, above all the men which were upon the face of the earth" (Numbers 12:3). He was teachable, submitted, and gentle, but none could call him weak.

The fruit of temperance is often the last "grape" in the cluster to fully ripen. I guess that fundamentally it adds nothing to the power of the life, but it becomes the governor that makes that power useful. All excess is dangerous. We are urged to be, "Temperate in all things" (1 Corinthians 9:25), and leaders in the church were required to be temperate (see Titus 1:8; 2:2).

All this fruit is the natural outgrowth of the abiding presence of the Holy Spirit within the life of the believer. Its abundance or scarcity will depend upon our yieldedness to the working of the Holy Spirit in our lives. It is His fruit, not ours, but He is both willing and anxious to transplant it into our being and behavior. It is impossible to bear this heavenly fruit without the abiding presence of the Holy Spirit of God.

Those who know anything about growing grapes know that grapes are propagated by grafting, not by seed. The purpose of bearing grapes, then, is not self-propagation, but for food and for the pleasure of others. Each branch must be grafted into Christ, but the fruit that results out of this uniting is a potential blessing to others. The fruit of the Spirit is produced in the lives of believers to give others a chance to "Taste and see that the Lord is good" (Psalm 34:8). How are others to know of the goodness of Christ if they cannot sample some of it in their relationships with believers?

With a little change of metaphor Jesus said: "He that believeth on me, as the scripture hath said, out of his belly shall flow rivers of living water. (But this spake he of the Spirit, which they that believe on him should receive: for the Holy Ghost was not yet given; because that Jesus was not yet glorified)" (John 7:38-39). Whether it is fruit for eating or water for drinking, each is a free sample of the goodness of our Lord.

The Activity of the Holy Spirit through a Believer

In his letter to the church in Corinth, Paul spoke of some special abilities [Greek: The Charismas] the Holy Spirit would give through Spirit-filled believers. He wrote: "For to one is given by the Spirit the word of wisdom; to another the word of knowledge by the same Spirit; To another faith by the same Spirit; to another the gifts of healing by the same Spirit; To another the working of miracles; to another prophecy; to another discerning of spirits; to another divers kinds of tongues; to another the interpretation of tongues" (1 Corinthians 12:8-10).

We normally refer to these as "the gifts of the Spirit". They are supernatural abilities that function beyond our own natural abilities. It is the person of the Holy Spirit operating at His level of ability rather than blessing us as we function at our limited levels of capability.

These gifts of the Spirit logically divide themselves into three triads of gifts, very much as the fruit of the Spirit is viewed as three groups of three. There are the supernatural enablings to know, to do and to speak.

The supernatural enablings to know are: a word of wisdom, a word of knowledge, and the discerning of spirits. These gifts are not the acceleration of a person's natural wisdom or knowledge; they are supernatural information given to meet a specific need at a precise time.

Then there are the three supernatural enablings to do: the gifts of faith, the gifts of miracles, and the gifts of healing. These charismas are far more than acceleration of natural or studied abilities. They are divine actions operating through the believer.

And finally, there are the supernatural enablings to speak: tongues, interpretation of tongues, and prophecy. Again, these gifts are beyond an acceleration of natural linguistic ability. It is the Spirit speaking through the individual beyond his or her natural abilities.

These gifts do not operate independently of the believer. It is a cooperative effort of the indwelling Spirit and the person who is indwelt. The individual becomes an active participant rather than becoming a robot. The gifts do not function through a trance-induced state. Every faculty of the individual is called upon when these gifts are exercised.

The Bible says that "The manifestation of the Spirit is given to every man to profit withal" (1 Corinthians 12:7). The gifts are not for display, nor are they spiritual measuring rods. They are manifested for the welfare of the Church. They are equally for the benefit of individual members of the Church, and they are also for the benefit of the world. Most importantly, the gifts of the Spirit are for the glory of God. This is the ultimate object. Their operation proves the presence of God, establishes the reality of God, and demonstrates the mercy and compassion of God.

These gifts are resident in the Holy Spirit as certainly as the fruit is the Spirit's fruit. The Word says: "Now there are diversities of gifts, but the same Spirit. And there are differences of administrations, but the same Lord. And there are diversities of operations, but it is the same God which worketh all in all" (1 Corinthians 12:4-6).

It is probably an error for any believer to brag that he or she has "the gift of ..." The indwelt person has the presence of the Holy Spirit and the Spirit has the gifts. Although some persons are more comfortable allowing the Spirit to function one gift more than another, this is an action of the faith of the individual far more than the possession of the gift.

It is proper that we want the operation of these spiritual gifts. Paul said, "But covet earnestly the best gifts: and yet shew I unto you a more excellent way" (1 Corinthians 12:31). The Greek word for covet means to desire earnestly; to long for with a passion. It seems that this is one route into the operation of the gifts. The second route is superior, because the "more excellent way" Paul speaks of is love, for the thirteenth chapter of 1 Corinthians is the chapter on love. Deep love for God and compassionate love for one another will open us to the ministry of the Spirit through our lives to others. It is obvious that prayer releases both of these channels, for both our strong desires and our love will cause us to ask the Father for the manifestation of the Spirit's power through our lives.

The Continuing Work of the Spirit

While the initial empowering of the Holy Spirit is seen as an experience, the Bible speaks of it as a continuing experience. It needs to be entered repeatedly. Paul exhorted the believers, "Be filled with the Spirit" (Ephesians 5:18). The Greek calls for a continuous action. Some versions of the New Testament translate this verse: "Keep being filled with the Spirit". Our human capacity is so small we need to be filled repeatedly. Our ability to yield to the Spirit grows through use.

The disciples learned the value of being refilled with the Holy Spirit. After the first persecution, and upon the release of the apostles from prison, we see them praying until there is a repeat of the initial experience of Acts 2:1-4. More than once we see them praying for a fresh outpouring — a renewed experience of the Holy Spirit.

After every ministry of the Spirit through us, there is a need for a fresh anointing. Energy expended must be renewed or we will be powerless. Persecution, pressure, spiritual battles, and spiritual ministries use up or deplete, the anointing. It is much like using a flashlight. At some point the batteries must be recharged or replaced. It is not that the Holy Spirit has been driven from our lives. It is that we need a renewing or refreshing from Him, just as the body needs the renewing of food and sleep.

Jesus speaks of the work of the Holy Spirit as "rivers of living water" (John 7:38). This implies a constant intake and outflow. If we do not have an inflow to balance the outflow, we will be depleted and dry. I live in Phoenix, Arizona, where we have the Salt River whose only source of water is rainfall. During most of the year it is a dry river bed. However, during a rainstorm it can become a raging torrent that washes out bridges. Some Christians flow only when there is a special rain of God's Spirit, but God's desire is that we have a constant source of the Spirit flowing through our lives so that we will never be dry river beds. We need to keep being filled.

The Compensations of a Spirit-filled Life

It would take a complete book to list the benefits of being filled with the Holy Spirit, but let me list some of the most obvious advantages. The Spirit-filled life is an abundant life. Jesus promised, "I am come that they might have life, and that they might have it more abundantly" (John 10:10). This abundant, full, satisfying life of Christ flows to us through the abiding presence of the Spirit of Christ. When Christ holds undisputed possession of us, He gives us a life that is open, strong, and filled with harmony. It is a life that shines forth and transmits itself to others. It is in complete contrast to the narrow, weak, unprogressive, pitiful, and sick life we lived before the Holy Spirit took residence in us.

I have also observed that the Spirit-filled life makes it possible to live a holy life. When He is dominant in our lives the Spirit frees us from the law of sin and death and brings us into true Christian liberty. He breaks the chains of sin asunder, brings freedom from slavery, and then nurtures within us spiritual fruit and spiritual gifts.

The Spirit-filled life becomes a life of power. Jesus said, "But ye shall receive power, after that the Holy Ghost is come upon you: and ye shall be witnesses unto me both in Jerusalem, and in all Judaea, and in Samaria, and unto the uttermost part of the earth" (Acts 1:8). This power is not only for ministerial success, but enables us to face trial and even martyrdom. Stephen, full of the Holy Spirit, died victoriously while praying for his executioners.

This Spirit-filled life is also a life of thanksgiving and praise. It is striking that Paul, following an exhortation to the Ephesians to "Be filled with the Spirit" added, "Speaking to yourselves in psalms and hymns and spiritual songs, singing and making melody in your heart to the Lord" (Ephesians 5:18-19). It does not come naturally to our human spirit to praise God; to thank Him for all things. However, when the Holy Spirit makes His home in our spirits, we find ourselves triumphing over difficulties in life with hymns and grateful worship. The Holy Spirit enables us to see the victory of God in all circumstances of life, and He empowers us to praise God in the midst of everything — positive or negative.

I have experienced that the indwelling of the Holy Spirit brings me into a life of joy and happiness. In speaking of the Spirit, Jesus told the woman at Jacob's well: "But whosoever drinketh of the water that I shall give him shall never thirst; but the water that I shall give him shall be in him a well of water springing up into everlasting life" (John 4:14). This "springing up" is the enthusiasm of joy and the pleasure of happiness. I have sought joy in possessions, position, and plenty of money, but the greatest joy I have ever experienced has been the joy of the Spirit as He abides in my spirit.

Believers who will allow the Holy Spirit to indwell their lives will also experience a higher level of continual peace than they have ever known before. There is the peace of a higher relationship with God through the presence of His Spirit.

There is the further peace of knowing that God accepts personal responsibility for the person He indwells with His Spirit.

I am convinced that there is no higher way to live life here on this earth other than to be filled with the Holy Spirit of God. It is the fulfillment of the promise of the Proverbs, "The blessing of the LORD, it maketh rich, and he addeth no sorrow with it" (Proverbs 10:22). At times this blessing is so generous that we need Christian ceremony to help us release it.

Chapter 5

The Basics of Christian Ceremony

It may be disturbing to some to speak of ceremony, especially if they prefer a free-form style of worship. But whether we choose to admit it or not, we all have our rituals. Some are just more polished in the way they handle their liturgy. Even spontaneous forms of public worship have their ceremonies. The Sunday service is usually opened about the same way each week, and the order of the service doesn't vary much, although there is always the liberty for modification, extension, or introduction of something new.

The true purpose of ceremony is to preserve a continuity with the past while extending a celebration for the present. To be totally disconnected from our past is to become an infant in our present. Our only hope of growth in any area of life is to learn from the past and grow into our future. The harmonizing of our past experiences with our present training is often some form of ceremony.

It is difficult to do things as a united group without some form of structure, whether it is worshiping together, playing baseball, or even a barbecue in the parking lot. The book of Judges tells us that the chaotic condition of Israel was because, "There was no king in Israel, and every man did that which was right in his own eyes" (Judges 17:6). Someone has to be the leader or a group soon becomes a mob.

Ultimately we look to the Lord as the leader of the church, but He works through human instruments. A conscientious pastor tries to offer leadership to the church that is consistent to what he feels the Holy Spirit wants for each service. There are some things God consistently wants from His people when they gather together. This means, of course, that there will be some repetition from service to service and when we repeat an action, it easily becomes a ceremony or a ritual.

There is nothing wrong with a ritual that expresses life. It is when the ritual is a substitute for life that it becomes useless. For instance, standing as an act of honor and respect for the Lord can become little more than conforming to function — everyone is doing it. Raising our hands in worship may be a release of praise or a sign of joyful submission to God, or it can become a religious action that we do in response to peer pressure.

We cannot throw out form and ritual just because it can be followed without personal meaning. We need to learn why the congregation is being led into a form of worship and join it from our heart.

Christians should not always be defending their faith; they also need to celebrate it. God certainly understands this. The Hebrews in the wilderness were given extremely detailed rules for daily behavior and worship of God. These were tied to their faith in God, but with them God provided for seven yearly feasts. Three of these were compulsory — every Hebrew male had to attend under threat of separation from the family of Israel.

Although these feasts generally began with sacrifices for past sins, they quickly evolved into joyous family reunions, feasts, and song and dance expressions of their enjoyment of God and of life. God gave these people far more instructions for feasting than for fasting. Through the ceremonies of these feasts, God gave a framework that directed the people to enjoy their God, their nation, their families, and themselves. Since God is unchangeable, He must still approve of whatever ceremonies will release our joyful response to life.

Most evangelical and Pentecostal churches observe seven ceremonies that enable the congregation of believers to respond to God and one another in sufficient variety as to fulfill the major experiences in their lives. These ceremonies or rituals are:

1. Water Baptism
2. The Lord's Supper
3. The Marriage Service
4. Baby Dedications
5. Prayer for Needs
6. Public Worship
7. Funerals

Perhaps these ceremonies can have increased meaning if I take a few pages to explain to you what they mean.

The Ceremony Of Water Baptism — Commencement

Even a person entering a service organization has an initiation. There is some form of public ceremony that states "He is one of us." Water baptism is an initiation into the Body of Christ. It has a far deeper meaning than mere church membership, for it is scripturally commanded, Biblically illustrated, and historically consistent. In the Old Testament it was part of the proselyte ceremony that enabled a Gentile to enter Judaism. It signified the washing away of the old religion and rising into the new. The proselyte entered into a new family and embraced the covenants of God.

In the New Testament, we do not build Christian fellowship on creed; but on Christ. It is not common "likes" that bring us together, but a common life. We are not bound by friendship, but by family. We don't even pick and choose those with whom we fellowship; we accept those whom God has chosen and learn to love them.

Being a Christian is not based on a change of mind; it is based upon a change of heart and inner life. Jesus spoke of it as being "born again" (John 3:7). No other descriptive term explains it better. Salvation is a drastic and radical change produced by the life of Christ in the new convert. Much as birth is a passing from one form of life in the womb to another form of life outside of it, conversion is a birth of a person's spirit into a totally new realm. Both the natural and the spiritual birth processes involve passing from the water.

The natural infant passes through the water in the mother's placenta to the air of the birthing room. Similarly, the spiritual infant passes through the waters of baptism. In the Old Testament after Moses led Israel out of Egypt (a type of our salvation), this new nation passed through the Red Sea. The New Testament explains: "[They] were all baptized unto Moses in the cloud and in the sea" (1 Corinthians 10:2). Consistently the Bible puts conversion and water baptism together. It is not the water experience that produces the conversion, but the conversion requires the outward confession of the inward change.

This is not baptismal regeneration, that is, being saved by the act of water baptism. Still we must acknowledge that the Bible puts conversion and water baptism together like bread and butter. They belong together. The one is substance; the other is demonstration. Conversion is God's inner work; water baptism is man's outer demonstration of that inner work.

Before Jesus entered His public ministry He went "From Galilee to Jordan unto John, to be baptized of him" (Matthew 3:13). When John first refused, saying that he needed to be baptized by Jesus, the Lord explained that this request was an act of obedience, so John accommodated Jesus. If the sinless Jesus obeyed the Word by submitting to water baptism, why do we transformed sinners find this act of obedience so distasteful and difficult?

On the day of Pentecost, Peter set the tone that the Church followed for succeeding generations when he said: "Repent, and be baptized every one of you in the name of Jesus Christ for the remission of sins, and ye shall receive the gift of the Holy Ghost" (Acts 2:38). After his sermon, his altar call produced 3,000 conversions, and we read, "Then they that gladly received his word were baptized: and the same day there were added unto them about three thousand souls" (Acts 2:41). That must have been some baptismal service!

When Philip entered the chariot of the Ethiopian eunuch and taught Christ to him, faith changed his heart and he exclaimed to Philip: "See, here is water; what doth hinder me to be baptized?" (Acts 8:36). They stopped the chariot and Philip baptized him. The conversion and baptism were almost simultaneous.

Similarly Peter obediently went to the house of Cornelius and preached Jesus to his household. When the Holy Spirit fell on them, to the amazement of both Peter and those who had accompanied him to Caesarea, Peter's immediate response was: "Can any man forbid water, that these should not be baptized, which have received the Holy Ghost as well as we? And he commanded them to be baptized in the name of the Lord. Then prayed they him to tarry certain days" (Acts 10:47-48).

Water baptism is an obedient response to a clear command in the Bible. It is the initiation ceremony into the family of God. In the New Testament the ritual was clearly immersion. They went "down into the water" and "came up out of the water". The convenience of sprinkling does not answer either of these actions.

Most Evangelical, Charismatic, and Pentecostal churches practice full immersion baptisms. Many churches have built baptismal tanks in their sanctuaries to make this more convenient. In the days of my father's ministry, I remember him taking persons to the ocean and rivers. In warm climates some groups use swimming pools as baptismal tanks. The people gather at someone's swimming pool and have a beautiful worship service as they watch persons allow their old life to be symbolically buried and rise to a newness of life in Christ Jesus. Where we are baptized is far less important than that we are baptized. God commands it; we must submit to it.

Most ministers do not preach that it is impossible to be saved if a person has not been water baptized, for the baptism is subsequent to that salvation, not the producer of it. We have no record of the thief on the cross being baptized, but Jesus assured him that "Today shalt thou be with me in paradise"

(Luke 23:43). Still, the disobedience of refusing water baptism puts the believer in a dangerous spiritual condition.

Even satan views water baptism as the final loss of a person. In India a person may attend a Christian school or church, and he or she may become an active participant in either program, without penalty. But once he or she submits to water baptism, each is cut off from their families and the government removes their names from the registration rolls. Technically, they no longer exist. The devil knows God's initiation rites better than we do. He also knows the rite of commemoration, and he hates it.

The Lord's Supper — Commemoration

Just before Jesus went to the Garden where He would be arrested and quickly led through a mock trial and a hasty crucifixion, He instituted what we call *The Lord's Supper*. Some prefer to call it *The Eucharist*. After Jesus and His disciples had eaten their meal, Jesus broke bread and shared it, saying that this was His body that was being broken for them. He also shared the wine with them, calling it His blood that was shed for the remission of sins (See Matthew 26:26-29).

Lest they mistakenly think this was a one time event, He added, "This is my body which is given for you: this do in remembrance of me" (Luke 22:19). He set no schedule for such observances, but the early church observed it daily. Later this observance was simply part of all public worship services. In our present day, some groups of believers observe it every Sunday morning, some but once a month, and others are very sporadic in obeying this command of Christ.

That Jesus instituted this ceremony on the Jewish Passover is more than accidental or incidental. He was giving His followers a ritual of commemoration very similar to the Jewish Passover that applauded their deliverance from Egypt.

Both ceremonies were commanded, constructive, commemorative, and celebrative. In the first passover, the purpose of eating was twofold: First, it afforded complete identification with the victim — the lamb. Second, it offered them strength for the coming journey. God is practical! It's time we were, too.

Similarly, Christians are instructed to eat of Christ, our "Paschal Lamb". Jesus told the Jewish leaders of His day, "Verily, verily, I say unto you, Except ye eat the flesh of the Son of man, and drink his blood, ye have no life in you. Whoso eateth my flesh, and drinketh my blood, hath eternal life; and I will raise him up at the last day. For my flesh is meat indeed, and my blood is drink indeed. He that eateth my flesh, and drinketh my blood, dwelleth in me, and I in him" (John 6:53-56).

As difficult as this passage is to interpret, it does teach that Jesus is the source of strength for our day to day living. Jesus called Himself the manna that Israel ate in the wilderness (see John 6:51). Later in the New Testament we read: "For we are made partakers of Christ, if we hold the beginning of our confidence stedfast unto the end" (Hebrews 3:14). Living the Christian life without the indwelling of Christ is not difficult — it is impossible. It is "Christ in you, the hope of glory" (Colossians 1:27).

The Passover and the Lord's Supper are equally commemorative. Commemorations are opportunities for review, and review is the first law of learning. It is one thing to be introduced to truth; it is another to rehearse, review, and reexamine that lesson until it is indelibly seated in our memories.

Commemorative review becomes an excellent way to introduce truth to another generation. God said through Moses: "Thou shalt shew thy son in that day, saying, This is done because of that which the LORD did unto me when I came forth out of Egypt" (Exodus 13:8). Each generation needs to personally experience the truth that so deeply affected preceding generations. Our children need to experience the power in the blood of Jesus.

Commemorations are also opportunities for renewal. Past experience can become impotent to meet present problems unless they are renewed. Even taking marriage vows a second time can renew a marriage. Commemorations are not duplications of the original event. We cannot relive life, but we can do things that renew the preciousness of what we lived.

The Feast of Passover was not identical with the first passover, nor is the Lord's Supper a reenactment of the crucifixion. Both, however, are powerful reminders of a divine provision and work of the blood of Jesus.

The Passover and the Lord's Supper are deliberate celebrations. At the Passover Feast, while the lambs were being slaughtered and the blood thrown at the base of the altar, the Levities led the people in hymns of praise. They sang the Hallel, the words of which were Psalms 113-118. Every first line of a Psalm was repeated by the people. To each of the other lines they responded by saying, "Hallelujah" or "Praise ye the Lord".

Passover was a joyous time in spite of the slaughter, blood pouring, and blood stained garments of the sacrificers. It may seem crude and primitive to us, but it was God's provision for them. They rejoiced in their deliverance; past and present. To many people, it was a repeated experience, and for others it was brand new. For all, it was joyous!

There was also joy at the institution of the Lord's Supper. It is true that Judas left on his mission of betrayal, and it is equally true that Peter did his bragging about protecting Jesus. But after Jesus proclaimed the truth about His death and resurrection, He led the disciples in singing a hymn — probably the Hallel. It was a hymn proclaiming victory.

Similarly, the Lord's Supper should be observed with rejoicing and gladness. It should not become a funeral. It is a time of celebration and rejoicing. "The blood of Jesus Christ his Son cleanseth us from all sin" (1 John 1:7). Why wouldn't we celebrate?

Charismatics and Pentecostals do not observe a "closed communion" that restricts participation to members of the local congregation. All who have received Jesus Christ as their personal Savior are welcome to share in the commemoration of the death, burial, and resurrection of the Lord.

The Ceremony Of Marriage — Commitment

Christians need to believe firmly in the time-honored celebration of marriage, especially while we live in a generation that belittles the commitment of marriage. From Genesis through Revelation, the Bible speaks of the union of a man and woman in the bonds of marriage as a holy, beautiful, and necessary provision of life.

God has sanctified marriage with His presence from the beginning of time until the present. In the Garden of Eden "The LORD God said, It is not good that the man should be alone; I will make him an help meet for him" (Genesis 2:18). The end of the Bible speaks of the Lamb's bride or wife (Revelation 21:9). God begins His book with a wedding and ends it with one. It is also fitting that the first miracle Christ performed was at the wedding at Cana of Galilee (see John 2).

We are very aware that in today's humanistic society marriages need not be solemnized in the church. Some merely use a justice of the peace, while others want to make a bazaar action of it. Almost daily our newspapers show weddings conducted in various places; while falling in parachutes, riding in boats, being on horseback, etc. I guess according to your god, be it unto you.

Christians who intend to live their wedded years in harmony with Bible principles should be married in the church. It is my personal position that the pastor should have an opportunity to do some pre-marriage counseling with every couple that plans to marry in the church. It is dangerous to try to blend two different lives without some guidance and scriptural foundations. It is not unusual for couples to allow such sessions to bring them to a personal acquaintance with Jesus Christ. While this is not the basic purpose of the sessions, it is sometimes a beautiful by- product.

During this counsel session with couples before marriage, it is wise to discuss with them the five basics that are necessary in a marriage:

93

1. Communication
2. God Concepts
3. Family Heritages
4. Money
5. Sex

A marriage can survive with compatibility in any three of the five, but it would be like sitting on a three-legged stool. You do it very carefully. You cannot, however, sit on a two-legged chair.

A marriage is already headed for trouble if there is not good communication between the partners entering the agreement. There will be so many differences to reconcile, so many decisions to be made, and so many compromises to make that without communication skills, there is a tremendous potential for mounting tension.

Couples need to take a good look at what planning the wedding may have done to them. It is a prelude to the future. If they cannot talk their way through the ceremony, it is unlikely they will talk their way through the marriage. Sometimes they simply need some guidance in communication skills. Having a totally silent partner in the marriage may seem to make things work smoothly, but it usually causes a repression of emotion that will eventually explode — often in a non-issue situation.

For a couple to learn to pray together is a good way of learning to communicate with one another. They also need to have a set time to discuss whatever is on their minds without repercussion. Couples need to learn the rules for argument and disagreement. No married couple agrees on everything. They have to learn to disagree without becoming disagreeable.

The second foundation for marriage is the couple's God concepts. A worshiper of Jesus is going to be hopelessly at conflict in spiritual matters if he or she marries a Buddhist. While it is advantageous for the couples to come from the same religious heritage, it is not absolutely necessary. Still, they need to have similar ideas of God or they are headed for division in their marriage. It is not by accident that the Bible commands: "Be ye not unequally yoked together with unbelievers: for what fellowship hath righteousness with unrighteousness? and what communion hath light with darkness?" (2 Corinthians 6:14).

The third foundation for marriage that I discuss with a couple seeking to be married in the church is family heritages. Our backgrounds deeply color our foregrounds. While some change is possible, we fundamentally live similar to the way we have been raised. Ideas of child raising come from the way our parents reared us. Attitudes toward possessions, use of our time, the way we view the opposite sex, and the respect or lack of respect the partners will have for one another come basically out of their family heritages. The more they are alike, the greater chance there is for a happy marriage. Where these heritages are vastly different, the couple must learn to do some big-time adapting or learn to live in a continual civil war.

It is wise to point out that each is leaving the home of his or her parents to build their own family heritage. Neither partner should allow the parents to unduly influence this new family unit.

The fourth foundation for marriage is money. It is not the abundance or lack of money that matters. It is the couple's philosophies of handling finances. Those concepts need to be similar, for when "sister spend-it-all" marries "mister thrifty", we can expect sparks to fly. It is healthy for the couple to talk seriously about who will handle the finances, how they will be distributed, and what their common goals are for their finances in the coming year. They need to see God's provision of the tithe, for that is His rent for our time on the earth.

The fifth fundamental in marriage that needs to be discussed with the engaged couple is sexual attitudes. Although sex is a very private issue, it is dangerous to wait until after marriage to discuss it. Since the biggest sex organ in our bodies is the mind, someone needs to point them to a similar mental image that will form a foundation for their sexual fulfillment through the years.

Often a good book on marriage can be an on going instruction book to the young couple. Usually they are so excited about the coming event that they hear only part of what is being said in the counseling session. The book can remind them and further reveal some of the mysteries of marriage.

God intends marriage to be a lifetime commitment. While the Bible does not classify divorce as an unpardonable sin, it should be considered a non-option by those entering into marriage. Running away is a poor answer to the problems marriage can impose upon a couple. God has made a provision to help us through the difficult times of adjusting to our partners, and Christian couples should seek direction rather than divorce.

In a day when "open marriage" is being more readily accepted, we must raise the question, "If marriage is wedlock, how can it be open?" God's plan in Christian marriage is to so blend a man and woman into a working team that there is no space for a third party to get between them.

Something as sacred as plans for a man and woman to spend the rest of their lives together while raising children in their own image, needs the sanctity and strength of the church. Marriage is the most demanding relationship we will ever enter. It needs not only the initial blessing of the church; it needs the continuing blessing, instruction, counsel, and comfort that the church can give to it. Marriage counseling before the wedding often needs follow up counseling for the rest of the marriage.

When members of a church get married, it is a joy for the congregation to share in their ceremony, help them establish their home with gifts, and continue to encourage and share in their marital growth. The celebration of marriage is one of the most joyful ceremonies of the church. Without them there would be no need for baby dedications.

Baby Dedications — Consecration

That night when the final plague came upon Egypt, God had spoken through Moses, "For I will pass through the land of Egypt this night, and will smite all the firstborn in the land of Egypt, both man and beast; and against all the gods of Egypt I will execute judgment: I am the LORD" (Exodus 12:12). This included the Hebrews, unless their firstborn was in a house with the sign of the blood on the door. These that were spared were considered the property of Jehovah for He said: "Sanctify unto me all the firstborn" (Exodus 13:2). After they came to Mount Sinai where God gave them the Law, God declared: "The firstborn of thy sons shalt thou give unto me" and "All the firstborn of thy sons thou shalt redeem" (Exodus 22:29; 34:20).

God considered these firstborn children His, but it was impractical for these sons to be literally brought to the Tabernacle to be raised, such as Samuel was much later. Instead, God made a double provision. The children could be redeemed — bought back — from God's service, and in their place God chose the entire tribe of Levi to be servants at the Tabernacle (and later the Temple).

To further underscore this sense that the children belonged to God, the law provided that they be presented at the Tabernacle or Temple for dedication, at which time the males would be circumcised. This provision of the law was really a codifying of a nearly universal practice. The Egyptians presented their children to the gods of the land. Later when Israel went into the promised land, they found the inhabitants well established in this practice. Repeatedly through the prophets, God rebuked Israel for dedicating their children to Molech and Baal. Often this dedication involved burning the children alive as a sacrifice to Molech.

Mary and Joseph fulfilled this command of the Law by bringing Jesus for dedication in the Temple. Luke records this event: "When the days of her purification according to the law of Moses were accomplished, they brought him to Jerusalem, to present him to the Lord; (As it is written in the law of the

Lord, Every male that openeth the womb shall be called holy to the Lord;) And to offer a sacrifice according to that which is said in the law of the Lord, A pair of turtledoves, or two young pigeons" (Luke 2:22-24). It was then that Simeon, a prophet, and Anna, a prophetess, blessed Jesus and Mary.

It is interesting that when the child was presented to God, God blessed the child and parents with a special word of comfort and guidance for His raising. This still happens today. There is often a transference of a special blessing and wisdom when parents present a child to the Lord.

The mystery of life is never more vivid than at the birth of a child — especially the first one. When a husband and wife stand before the minister of the Lord with their baby in their arms and dare to pass that baby to the minister to present it to God on their behalf, they are expressing their awe and wonder at the miracle of birth. Sensing that life can come only from God, they want to thank God and offer back to Him what He has given to them.

Charismatics, Pentecostals, and most Evangelical churches do not baptize babies, for they feel that water baptism must be preceded by conversion. They do, however, dedicate or present babies to the Lord. It is a consecration of God's gift, and it becomes a time of parental consecration to raise their child to serve the Lord.

One of the happy by-products of baby dedications is the sharing of the joy of life with the church family. All parents vicariously share in the occasion as they remember the gift of life that God gave to them some years earlier. It is like the moment when the wife lays the newborn baby in the arms of the father, or he hands his child to the new mother. It is a visible and emotional extension of family life. Everyone, from the children to the grandparents, enjoys the ceremony of baby dedications.

The Ceremony Of Prayer For Needs — Compassion

Some congregations make a break in the worship service to invite those with needs to come forward for prayer. The congregation silently prays or sings while the pastor and his co-laborers briefly ask the nature of the need and then pray with the individual. Sometimes the need is for physical healing, but not always. Life is full of complexities and problems that are beyond a person's ability to handle the situation by themselves. They need the help and faith of others to pray them to victory.

The New Testament authority for congregational prayer for the needs of those attending public worship is: "Is any among you afflicted? let him pray. Is any merry? let him sing psalms. Is any sick among you? let him call for the elders of the church; and let them pray over him, anointing him with oil in the name of the Lord: And the prayer of faith shall save the sick, and the Lord shall raise him up; and if he have committed sins, they shall be forgiven him" (James 5:13-15). This passage lists three areas of needs the church should pray over:

1. Afflictions — "Is any among you afflicted?"
2. Illness — "Is any sick among you?"
3. Iniquity — "Sins shall be forgiven him."

There are many forms of affliction. Some are physical, some are emotional, others are mental. Life is not all pleasant; sometimes it isn't even fair. Financial crises arise. Homes break up. Children go astray. Jobs are forfeited and change is fostered upon us. These and many other similar afflictions, are threatening to our security, our inner peace, and even our ability to cope with life.

Bearing these afflictions or burdens alone can be a load far too heavy for some persons to bear. One asset of being related to a church family is having someone to share these ordeals with us. This is not only a privilege of the church family, it is a command of God. The Bible tells us: "We then that are strong ought to bear the infirmities of the weak, and not to please ourselves" (Romans 15:1). If this seems optional for you, look at this verse: "Bear ye one another's burdens, and so fulfil the law of Christ" (Galatians 6:2).

If there were no ceremony for praying for needs, how would the congregation know of a member's situation? Just how would they go about expressing concern or offering prayer? This simple ceremony of praying for the afflicted is a double blessing. It gives the non-afflicted an opportunity to reach compassionately to those who are, and it lets the distressed individuals renew their hope, receive a blessing, and often find a solution to their need. It is another of God's win/win situations.

Not only does this ceremony allow the congregation to obey the Bible in sharing care and compassion with others, but it also allows the afflicted persons to obey the instruction of the Bible that says: "Be careful for nothing; but in every thing by prayer and supplication with thanksgiving let your requests be made known unto God" (Philippians 4:6). The word "careful" in this verse actually means anxious. Rather than live in the limiting power of anxiety, God urges us to let our requests be known to God (directly or indirectly through the prayers of others) that God can intervene and bring a victory into the life.

This same ceremony allows those with physical problems to ask the elders of the church to anoint them with oil and pray the prayer of faith over them. Repeatedly this simple obedience to God's Word has brought glorious healing to them.

James assures us that in the midst of this ceremony designed to help the afflicted and heal the sick, God would deal with iniquity and sin. There are times when a person's problems or sickness is the direct result of sin. In bringing an answer to their lives, God deals conclusively with that sin. Other times the problem is sin related, but when persons receive a touch of God's presence, they often choose to release the sin in their lives and accept God's cleansing. Some persons need this concerned touch and prayer of another to find their way out of their negative situations into the positive presence of the Lord.

We find a strong precedent for this ceremony in the ministry of Jesus. In several portions of the Gospels we read: "Jesus went forth, and saw a great multitude, and was moved with compassion toward them, and he healed their sick" (Matthew 14:14). Christian compassion is part of the Christ-life.

This ceremony can be exercised in several different ways. We can call the needy forward to the altar. Sometimes, however, we can merely have them raise their hands and persons seated near them can lay hands on them right where they are standing. This frequently gives persons, who would hesitate coming forward to pray for others, a chance to release their compassion and faith without leaving their pew.

Besides this, many congregations conduct special prayer meetings where they pray unitedly for needs that have been written out as prayer requests. Most of them also accept vocal requests. It is a way of saying that they are concerned enough to lift their faith to petition God for a change in the circumstances of another person.

Other groups have a prayer chain that operates over the telephone. When an emergency arises, the afflicted person can call the church office during office hours and that need will be passed on to praying persons by phone contact. No needy person need wait for a public service to share his or her burden and receive prayer help. This sensitive praying for others can be one form of worship, for all prayer should be a renewed contact with God.

The Ceremony Of Public Worship

While worship is really a private involvement with a person and his or her God, the united worship in a public gathering needs some ceremony to give form and direction to it. Although we urge each individual to reach worshipfully toward God, it is important that some guidance be offered to the congregation to avoid confusion. If having worship leaders seems too ritualistic for some persons, imagine the chaos Sunday morning if each person sang the song of his or her choice.

Although we commonly accept a vocal freedom during praise, when each person gives vocal expression to his or her heartfelt thanksgiving, the ceremony of the pastoral prayer gives a common message of expression to God. While this prayer is being offered from the pulpit, our thoughts can flow with it, our faith can be expressed in it, and we can give an honest "Amen!" at its end. It enables the entire congregation to join in a united prayer in a way that would otherwise be close to impossible.

Worship is more than prayer and praise. Giving is equally an act of obedient worship. I know that it is popular for skeptics to charge the church with being too money oriented — always asking for offerings. Yet these same persons willingly pay from $50 to $200 for tickets to the sporting events of their choice. Somehow they forget that the services of the church call for personnel, buildings, and equipment.

From the days of Abraham until the present, God has consistently financed His program on earth through the tithe He requires of believers. It is not that He needs the money. We need it to make it more convenient for us to gather in worship, and we need to learn to give. God ended the Old Testament with the conditional promise: "Bring ye all the tithes into the storehouse, that there may be meat in mine house, and prove me now herewith, saith the LORD of hosts, if I will not open you the windows of heaven, and pour you out a blessing, that there shall not be room enough to receive it" (Malachi 3:10). It is the Old Testament version of the words of Jesus: "Give, and it shall be given unto you; good measure, pressed down, and shaken together, and running over, shall men give into your bosom. For with the same measure that ye mete withal it shall be measured to you again" (Luke 6:38).

The tithe is God's rent on His earth. We owe it to Him. It is an act of His mercy that He prefers we bring it to Him instead of Him having to collect it. Since God makes giving an act of worship, we need to incorporate it in our worship ceremony.

For logistic reasons, passing the offering plates while singing unto the Lord is better than having individuals walk to the front during various segments of worship to hand their tithe to the pastor. By having the ceremony of receiving the offering, we provide a convenient and private opportunity for persons to give unto the Lord what is due His name.

Even the preaching of God's Word takes on some aspect of ceremony. While the necessary information could be passed out in printed form or handled by question and answer sessions, there is a dynamic blessing in preaching what God has ordained. The Bible reminds us, "It pleased God by the foolishness of preaching to save them that believe" (1 Corinthians 1:21). If preaching pleases God, it should certainly please us. Preaching informs, instructs, and inspires us. Some church congregations give more place to ritual than to preaching, but most dynamic churches are very proclamation oriented. Many congregations give at least half their worship sessions to the preaching of the Book. It is a ceremony oriented to the daily life of believers. Preaching prepares believers for their future life.

The Ceremony Of Funerals — Completion

During our lifetime we will avoid, postpone, or turn over to others many appointments, but there is one inescapable assignment none of us will escape. The Bible says, "It is appointed unto men once to die, but after this the judgment" (Hebrews 9:27). Death is even more certain than taxes.

We know that death is as much a part of the life cycle as birth. It is all around us. Some have said that we enter the world with joy and depart from it in sorrow, but this is not necessarily true. We enter the world through the pain of another, and our parting causes pain to others, but both experiences are a passing from one realm into another.

Just as the baby finds passing from the comfort and security of its mother's womb traumatic, so leaving the human body to step into another world is also distressful. Happy is the person who has prepared himself or herself for this passing before the time to die arrives.

In the final struggle with the grim reaper, it is comforting to know that the estate has been cared for, the funeral arrangements have been made and, perhaps, even prepaid, and the loved ones we leave behind know all that they need to know to care for the details of life that have been left undone. Also, it is a little late, but not impossible, to make peace with God while fighting the intrusion of death to the body.

When the last breath has been taken, attention is turned from the dying to those who remain. They must make a series of adjustments that are very difficult. It is likely that those close to the deceased will go through four distinct seasons of adjustments: denial, grief, anger, and acceptance.

First there will be denial of what has happened. It may be viewed as a great dream, and they hope to awaken soon. "This didn't really happen" is the mind-set.

Once they realize that the deceased loved one will not return, grief sets in. It is nothing to be ashamed of; it is part of the process of handling this deepest of wounds that come to our lives. Tears will be close to the surface, and the mind can think of nothing other than the great loss.

When grief has run its course, anger often replaces it. "How dare he (or she) do this to me", is the feeling. Very frequently Christians vent this anger at God; making Him responsible for the death of the loved one and the pain this has caused in others.

Eventually these negative emotions will be replaced with acceptance of this turn in life. Not until the death is fully accepted emotionally can a person really pick up his or her life and go on with it.

The law does not demand a funeral, and many persons are buried without one. It is not likely that the deceased one cares one way or the other, for the purpose of the funeral is not for the dead, but for the living. It is a ceremony that allows loved ones to gather for mutual comfort and strength, and it affords them a channel for saying goodbye to the deceased.

In some communities it is quite customary to have a wake where the mourners gather in the funeral parlor to view the deceased before the funeral. This gives the pastor a chance to meet with the family at this time and explain five things to them.

First, the family needs to admit that this day is a black day for them. Clouds have blocked out the sunshine. It is a time to mourn, weep, and express their loss. This will carry into tomorrow during the funeral ceremony, but after the body is buried and the family gets together to talk about better days, there will come a temptation to laugh at some memory. They need not feel guilty about laughing on the day of the funeral. Life is for the living, and we must pick up the pieces and go on. It is likely the person in the casket would want us to find something amusing on this day of inner tension.

Second, someone needs to tell them that the days following the funeral will be brighter days, but the family will need one another, for anniversaries (birthdays, wedding anniversaries, Christmas, etc.) will bring a stabbing pain that can best be healed by the family. First anniversaries will be the worst. Send cards. Call on the phone. Undergird one another until the wound has fully healed.

Third, they need to be told that if the person in the casket has left any of them with debt, either emotional or financial, to go to the casket and say, "I forgive you." Don't carry emotional wounds or grudges from the graveyard.

Fourth, they need to be reminded that if they've been blessed through an inheritance left by the deceased, to not feel guilty in using it. It was his or her love that made it available to them. Use it wisely, but totally without remorse.

Fifth, someone should remind them that they may well need the strength and guidance of a pastor for the early months following a funeral. The surviving family members need to get close to their pastor during these months of adjustment.

At the funeral of a believer, my pastor, Jim Cornwall, likes to tell the gathered loved ones, "We who are candidates for heaven came to celebrate the life of one who is a resident of heaven. He (she) cannot come to us, but we can go to him (her)."

Either at the wake or at the conclusion of the funeral, my pastor encourages the close family members to touch the corpse, or at least the casket, and say goodbye. It helps them realize that he or she is not there and will not be coming back. It is a step toward facing the reality of death.

From birth to death, ceremonies become channels to celebrate different stages in the life cycle. Much as we have the ceremony of baby dedications to consecrate entrance into this world, and we offer the ceremony of water baptism to celebrate the commencement of the Christian life, so we offer the ceremony of the funeral to celebrate the completion of a life. Certainly Christian ceremonies help adjust our lives from the cradle to the grave. They are channels through which we can express our faith.

Chapter 6

The Basics of Faith

When Paul summarized the three great elements of life, he said: "Now abideth faith, hope, love, these three; but the greatest of these is love" (1 Corinthians 13:13). It was no accident that he listed faith first, for without it there can be no hope or love.

Even in natural realms far removed from anything spiritual, faith is vital to life. Where faith in a monetary system fails, depression follows. When faith in a governmental system fails, hope perishes, and when faith in a person falters, love is set aside. Love may be the greatest in the list, but it rests upon the foundation of faith and hope. Without them, love falters.

We cannot sit in a chair without exercising a measure of faith in the person who built it. Driving a car would be more than nerve racking if we did not believe that other drivers would obey the traffic regulations. Faith is essential to life.

Similarly, the Bible teaches us, "Without faith it is impossible to please him: for he that cometh to God must believe that he is, and that he is a rewarder of them that diligently seek him" (Hebrews 11:6). Faith is the first step toward God, and it is the final step in pleasing Him. It is the channel by which we receive from Him, and it is the vehicle through which we serve our Lord. The Christian life without faith is not merely difficult; it is impossible!

The revelation God gave to Martin Luther was, "For therein is the righteousness of God revealed from faith to faith: as it is written, The just shall live by faith" (Romans 1:17). It became the backbone of the Protestant revolution. Luther believed that righteousness came by faith not fiat and that we live by faith, not by works.

Faith is a New Testament word that appears 247 times in 231 verses. It is a translation of the Greek word *pistis* which means persuasion, credence, conviction, or reliance. By extension it speaks of the system of religious or Gospel truth usually called "The faith". While faith is not an Old Testament word, occurring but twice in its pages, trust is used over 140 times in the Old Testament, but it appears less than 40 times in the New Testament. Even though the eleventh chapter of Hebrews credits many Old Testament characters with faith, the Old Testament speaks of their trusting in God. They were men and women who had a confident reliance upon God that radically affected their attitudes and actions in life. It is not so much that they were people to be trusted, although with our hindsight we can affirm that they actually were; it is that they were people who trusted in God. May the same thing be said of us.

Faith Discovered

God is the only source of true faith. Mental assent, emotional stirrings, and misdirected zeal are often substituted for true faith, but when the test comes, these expedients always fail. No matter how strong the emotions or how fervent the zeal, they never metamorphose into faith, any more than an incubated hen's egg can ever produce a calf. They are distinct and separate, and neither can be transformed into the other.

Seeking to create faith will not only be frustrating, but fruitless, for, of course, only God can create faith. The Bible calls it "precious faith" (2 Peter 1:1) and "holy faith" (Jude 1:20). Neither of these terms fit the mental assent we produce and call "faith".

The heartbreak of attempting to produce our own faith is the absolute needlessness of it. Divine faith is abundantly available, thereby nullifying the need for spurious or substitute faith. The Bible tells us, "So then faith cometh by hearing, and hearing by the word of God" (Romans 10:17). Faith flows when God speaks, for God Himself is the source of our faith, and His quickened word is the channel through which that faith is transmitted to men. God has never been known to have a shortage of faith, but men and women have been known to be deficient in hearing the voice of God, thereby depleting their faith.

True, pure, holy, precious faith that is unadulterated, undisguised, unalloyed, unqualified, and without hypocrisy is God's never changing goal for His church and every member in it.

Faith's source is in God the Father, God the Son, and God the Holy Spirit; not in the Bible, not in theology, not in doctrine, although sometimes doctrine is called "the faith". The Bible, theology, and doctrine will direct faith, but they do not produce it.

Not only is God the source of our faith, He must be the object of that faith, for faith comes from God and must return to Him. When faith's object is God, it will also envelop God's power. When Peter and John explained the miraculous healing of the lame man at the temple's Gate Beautiful, they preached Jesus, declaring, "His name through faith in his name hath made this man strong, whom ye see and know: yea, the faith which is by him hath given him this perfect soundness in the presence of you all" (Acts 3:16).

When God is known, His power is shown. It may be difficult to develop faith in the power of God, apart from a knowing of God, but those who know God best, easily find faith for His demonstrative power. Knowing Him will involve knowing what He can do, and once there is an assurance that He desires to do it, faith readily grasps the exercise of power as a natural extension of God's Person and promises. To really know God as omnipotent is to never be surprised at a display of that Almighty power.

The saint who has channeled faith directly to God's Person will find that faith in God involves faith not only in God's promises and power, but also in God's provision. That God is *able* to do is one thing; that God has *provided* to do is still another. Israel lived for forty years on God's provision of manna, not merely on His promise of manna or His demonstrated ability to produce that manna.

God, our loving heavenly Father, has made lavish provision for His children. There need be no lacking of any good thing, nor need there be exertion of great pleadings or spiritual energy to be the beneficiary of these provisions. When seated at the Father's table you merely say, "Pass the potatoes, please." They are on the table as His provision, so "Ask, and it shall be given you" (Matthew 7:7).

Faith is not fact; it precedes fact. Using the word "hope" rather than the word "faith", Paul asks: "Hope that is seen is not hope: for what a man seeth, why doth he yet hope for?" (Romans 8:24). I think it is safe to say that hope originates in a person's heart when a promise is given, but faith flows from God at the giving of the promise. In either case, we need neither hope nor have faith after the fact. They are needed before the promise is fulfilled. When God speaks, it is like cash in the bank or food on the table. His faith is sufficient evidence that the fact will be accomplished.

Faith Defined

The most quoted verse used as a definition of faith comes from the great chapter on faith: "Now faith is the substance of things hoped for, the evidence of things not seen" (Hebrews 11:1). True faith — God's faith — gives us something to stand on (sub = *beneath*; stance = *to stand*). Simplistically we could say that there is natural faith and divine faith; faith that has its origins in man and faith that has its origins in God. All men have faith. The farmer would never plow the soil if he didn't have faith for a harvest. But not all men have divine faith, for while natural faith is a thing of the head, divine faith is a thing of the heart. Even the demons have the head faith (natural faith), for they believe the reality of God and the veracity of His Word and tremble (see James 2:19), but this is not redemptive for them. Saving faith is not a matter of the head; it is an energy in the heart, for "The word is nigh thee, even in thy mouth, and in thy heart: that is, the word of faith ... For *with the heart* man believeth unto righteousness" (Romans 10:8,10, emphasis added).

But God has not revealed faith to be utterly simplistic. There is natural faith, divine faith, and saving faith, but beyond this there is what we could call "basic" or "general" faith. It is the energy by which we live the Christian life, love our faithful God, obey the written Word, and minister in the earthly Church. This "general faith" can be passive or very active. Christians usually have this "basic" faith in mind when they speak of faith. It is the normative definition of faith, and is often spoken of as our faith.

Beyond these aspects of faith, however, the Bible speaks of faith as a fruit and faith as a gift. The fruit of faith deals with our character, and the gift of faith deals with our competence. Faith develops silently as a result of an abiding relationship, and faith also develops charismatically as a result of special energizing of God's Holy Spirit.

Nevertheless, saving faith, "basic" faith, faith as a fruit, and the gift of faith do not give a complete representation of faith. There is also the major aspect of divine faith to be considered, for although all but "natural faith" have their origins in God, there is a form of faith that is merely called the "faith of God".

Jesus challenged His disciples to "Have the faith of God" (Mark 11:22, marginal reading). Admittedly most translators have chosen to say "faith in God", but in the Greek, "God" is in the genitive case, which allows either translation with equal justification. The issue lies in whether God is the object of the faith or the subject of that faith (where it is possessive and represents God's own faith). Obviously, the context must determine the issue, and in the verses surrounding this text, Jesus had cursed the fruitless fig tree that withered and died overnight. When the amazed disciples marveled at this miracle, Jesus said, "Have the faith of God", and then proceeded to explain to them that when God's own faith was operating through them, they could cast literal mountains into the sea with a verbal command (see Mark 11:20-24).

If we have mountains to move, then we would do well to stop examining the mountains, call off the surveyors, and spend our time and energy getting in and staying in God's presence. That was where David received new faith when it seemed that everything had failed. That is where Paul and Silas received new faith when jailed at Philippi, and that is where we will obtain a new, energetic, dynamic, totally supernatural faith.

Paul seemed to grasp this concept of possessing the faith of God, for he wrote: "I am crucified with Christ: nevertheless I live; yet not I, but Christ liveth in me: and the life which I now live in the flesh I live by the faith of the Son of God, who loved me, and gave himself for me" (Galatians 2:20). Paul clearly testified that he did not live, move, minister, and function in his faith, but in the "faith of the Son of God". Paul had learned to lay hold of God's faith as the energy and force of his life. Everything that issued from his carnal nature had been crucified with Christ, and in exchange he lived a quickened life sustained and energized by God's own faith. What a glorious exchange: Christ's life for ours; His faith for ours; His love for ours.

How great this level of faith must be — to have "God-like faith!" Imagine having access to the unlimited, unwavering, inexhaustible faith of God. It was that faith that spoke the worlds into existence, formed man out of the dust of the earth, and continues to control everything He has created. "Have God's faith" must have been a command beyond the disciples' mental comprehension or volitional ability to respond. But it was available.

Did Jesus command them to have God's faith or did He offer it to them as a commitment? When Christ says "Have ..." it is an offering of a gift, similar to our saying "Have a mint" as we stretch forth our hand to make the candy available to the recipient.

"Have the faith of God" is an offer of limitless faith. Jesus had it, Paul had it, and we, too, may have it, for Jesus is "The author and finisher of our faith" (Hebrews 12:2). The faith of God does not have its origin in the beliefs of men and women, but in the very nature of God Himself. It begins and ends in Him, so nothing we can do will manufacture it; it must be imparted by Him.

Faith is the key to our entire relationship with God. We are "saved through faith" (Ephesians 2:8), "sanctified by faith" (Acts 26:18), "justified by faith" (Galatians 2:16), and we are "kept ... through faith" (1 Peter 1:5). All the graces of God are entered into through the doorway of faith, for Paul wrote, "Therefore being justified by faith, we have peace with God through our Lord Jesus Christ: by whom also we have access by faith into this grace wherein we stand, and rejoice in hope of the glory of God" (Romans 5:1-2).

Faith Embraced

This Bible imperative — faith — is a gift of God. We need but receive it and release it. Being surrounded by it is insufficient. We must appropriate it and use it. As a powerful Bible example of this principle, remember that no nation on the face of the earth has ever been more aware of the direct intervention of God in her national affairs than Israel. Emancipated from slavery and led to the Red Sea, where God could liberate them from their former captors once and for all, Israel became a nation under God in a day.

In the years that followed, God faithfully defended His people, defined His laws, demonstrated His power, and devoted Himself to supplying every physical and spiritual need among them. He designed a tabernacle as a meeting place and He consecrated Aaron as their priest; giving him the entire tribe of Levi to assist the people in their worship. They were declared to be His people, and they submitted to complete dependence upon Him in everything. God surrounded them with faith-producing interventions and activities.

Israel lacked nothing from the day she left Egypt to the day she entered Canaan — nothing, that is, except faith. The Lord said, "I will hide my face from them, I will see what their end shall be: for they are a very froward generation, children in whom is no faith" (Deuteronomy 32:20).

The children of Israel did not lack a provision of faith, but they neither embraced that faith nor functioned in it. The parting of the sea, the sweetening of Marah's waters, the daily manna, the guiding cloud, the smitten rock that provided continuous water, plus the voice of God were all faith-producing. They were incontestable evidences of God's goodness, grace, and glory. Still, Israel murmured ten or more times, sought to return to Egypt's slavery several times, made a golden calf as a replacement for God, and secretly carried images of Egyptian gods throughout all of her wanderings.

God's great provision of faith did not find a place in the hearts of the Israelites no matter how many ways He tried to impart it to them. Unfortunately, Israel never admitted her lack of faith. Instead, the people functioned as though they had it. Tabernacle services never ceased, sacrifices were never discontinued, feast days were faithfully observed, and the cloud was dutifully followed all the days of the wilderness wanderings. The people performed as though they had faith, but they were hypocritically pretending.

We can relate to that, can't we? We can delude ourselves into believing that we are acting in faith as long as we are religiously busy. We can even pray, praise, and worship without flowing in God's faith, but none of it will be acceptable to God. Sometimes being in a church where faith flows to God on a regular basis makes us believe that we, too, are acting in faith. Perhaps we are, but it is also possible to coast on the faith of another. The test comes when we are by ourselves. Do we have faith in the night hours? If we have a personal relationship with God, His faith can flow to and through us no matter where we are or what we are doing. His faith does not flow as a result of community effort. It flows as a response to a personal relationship with God.

Either "Now faith is ..." (Hebrews 11:1), or it is not. All the right words and religious ritual can never successfully replace true faith, for faith alone accomplishes divine results.

Faith is the normal atmosphere of Heaven. Certainly, then, it would be an abnormal atmosphere on earth, for sin has so defiled the place of our residence that it no more resembles God's homeland than darkness resembles light. For one on earth to live in the atmosphere of heaven requires a transfusion, a transference, or a transmission of God's atmosphere into man's environment. It cannot be synthesized or produced by man any more than darkness can produce light, but light can be beamed into the darkness, transforming it into brilliant brightness. The more the light, the greater the brilliance.

While men and women are not inactive in the production of faith, they are not the initiators of it. Faith does not have its origins in the hearts of people, but in the Word of God. Faith is a heavenly grace made available by God's mercy through His Word.

Faith Increased

Faith far more than stabilizes the Christian life; it gloriously animates it. Faith draws from the soil of the Word of God, converts it to an usable energy, and then transports it to the uttermost extremes of our lives.

Fortunately, faith need not be understood to be experienced. Paul speaks of "the mystery of faith" (1 Timothy 3:9). It is a force beyond our natural lives, but it always works both in and through our lives to such an extent that we can be "full of faith" (Acts 6:8), "strong in faith" (Romans 4:20), and "steadfast in faith" (Colossians 2:5).

We can be repositories of faith, we just cannot be producers of faith. Neither can we be farmers of faith. The popular concept of "seed faith" does not fit the Bible's presentation of faith. Faith does not grow. It is received fully developed. If we need more faith, we return to the source. We don't plant what little faith we have and expect it to put down roots, sprout, and produce a crop of fresh faith.

While we cannot, by human effort or emotional activity, enlarge our faith, we can add Christian graces to it. Peter addresses his second epistle "To them that have obtained like precious faith with us" (2 Peter 1:1). Then he adds, "... giving all diligence, add to your faith virtue; and to virtue knowledge; and to knowledge temperance; and to temperance patience; and to patience godliness; and to godliness brotherly kindness; and to brotherly kindness charity. For if these things be in you, and abound, they make you that ye shall neither be barren nor unfruitful in the knowledge of our Lord Jesus Christ" (2 Peter 1:5-8).

These seven Christian graces can be added or blended into and harmonized with the divine faith that has been "obtained" from God, but they do not increase that measure of faith; they merely flavor it, give it texture and color, and become its fragrant aroma. They are not so much the bread crumbs in the meat loaf of faith as they are the salt, pepper, and spices.

Furthermore, none of these Christian excellences can ever substitute for faith, for while they are attracted to faith as steel is attracted to a magnet, they no more possess the energy of faith than nails possess the energy of a magnet. While faith may flow through all these additions, lending its energy to and through them, they never become faith — only channels of faith.

Only the most despicable rebel can claim to be without faith, for the Bible declares: "God hath dealt to every man the measure of faith" (Romans 12:3). It is obvious that some persons have a higher level of faith than others. How did they enlarge God's gift? We cannot enlarge this faith, but we can come back to God and His Word for another allotment of faith.

When the father of the demonized son brought his child to Jesus for deliverance, "Jesus said unto him, If thou canst believe, all things are possible to him that believeth. And straightway the father of the child cried out, and said with tears, Lord, I believe; help thou mine unbelief" (Mark 9:23-24).

The simple fact that this father had brought the son, even though it must have been humiliating for him to do so, shows that there was a measure of faith. Christ's scrutiny revealed that the level of this faith was far too low. The man, in simplicity, merely asked the Lord to increase the measure of faith to a level that was workable. It worked. Jesus delivered the son.

We do not work small faith into large faith. We simply come to Jesus to receive a large measure of His faith.

Faith Released

Faith is a divine energy, not a religious one. It flows to us from God through His Word, both written and spoken. It is far more than an emotional attitude, and it goes far beyond mental assent to what is spoken. It is a divine force that always produces. Something happens when faith is released. Faith saves, faith heals, faith obeys, and faith cleanses. Faith reaches into the unseen world and brings visible evidence into the seen world. Faith is active, not passive.

When Jesus exercised faith, the fig tree dried up from its roots, bread and fish were multiplied to feed vast multitudes, blind eyes were opened, demons were cast out, and even the dead were raised. Christ's faith was potent and productive. It was rooted in God and released to men. It calmed the storm, walked on water, turned water into wine, and rode an untrained donkey in a parade of shouting people waving palm fronds.

When Jesus spoke faith, people responded in action, not merely in attitude. When He told the lame man at the pool of Bethesda to "Rise, take up thy bed, and walk" (John 5:8), "Immediately the man was made whole, and took up his bed, and walked: and on the same day was the sabbath" (John 5:9). Faith produced immediate action.

The same can be said of the blind man Jesus sent to the pool of Siloam to wash out the clay Jesus had put in his eye sockets.When Jesus spoke, faith was released and the blind man received and responded to that faith.

The entire ministry of Jesus released faith to needy persons and when they acted on that impartation, the results were immediate. No miracle occurred until there was some form of faith response by the participants. In Christ's very first miracle (John 2:1-10), huge water pots had to be filled with water and then this water was delivered to the governor of the feast. At that point it became wine. Had the servants refused to act on Christ's word, the wedding feast would have been an embarrassment to the bridegroom for they had run out of wine.

The word "faith" is more often used as a verb than as a noun. A very common expression in the Bible is "by faith". It is the faith that gives action to the sentence. This is the way faith is presented in Hebrews 11. Faith was the producing force, never a latent attitude. Faith gets things done. Faith cooperates with God and His program. Faith is always dynamic; it is never latent. Faith produces; it does not pontificate.

The provision of faith is entirely up to God, and He has never failed in any covenant He has ever made with people. God mercifully has not demanded faith of men and women and then left it up to them to produce it. He merely asks us to receive and release it. God speaks the faith into existence, requiring only that we hear it with our hearts and speak it with our mouths. We are not the producers of faith; we are the consumers. We do not speak faith into existence; we speak the existing faith. What we hear becomes what we speak, and when we say what God is saying, marvelous things happen. But if we have been exposed to faith through the hearing of the Word and do not respond, nothing will be produced.

Faith Focused

Faith not only issues from God, it should return to Him. It is the failure to see that the ultimate object of our faith is God Himself that causes many persons to prostitute their faith rather than progress in it. The measurement of faith is not only its strength, but its object. It is possible to have faith in faith. Some have almost deified faith itself, believing that their faith can do all things, provide all things, and solve all mysteries.

Perhaps the resurgence of ascribing God-like qualities to faith instead of letting faith bring us to God in this twentieth century is rooted in America's nearly wholesale embracing of the philosophy of humanism, which puts man at the center of all things instead of God. Whenever we espouse the deity of man, we automatically forsake the deity of God. It is natural, then, that we subconsciously think of faith as a possessed force that will, of itself, produce or perform whatever we direct it to do, instead of seeing it as a channel to bring us into a walk with God who, the Scriptures affirm, is to be the object of our faith.

If we do not heed the testimony of the early apostles that we must have "Repentance toward God, and faith toward our Lord Jesus Christ" (Acts 20:21), we may fall into the trap of having faith in formulas more than having faith in God and His Word. Our scientifically minded society is formula oriented, and we love to bring the exactness of mathematical equations into our religious experiences.

When we do this, we find ourselves dealing with phrases, texts (sometimes out of context), clichés, and specific recipes in preference to dealing with the living God. However, it is not formula but faith that pleases God. He sometimes follows a known formula, but oftentimes in His omniscience, He functions beyond our limited, finite understanding of His principles, power, and purposes.

When we shift the focus of our faith from God to anything else, we tend to think and exercise faith *for* rather than faith *in*. Faith *for* makes us *things* oriented instead of *God* oriented. With a "faith for" mentality, we become the source, possessions become the object, and faith is viewed as the force that brings the desired thing or end result into our experience. Actually we unwittingly seek to become the creators rather than the creatures who have access to the Creator.

God's ultimate purpose in giving us faith was to make us dependent upon God, not independent from Him. Faith is given to make the heavenly realm real and available to us, not to make us self-sufficient and apart from God's domain.

Repeatedly the New Testament speaks of our faith in God or in the Lord Jesus. God is the accepted and expected object of our faith. God's faith has been imparted to men and women to bring them to God, for God created them to have intimate fellowship, union, and communion with Him. Although sin separated persons from God, salvation reunited the creature with his Creator, and faith is the divine channel of both that salvation and that companionship.

Without faith, God can be neither appreciated nor apprehended, for, "He that cometh to God must believe that he is, and that he is a rewarder of them that diligently seek him" (Hebrews 11:6). God cannot be discovered by persons; He must be revealed to them, and faith is the vital key that unlocks the door to the knowledge of God.

To seek God apart from faith is to seek in vain, but "Ye shall seek me, and find me, when ye shall search for me with all your heart" (Jeremiah 29:13). The search that finds God is the search of the heart, and faith is a matter of the heart, not of the head. Faith, when released from our restraints, ascends toward God's presence as naturally as a gas-filled balloon rises when its string is released. Perhaps if we would cease grasping our faith so tightly and just relax in the faith that God has given to us, we would find ourselves being lifted into His presence.

Faith in God's Person will always involve faith in God's promises, for God and His Word are inseparable, as John expresses: "In the beginning was the Word, and the Word was with God, and the Word was God" (John 1:1). Faith is the force that not only enables us to believe the veracity of God's promises, but also helps us to grasp them and bring them into fulfillment in our lives. To know the Word and to believe that it is actually the Word of God does not change either our condition or our circumstances. We need to mix faith with the promises to effect the desired results.

We need to focus all faith on God. Many years ago in England, Harold Horton, a pastor and a conference speaker, wrote:

> *Faith touches God and brings Him to our aid in every time of need for spirit, soul, or body. Faith invades God's armory for weapons in the fight against sin, storms heaven's strong room for God's promised bestowals. Faith takes God's righteousness for man's sin — and that is salvation. Faith seizes God's fullness for man's emptiness — and that is the baptism in the Holy Spirit. Faith snatches God's health for man's sickness — which is divine healing. Faith grasps God's holiness for man's failure — which is sanctification.*

These are not different forms of faith. They are different focuses on faith.

The minor prophet Habakkuk, standing in his watchtower, was granted a vision involving the end times. In this divine visitation he was told, "The just shall live by his faith" (Habakkuk 2:4). Following the vision, he offered a prayer that was to be sung to a double harp, so great was the excitement of this revelation.

It is not merely that those whom Christ has justified shall be possessors of faith, but their lives will be lives of faith. Faith, therefore, becomes more than a force; it is a focus. Faith is far more than a channel through which we receive gifts; it is a calling in which we respond to God. We live, not lust, by faith. Faith is far more a walk than a work; it is a way of living that is assured in the Old Testament and reassured repeatedly in the New Testament.

Faith Activated

While it is common to say that Hebrews 11 is the faith chapter of the Bible, it really is far more about men and women who received faith and exercised it in a remarkable way. We learn from them that there is but one divine faith, but it can be manifested in many ways. It is somewhat like electricity. The action the electricity produces is determined by what is plugged into it. We can have heat, cooling, motion, or illumination from the same electricity. Similarly, the product of faith depends on what was plugged into it.

I urge you to read Hebrews 11. Nowhere in the entire Bible will you find such a summary of faith at work. Look at what you'll discover:

Verse 2:   Faith to understand what God says.
Verse 4:   Faith to offer to God (Abel).
Verse 5:   Faith to walk with God (Enoch).
Verse 7:   Faith to escape judgment (Noah).
Verse 8:   Faith to obey (Abraham).
Verse 11: Faith to conceive (Sarah).
Verse 17: Faith for the future (Isaac).
Verse 21: Faith to worship (Jacob).
Verse 22: Faith to die (Joseph).
Verse 27: Faith to forsake (Moses).
Verse 30: Faith for conquest (Jericho).
Verse 31: Faith for salvation (Rahab).
Verse 33: Faith to subdue kingdoms (Gideon).
Verse 33: Faith to work righteousness (Samson).
Verse 33: Faith to obtain promises (David).
Verse 34: Faith for battle.
Verse 35: Faith for imprisonment.
Verse 37: Faith for martyrdom.
Verse 38: Faith for exile.
Verse 39: Faith for a good report.
Verse 39: Faith for a divine "No!"

Remember that the Bible was written without chapter and verse divisions. This great listing of heroes and heroines of faith is followed with: "Wherefore seeing we also are compassed about with so great a cloud of witnesses, let us lay aside every weight, and the sin which doth so easily beset us, and let us run with patience the race that is set before us, looking unto Jesus the author and finisher of our faith" (Hebrews 12:1-2).

These men and women of faith are not only a testimony to what God's faith can do in an individual's life when he or she activates it against a promise or problem, but they are looking down on us as witnesses. They are crying from the grandstands, "Come on! You can do it. We did, and you have access to the same faith we had."

Faith is not merely doing something; it is receiving something. It is not the earning of a reward, but the acceptance of a gift. Living by faith does not mean doing without or not doing at all; it means doing His will. It is a walking with God into new territory as Abraham did. It is obeying God when the request seems incongruous to all known facts, as in Noah's life.

The life of faith is not optional; it is obligatory. It was never offered as an elective for the super saints. "The just shall live by His faith." I dare you to try it. You'll find yourself headed for abundant living.

Chapter 7

The Basics of Worship

Every gathering of Christians for worship services needs to include a time not only of singing, but of praising God vocally and physically. The Bible declares: "Lift up your hands in the sanctuary, and bless the LORD" (Psalm 134:2); "O clap your hands, all ye people; shout unto God with the voice of triumph" (Psalm 47:1), and "Praise him with the timbrel and dance: praise him with stringed instruments and organs" (Psalm 150:4).

It may be comforting to you to know that my first reaction to a praise based worship service was one of distress. I had many mixed feelings because the style of worship was so different from mine. As I watched, however, I soon realized that I was among people who truly knew how to worship God. I sensed they had moved to a level far beyond my own experience.

In all honesty, I finally cried out to the Lord, "I don't know how to worship!"

"But *I* do," the Holy Spirit seemed to say to me, "and I will teach you if you will let Me."

I must confess I didn't learn how to worship in just one service, but the Holy Spirit was very patient with me and I was willing to learn. I found my level of worship rising as the months went by. The more I saw of God's loving and holy character, the more I wanted to worship Him with greater freedom. Sometimes we are unaware of the effect that our nature, culture, and training can have on our spiritual lives. The essence of this world and our old sin nature strongly resist and resent real freedom in worship. We feel strange and uneasy about any outward display of devotion to God.

True, we may be comfortable with certain forms of worship if we are familiar with them. We hold back, however, when faced with a freedom in worship that goes beyond our past religious training or experience.

The Holy Spirit is the Spirit of worship. As our teacher and motivator, He deeply wants to move us on to higher levels of worship. It is God's Spirit that enables us to cry, "Abba Father;" the happy cry of a little child to his father. It is hard, however, for the proud minds of men and women to take on the humble, obedient attitude of a little child. Let me discuss with you the who, when, and why of worship and four basic factors of worship.

The *Who* of Worship

God declared through the prophet: "All flesh shall come to worship before Me, saith the Lord" (Isaiah 66:23). This is not merely a declaration of universal worship; it affirms that God will be the sole object of that worship.

"To worship or not to worship" has never been the question, for all God's created beings are inherently worshipers. Heaven is full of worship. It is the stuff of which heaven is made. The book of Revelation progressively shows worship being performed by every inhabitant of heaven, including mankind.

No matter how vehemently he or she may deny it, each person on earth is instinctively a worshiper. It is in his genetic strain! No, the issue has never been shall we worship or not? It is more consistently a question of who, when, and why shall we worship?

The object of our worship is the greatest point of controversy in worship. According to Isaiah 14, Lucifer's fall was perpetrated because of high level pride that caused him to desire to become the object of heaven's worship. He has never lost this aspiration. From his temptation of Eve in the Garden of Eden to the temptation of Christ in the wilderness, satan consistently recruited worshipers from among earth's inhabitants and he still does.

Satan so greatly desired the worship of Christ that he offered Him full control of this earth and all of its inhabitants in exchange for it. Some have seen an opportunity for Christ to have bypassed the cross through this act; restoring man to God's dominion without the ignominy of becoming sin and suffering Calvary. This proposed "shortcut" was probably the root of that temptation.

Jesus beautifully withstood the temptation by paraphrasing Deuteronomy 6:13: "Thou shalt worship the Lord thy God, and Him only shalt thou serve" (Matthew 4:10). These few words of Jesus cut right to the core of our main problem with worship — the person to be worshiped and the priority of worship.

As to the person of worship, all fundamental Bible believing Christians agree with Jesus that God the Father is the only acceptable object of worship. They know about God's expressed hatred of idol worship and have read in the Old Testament of God's repeated punishment of those who worshiped anything besides the true and living God. They accept, intellectually at least, God's demand for a monopoly upon their worship.

Most of these have also memorized Christ's pointed statement on worship from John 4:23: "The hour cometh and now is when the true worshippers shall worship the Father in spirit and in truth." And yet for all their mental acquiescence to God's exclusive rights to their worship, even a casual observer will discover fundamental Christians offering worship to lesser gods in their lives.

If we will accept the dictionary's definition of worship as: "to adore, to revere, to exalt, to magnify, to dote, to admire, or to esteem", then it becomes quite obvious that many Christians worship, to a lesser extent perhaps, many things that are beneath the image of God.

Some exalt their denomination in a manner that at least borders on worship. Others dote dangerously on their pastor, while still others magnify a doctrinal truth almost to the place of God himself.

We've all seen people, even God fearing saints, who so loved their possessions as to become worshipers of them, and others have disgusted us as they became worshipers of themselves. Not that anyone intends for his affections to get out of control and direct his or her worship to something less than God, but still it happens all too frequently. For what we love will soon become what we worship, since worship is merely an expression of love in its highest form. Perhaps this is why the Bible so clearly commands us: "Love not the world, neither the things that are in the world. If any man love the world, the love of the Father is not in him" (I John 2:15).

So the key to maintaining the Divine monopoly in worship is to: "Love the Lord thy God with all thy heart, and with all thy soul, and with all thy mind, and with all thy strength ..." (Mark 12:30). When everything within us loves God fully, He alone will be the object of our worship. Otherwise, we will be as vacillating in our worship as we are in our loving. To worship the Lord exclusively leaves no room for other objects of homage. He will be Lord of all or not Lord at all.

When the Anglican marriage ceremony asks the man to vow to his bride: "and with my body I worship thee ...", it exemplifies how easily we can move from love and adoration to reverence and veneration — worship! It seems that idolatry is inherent in each of us, for worshiping something short of God is always easier than worshiping God Himself. We find it easier to relate and respond to the tangible; to the seen rather than to the unseen. Yet God is the only truly acceptable object of our worship — "Him only."

Twice an angel forcefully told John, "Worship God! for the testimony of Jesus is the spirit of prophecy" (Rev. 19:10; 22:9). God the Father and God the Son are the designated objects of our praise. It is Christ's person, not His performance, that becomes the object of our worship. Thanksgiving and praise are often based on Christ's deeds, but worship is always concerned with His person. Worship is a person responding to a person. We cannot worship until we get a glimpse of God.

If God is not the object of our worship, we are involved in idol worship, no matter where it takes place or how we are performing that worship. Anything short of God that becomes an object of our worship is an idol to us. Worship of pleasant religious sensations is self-worship. Worship of doctrine, creed, theology, or experience is tradition — the very thing that Christ condemned so severely. Worship of a pastor or leader is hero worship — equal to the world's worship of their sports figures or singing stars. Veneration of power, position, or prestige is idolatry ipso facto. Only God is worthy of our worship.

We serve in the kingdom, but we worship the King. Our response to position or power in the kingdom of God will hinder our worship of the King of kings. The disciples who squabbled over their positions of power and greatness in the coming kingdom were not worshiping; they were lusting. It is the King, not His kingdom, that is the object of our worship.

Worship without an awareness of Christ is impossible. The greater our self-awareness, the greater the hindrance to worship. Even "place" awareness hinders worship. Undue consciousness of the style of worship hinders true worship. We must have a consciousness of Jesus and His Father to be able to worship.

The *When* Of Worship

Still, in reminding satan that God the Father was the exclusive object of worship, Christ also established the divine priority of worship over service in saying: "Thou shalt worship ... and thou shalt serve." Worship first; service second. Until we have fulfilled the worship requirement, we cannot serve properly. All service must flow out of worship lest it become a substitute for worship. We learned long ago that God will curse a substitute, but may well bless a supplement.

Nothing can acceptably substitute worship. Consider the plight of the widower who hires a housekeeper, a cook, and a nurse for his children. He is being served very acceptably, but does this substitute for the love of his deceased wife? Of course not! Neither does our service substitute for loving God in worship.

Still, service is part of our Christian walk. It is not an either/or situation; it is both/and. We will worship and serve the Lord God in that order!

Christians need to be careful lest they get so busy working for God that they have no time for God. Activity can become the enemy of adoration, as surely as service can become a substitute for submission and supplication.

How many marriage partners become so engrossed in doing for his or her mate that he or she no longer takes the time to love and adore her husband or his wife? The wife is so busy with the house and the children (or maybe she has a job outside the home) while her husband is so taken up with his business and activities that they become strangers to each other. The love that drew them to one another is consistently neglected and has been replaced with service to each other. But no amount of service, however devoted it may be, can replace the interpersonal relationship so needed to maintain a viable marriage. The home needs the constant undergirding of expressed love, and out of this love flow will proceed all needed service.

The same principle is true regarding our relationship to the Lord Jesus Christ. He is repeatedly called "our husband", and we are called "His wife". We were drawn to Him by His love, and He responded to us because of our love for Him. If we let this love relationship diminish because we are so busy serving Him, we will jeopardize everything that this relationship has produced. Jesus told His disciples: "Henceforth I call you not servants ... but I have called you friends" (John 15:15). We have not been chosen merely to serve, but He has ordained us to be with Him (see Mark 3:14). He enjoys our service unto Him and invites us to serve with Him, but He cannot accept service that is offered as a substitute for worship. He did not die to present to Himself a fully trained servant, but a spotless bride. Out of that marriage will come beautiful service!

Not only must our worship precede our work we should worship while we work. In a very real sense, the way we live should express worship to God. If we have not been singing to the Lord during the week it is unlikely that we are prepared to sing to Him Sunday morning.

The *Why* Of Worship

By observing Christ's statement to satan, we automatically settle the who and the when of worship, which leaves only the all important why of worship.

Just why do we worship? Is it to fulfill a command of God's Word? Is it done to meet needs in our spiritual nature or do we do it because it gives such pleasure to God? Hopefully, we worship for all these reasons and many more. But perhaps the two major reasons for worship are:

1. Worship brings us into a right relationship with God and with ourselves.
2. Worship brings us into a right expression of ourselves to God.

Worship teaches us much about ourselves, about our God, and about our responses.

Matthew tells about a Syrophenician resident of Canaan who seems to have heard that Jesus was preparing to visit her area of Tyre and Sidon. She practically met the boat at the shore, and the moment she saw Jesus she cried: "Have mercy on me, O Lord, thou Son of David; my daughter is grievously vexed with a devil" (Matthew 15:22). She may have heard that blind Bartimeus was healed by yelling a similar cry (see Mark 10:47), or that two pairs of blind men, on widely separate occasions, had been restored to sight by crying this plea (Matthew 9:27 and 20:30). Somehow this formula seemed to crop up repeatedly in the stories that had come out of Jerusalem. It had always seemed to work. Until now, that is, for no matter how earnestly, loudly, or passionately she cried this formula, Jesus "answered her not a word" (Matthew 15:23).

The actions of the disciples proved that she had been heard, for they pled with Jesus to send her away to get rid of the disturbances. But instead of complying with their request, Jesus replied: "I am not sent but unto the lost sheep of the house of Israel" (Matthew 15:24). In this one stage whisper, spoken loudly enough for the woman to hear, Jesus unmasked the deceit and hypocrisy of her petitioning. She had been claiming a non-existent relationship with Christ. In imploring Him as the "Son of David", she was apparently claiming to be an Israelite. This was untrue, for the gospel writers clearly identify her as a Gentile. But because she did not feel that Gentiles had any claim upon Christ, she masqueraded as a daughter of Israel who had covenant claims on the "Son of David". All this pretense got for her was total silence.

When God gives us the silent treatment, it is usually because we, too, are claiming a non-existent relationship. We, like her, pick up formulas that have worked beautifully for others and cry them religiously, whether they work or not.

How many who have never been born again pray, "Our Father which art in Heaven?" Carnal Christians use the prayer language of the true bride, while the rebellious plead with God in their hour of trouble with the same expressions as the submitted saints. This will always be met by divine silence. God does not respond to hypocrisy, since He is truth by nature. We have been instructed to "draw near with a true heart" (Hebrews 10:22). Any form of deceit will deny us an audience with God. Someone has been quoted to say: "Either live it or don't lip it."

Nevertheless, we go on giving lip service to the words that meant life to our fathers and to the founders of our denominations, often unaware that we have only the liturgy, not the life, of these men. We have expressed the words as fact for so long that we are unaware that they have become a fable. We have claimed a non-existent faith until we cannot recognize our fraud. What can bring us out of our deceit and back into His grace? Worship!

Immediately after Jesus unmasked this imposter, "Then came she and worshiped Him, saying, Lord, help me" (Matthew 15:25). Likely, she prostrated herself before Him, perhaps even grabbing Him by the ankles and kissing His feet. She completely submitted herself to Him and poured out both her worship and her plea for help. And it worked. It always works! Worship is a door opener that gives the supplicant ingress to God. All men have been invited to worship God, converted and unconverted alike.

The psalmist sang: "My mouth shall speak the praise of the LORD: and let all flesh bless his holy name for ever and ever" (Psalm 145:21), and John saw a great company in Heaven singing the song of Moses and the song of the Lamb ending it with these words: "For all nations shall come and worship before Thee" (Revelation 15:4). Even if we can claim no covenant that will afford us entrance to Christ, we can open the door to His presence with worship. When our faith has failed and we falter in our approach to Him, we can always fall back on worship, for worship is a consistent door opener.

It is only fair to point out, however, that this door opener to Christ automatically becomes an open door that allows Him to get to us. Immediately after she began to worship Jesus, Jesus began to probe into the depths of her heart. "It is not meet to take the children's bread," He said, "and cast it to the dogs" (Matthew 15:26). In other words, He said: "You've claimed to be a daughter of Abraham, but in their eyes you're nothing but a dog." These have always seemed like harsh words, but they were spoken by the world's greatest example of a perfect gentleman. Christ was not condemning her, He was merely unveiling her to herself. He was bringing her, "not to think more highly of herself than she ought to think" (Romans 12:3). J.B. Phillips translates this verse: "Don't cherish exaggerated ideas of yourself or your importance, but try to have a sane estimate of your capabilities by the light of the faith that God has given to you all" (The *New Testament In Modern English*, J.B. Phillips).

Our Lord was merely helping to adjust this woman's self-concept, and He did it while she was worshiping. As she exalted Him in worship, He exposed her worthlessness. While she spoke of His Majesty ("Lord"), He spoke of her hypocrisy. His goal was not to depreciate her, but to help her appreciate her true relationship to Him, for until she did, He could not respond to her without condoning her falsehood. If she would accept His appraisal and respond accordingly, He could and would minister to her need. Truth can relate to truth.

Isn't it when we are worshiping that God reveals us to ourselves? It was so with Isaiah. He, who was likely the most godly man of his generation, when caught up into God's presence cried out: "Woe is me, for I am undone! Because I am a man of unclean lips, and I dwell in the midst of a people of unclean lips; For mine eyes have seen the King, the LORD of Hosts" (Isaiah 6:5).

At this season of his life, Isaiah was a counselor and tutor in the courts of earthly kings, but when worship brought him into the presence of the Heavenly King, he not only "saw the Lord sitting upon a throne, high and lifted up" (Isaiah 6:1), but he saw himself defiled and dirty. It is only when we are in the presence of Heaven's majestic King that we gain a true picture of ourselves. Compared with another, we may look great, but contrasted to Him, we lose all artificial glory.

So the Lord's response to the woman's worship was to call her a dog. How did she handle that? The only sensible way we can ever handle His evaluation of us — she said: "Truth, Lord" (Matthew 15:27). For until we acquiesce to His appraisal, communication with Him is ended. He has revealed our position and our condition; the next move is ours.

But admitting the truth that she was as separated from a covenant relationship with Christ as a dog is beneath his owner did not devastate this woman. She wisely changed her style of approach to match His estimate of her and gained everything she desired. She merely told Jesus, "Yet the dogs eat of the crumbs which fall from their masters' table" (Matthew 15:27). She simply said: "If I am a dog, don't deny me a dog's privileges!" We can learn no greater principle than to approach Christ consistent to our true nature. If we are "a dog", our nature has not yet been changed by a Divine transformation; we can sit up, wag our tail, and lick the hand of the Master. If we're an infant in Christ, we can make pleasant "gooing" sounds and smile a lot. If we're a toddler, we can crawl to Him, pat Him, and say "da-da".

But for a mature saint to do this would be ridiculous. He should approach Christ as a Christian adult. In worship we must approach Christ, consistent with our current relationship with Him.

We need not wait for a voice from Heaven saying, "This is my beloved Son in whom I am well pleased" (Matthew 17:5), before praising and worshiping God. We can come just as we are. He can cleanse us as surely as He cleansed Isaiah, and change us as completely as He changed Nebuchadnezzar or Saul of Tarsus. We merely need to respond to Him as we are and from where we are, and it is worship that opens the door for this revelation to come.

It is, indeed, worship that brings us into a right relationship with God and with ourselves. But it also brings us into a right expression of ourselves to God.

Perhaps as dramatic an example of worship to be found in the Bible is the story of Mary washing the feet of Jesus. All four Gospels record the event, and Jesus said that wherever the gospel would be preached, her deed would be spoken of as a memorial to her (Mark 14:9). Remember that Mary still overflowed with gratitude to Jesus for raising her brother, Lazarus, from the dead. Her whole way of life was rescued in that resurrection, for the lot of the widows and the unmarried woman was tenuous. Too frequently, they were exploited and stripped of all possessions. When she looked into the home of Simon, the leper, and saw that Lazarus was being highly honored at the banquet, but that Jesus was being treated like any other guest, it broke her heart. He was not being properly appreciated. Simon's expression of thanks to Jesus was grossly insufficient.

Slipping quickly to her home nearby, she sought out an alabaster box full of liquid nard and returned to Simon's house where she broke it, allowing the spikenard to flow over Jesus' head, down His beard, and onto His garments. Then she bathed His feet with her tears, and wiped them dry with her hair.

In contrast to the others who had merely taken Christ's presence for granted, she made a right expression of herself to her Lord. She worshiped. She loved, not from a distance, but in intimate fellowship. She was not content to say thanks with a dinner; she had to worship with a deed that pleased her emotions of love, adoration, thanksgiving, and reverence. She had to touch, to kiss, to weep, and to bow in order to thoroughly pour out herself on Jesus. The spikenard was merely a symbol of what was really being poured out on Jesus — Mary herself! This is the heart and core of true worship; the unashamed pouring out of our inner self upon the Lord Jesus Christ in affectionate devotion.

Factors In Worship

Mark's account of Mary's selfless act of worship (Chapter 14) demonstrates four distinct factors in worship. The first of these is that worship is costly. The disciples quickly calculated that this liquid nard could have been sold for at least three hundred pence, which equaled a full year's salary for a working man. Translated into today's earning power, it would be closer to thirty thousand dollars. That's quite a price to pay just to worship Jesus acceptably.

But the monetary value was probably the smallest part of the price. This costly oil had been saved for one of two reasons: either as a dowry for marriage or to assure a proper burial. Both were vitally important to this Jewish maiden. When Mary poured out the ointment, she was surrendering all her plans, ambitions, and aspirations for the future. Worshiping in the present was far more important than longing for the future. In Verse 8, Jesus said of her act, "She is come aforehand (Greek 'now') to anoint my body to the burying." True worship often costs us some of our self-centered plans and ambitions. It requires us to put God's glory above our goals.

A second factor of worship that is illustrated here is that worship invokes criticism. The fragrance of this perfume had scarcely reached the nostrils of the disciples until they were vocally critical that the ointment had not been sold and the money given to the poor. While social service is laudable, and Jesus even required it, there is also a time and place to minister unto the Lord.

I've received more criticism because of worshiping than any other activity into which I've ever led a congregation. Somehow people still seem to feel that it is a waste to pour out anything directly upon the Lord. I've seen husbands, who had never complained because their wives worked at the church supper or served as volunteer secretary to the staff, become incensed and prohibit their wives from attending worship sessions. We should be prepared for and expect criticism if we become worshipers.

The third factor of worship that Mary illustrates is the need for brokenness. The liquid nard was permanently sealed in a stone container; the bottle had to be broken to release it. Similarly, worship, which is resident in the spirit of every saint, is sealed in by the outer container of the soul and body. Worship can never be released until something happens to rupture this stony container. Presenting the bottle would not have been worship; it would have been an offering. Fracturing the alabaster box allowed the oil to flow as an anointing to the body of the Lord.

David, who knew much about being broken before the Lord, wrote: "The sacrifices of God are a broken spirit; a broken and a contrite heart, O God, Thou will not despise" (Psalm 51:17). The Hebrew words he used are extremely strong. For the "broken spirit", he used the word *shabor* which means to *shiver*, to *break to pieces*, or to *reduce to splinters*. For "the broken heart", he used the Hebrew word *dakah* which means to *crumble*, to *beat to pieces*, to *bruise*, to *crush*, or to *humble*.

Spiritual worship requires a splintering of our prides, a crumbling of our natural reserves, a bruising of our self- sufficiencies, as well as a crushing of our self will. The beating to pieces of our carnal nature will release our emotions to flow out in tears of repentance, submission, and love. I am not calling for us to become sadistic or cruelly introspective, but we need to break and crush everything we have developed in our lives that prevents true humility and love from flowing out. Very often hardness of heart is a defense built up against being wounded by others. We need no such defenses when with Jesus. He will never wound; He is the healer of wounds!

The hard hearted person cannot worship; he or she must be content with mere rituals of worship. It is the tender hearted, the gentle spirited people who can pour out their inner spirit upon God. One must be able to respond positively to projected love, for the true essence of worship is love responding to love. We may express our love to God in praise, but in worship we respond to His expressed love for us.

When David was hiding in the cave of Adullam, fully reduced to splinters by Saul's murderous pursuit, he wrote: "The Lord is nigh unto them that are of a broken heart" (Psalm 34:18). Brokenness, which is necessary to worship in order to release our inner man, also assures us the nearness of the Lord, without which worship is impossible, for worship can only be performed when we are in His presence; when we are conscious of His love flowing out to us. Worship, you see, is a response.

A fourth factor in worship that is alluded to in this story is that worship is reciprocal; we get something in return. When Mary held the alabaster box over the head of Jesus and broke it with a hammer or a stone, the oil gushed out over His head. She quickly rubbed it into the hair and beard, and transferred the drippings to His feet. Then she let her long tresses fall and used her hair to wipe up the residue. When she left the banquet room, people could sniff and say, "She's the one; I can tell, for she smells exactly like Jesus does."

When we pour worship out on the Lord Jesus Christ, we also get it all over ourselves. As we go out from His presence, we carry the fragrance of Christ everywhere we go. Paul recognized this when he wrote: "God ... maketh manifest the savour of His knowledge by us in every place" (2 Corinthians 2:14). Worshipers tend to smell like the love of God.

Just as the Old Testament priest carried the fragrance of God's incense in his hair and clothes after he had tended the golden altar, so we give the world a demonstration of the sweetness of our Lord after we have worshiped. The worship permeates our very nature and is as pleasant as a rare perfume. Worship is very reciprocal, for we benefit as much from it as He does.

The Mood For Worship

It is the Holy Spirit who sets the tone or mood of worship. By "mood" we mean a state of mind or feeling. God is a Person. He always has a purpose which is upon His heart and mind for His people whenever they come together. The Holy Spirit always knows the will and mind of God. Therefore, He will seek to set the tone and theme of a service in line with God's purpose.

Sometimes the tone or mood of a meeting may change. There may be a heavy spirit of grief for those who are away from God. After repentance, the mood of the meeting might change to one of great joy. It is important, therefore, for us to be sensitive to the leading of God's Spirit.

The Spirit of God will always bring a sense of expectation to our services of worship. He is always ready to move in the fresh, new ways of ministry. Even familiar forms of worship, therefore, should never become old or boring.

We cannot successfully copy Mary's act of worship. Expressions of worship are unique and varied. We may look on the blessings of last week and say: "This is how it worked then; so

139

let's try it again today." However, in trying to make it "work again", we lose the freshness and life of God's Spirit.

For this reason, we must be careful to follow after the new ways of the Spirit — even if He wishes to lead us beyond the set form of our liturgy. Rather than conform to the pattern of another or to repeat what has been done before, we need to be sensitive to the leading of the Holy Spirit. He understands worship far better than we do. The Spirit of God is a person, and has many different moods. We need to be sensitive to the mood He brings to a meeting, and move in that direction. If He is in a mood of rejoicing, we also should rejoice. If He is in a giving mood, we should respond wisely by giving to God. Whatever He is doing, we should do it with Him. This is the only way we can really worship the Father as we have been created and called to do! The Holy Spirit keeps our worship from becoming dull and routine. The Spirit of God always blows where He wills and in fresh, new ways. It is a glorious thing!

In a way, we have to "open the windows" at the beginning of a service, and ask the Holy Spirit to "blow upon us". In our hearts, we want to be led by God. Sometimes, however, we may be afraid of anything new and different. In that case, sadly, we may try to keep the windows tightly closed.

We are responsible to be open to the Spirit and be aware of where He is taking us. The Holy Spirit wants to glorify Jesus; and we do too. That means He will faithfully lead us into worship which will be new and different every time!

David wrote, "Listen, O bride, and bend your ear! Forget your own folk and your father's house; and when the king desires your beauty, yield to him — he is your Lord" (Psalm 45:10-11, Moffatt translation). Most worshipers desire the King's beauty. Their approach is based upon their need. Their worship is an expression of their desires. True worship is a willing response to our Bridegroom. It is a willingness to meet His needs. It is a response to His wooing and expressions of love.

Many men have difficulty in worshiping because they fail to take the feminine role; the submissive response to the Lord.

God is always the husband and we are always the bride. Worship is more a response to God's desires than an expression of our own desires. Submission, rather than aggressiveness, is the key to worship. We don't lead God in worship; He leads us. God can set the mood and tempo of worship; He is a great Lover. Worship becomes a relaxed responding to God's expressions of love when we let Him be dominant. Our worship is a response to a Person, not a religious performance. Worship is love responding to love or, better yet, two lovers responding to one another. Worship is recognizing that the King desires your beauty and your submission to Him.

Since it is inherent in our natures to be worshipers, may God clearly lead us to know the true "who", the correct "when", and the manifold "why" of worship as we embrace the factions of worship and the mood of the Holy Spirit for the service. Both God and we will greatly benefit from this!

Chapter 8

The Basics of Healing

One characteristic of Jesus' ministry when He was here on earth was His compassion for the sick and afflicted. Matthew, who walked with Jesus during His three years of ministry wrote: "Jesus went forth, and saw a great multitude, and was moved with compassion toward them, and he healed their sick" (Matthew 14:14). He also reports that when two blind men called out to Jesus for healing, "Jesus had compassion on them, and touched their eyes: and immediately their eyes received sight, and they followed him" (Matthew 20:34).

The apostles who were eye witnesses to the ministry of Jesus reported repeatedly that people brought sick, infirmed, and demonized persons to Jesus and He healed all of them. Jesus had pity on the afflicted. He not only had the ability to heal; He had the empathy that moved Him to release divine power to deliver these afflicted ones.

The writer of the book of Hebrews happily reminds us, "Jesus Christ the same yesterday, and to day, and for ever" (Hebrews 13:8). Our sicknesses so affected Jesus that He healed all who reached out to Him. Our physical limitations still touched Him. Jesus was touched with feelings of infirmities, and He is still touched with those limitations. He healed those who were oppressed and He still heals the oppressed.

Jesus did not leave His compassion in the tomb when God the Father raised Him from the dead. This same writer assures us, "For we have not an high priest which cannot be touched with the feeling of our infirmities; but was in all points tempted like as we are, yet without sin" (Hebrews 4:15).

The double negative in this sentence assures us that we actually have a high priest (Jesus) who feels our feelings of infirmity. He is still compassionate toward the sick of spirit, soul, and body.

Jesus once lived in a body as we do, and He felt the pressure of pain, anxiety, and suffering. Not all of it was by observation. When He hung on the cross all the sicknesses and diseases of the world were thrust upon Him. The prophet declared, "Surely he hath borne our griefs, and carried our sorrows: yet we did esteem him stricken, smitten of God, and afflicted. But he was wounded for our transgressions, he was bruised for our iniquities: the chastisement of our peace was upon him; and with his stripes we are healed" (Isaiah 53:4-5). No one dare say that our Lord doesn't understand how he or she feels. He once felt it as you now feel it. It has made Him merciful and compassionate.

Out of this mercy and compassion, Christ Jesus has made multiple and bountiful provision for cleansing our spirits, renewing our souls, and healing our bodies. Sometimes His provisions work cooperatively, and other times they work independently, but all are provisions of our Lord. Look at them.

Natural Healing

Even the most prestigious automobile manufacturer has never produced an automobile with the ability to fix itself that is equal to our body's ability to heal itself. The law of self-preservation is fundamental in each person born into this world. The life that God gives us at conception has an amazing ability to mend physical wounds and fight off invading germs and viruses.

Some years ago a close associate of mine worked as a medical assistant in a small prison hospital. During the time he was there, he lost count of the gunshot and stabbing victims they treated. My friend told me that he was amazed at how little the doctor did for most of these, and yet how completely these victims recovered from their wounds. When he dared to ask the doctor why he gave such insignificant treatment to these patients, he merely said, "The body, if given half a chance, will heal itself." Fortunately, he was correct.

Through the long history of medicine, we have repeatedly discovered that persons often got well in spite of the treatment they received than because of it. For many generations surgeons did little, if any, sterilization of their instruments or their hands. They often introduced more illness to their patients than the surgery could cure. Still many of these patients recovered.

Similarly, for a long time it was felt that reduction in the blood supply of an ill person would hasten his or her recovery. Even barbers used to slit a vein and catch a flow of blood from their customers to cure a variety of maladies. Interestingly enough, that is the reason for the red strip on a barber pole.

In spite of such malpractice, many of these patients got well. No wonder David said, "I will praise thee; for I am fearfully and wonderfully made" (Psalm 139:14). We can all join David in this rejoicing, for God has given us bodies that have amazing abilities to cure illness. The life force in each of us urgently resists the invasion of anything that threatens the body.

Medicinal Healing

In spite of this amazing capacity, there are times when the invading illness is greater than the body's defenses. Modern medical science has gone a long way in producing medicines that can help the body's healing powers. Sometimes the basic problem is a chemical imbalance in the system. Doctors can often give prescriptions that correct this imbalance; enabling the body to function normally.

I have met some Christians who refuse to take any medicine and boldly declare: "The Lord is my healer." I know that He is. I have also learned that He offers different channels for this healing grace. In describing the New Jerusalem where the saints will live after the coming of our Lord, John observed, "In the midst of the street of it, and on either side of the river, was there the tree of life, which bare twelve manner of fruits, and yielded her fruit every month: and the leaves of the tree were for the healing of the nations" (Revelation 22:2). If God provides leaves of medicinal benefit for the people who live after His coming, would we not suspect that He has provided such benefits for those of us who await His coming?

Coupled with medicinal healing, the science of medical surgery has come a long way. A medical practitioner of the 1920's would be astounded at the technology of the modern hospital. The cat-scan, laser-beam technology, and a thousand other machines of medicine that were totally unknown in his day would overwhelm him as much as it would a medicine man from the bush country of Africa.

All branches of medicine have advanced at high speed over the past twenty years. Procedures unheard of a decade ago are common to doctors today. While doctors still admit that they are "practicing medicine", it is amazing how skillful they have become in their practices.

Is this totally the result of keen minds and lucky discoveries? It is more than interesting to realize that the major advances in medicine have come to "Christian" countries. The nations that do not acknowledge the supremacy of God seem to be locked into the dark ages of medical practice unless they learn it from the Christianized nations. Doesn't this speak of God's intervention even in the field of medicinal healing?

Attitudinal Healing

The cause of the illness usually determines the cure. If it is an invading wound, it is treated differently than indigestion. Infection calls for a different action. If the cause of the sickness is in the soul, it is not likely that it can be cured in the body, even if that soulish problem has produced a physical reaction.

My daughter, who now teaches nursing, used to work for a doctor in Phoenix, Arizona, who had his own laboratory. After repeatedly running a series of diagnostic tests, he would ask my daughter to come into his office while he filled out a prescription for the patient. To the shock of the patient, he handed him or her a prescription with the statement, "This is for your symptoms. Take it as directed." Then he would ask, "Now, whom do you hate?"

"I don't hate anyone," the patient usually responded.

"My tests indicate otherwise," the doctor said. "You are filled with anger, resentment, and hatred."

Picking up his prescription pad again, the doctor wrote down a couple of Scripture references. As he handed it to the patient he said, "Read these passages three times a day. I want to see you again in a week."

This Christian doctor realized that some illnesses have their roots in attitudes. Until there is a change in these attitudes, curing the symptoms will not effect a cure. The symptoms will simply reappear. Perhaps this is what Jesus meant when He spoke to the lame man He had healed at the pool of Bethesda and told him, "Behold, thou art made whole: sin no more, lest a worse thing come unto thee" (John 5:14).

Maybe this is why the Bible repeatedly talks about dealing positively with forgiveness, anger, bitterness, and interpersonal relationships. Our Creator knows these negative attitudes put a stress overload on the physical system and the human body breaks down. Sickness that is the result of sin cannot be cured until the problem of sin is solved at Calvary.

Unforgiveness, bitterness, inner strife, and uncontrolled anxiety are all sickness producers. These attitudes of the soul need correcting before healing can come, otherwise we will merely be treating the symptoms rather than cure the sickness. Tremendous pressure is exerted upon the body by what is in the soul or spirit.

This is an excellent reason for praying for sick persons, for prayer often makes us conscious of our inner being while we are in the presence of Jesus who forgives sin and cleanses our lives. We do not know how old this proverb is, but we do know that it is as true today as the day it was written: "A merry heart doeth good like a medicine: but a broken spirit drieth the bones" (Proverbs 17:22). We read frequently of the curative powers of laughter, and the value of reaching beyond ourselves in expressing our joy. Actually, we are merely redefining the curative powers of celebration. Persons who have learned to thank and praise God with worshiping spirits have discovered how healthful a positive appreciation of life can be. They generally outlive those who are introspective, critical, and condemnatory.

Still, while both theologians and doctors better understand the healing power of living in right relationship with oneself and with others, neither group would blame all sickness on negative inner attitudes. The medical field declares that much sickness is the result of microbes, viruses, and organic malfunctions.

Because prior to the introduction of sin, there was no sickness and after the eradication of sin, there is no more sickness, we see a cause/effect relationship between the two. Sickness is an irrevocable part of the curse of sin. Sin and sickness are so intertwined that it is difficult to see one without the other. The Bible declares that the foundational root of sickness is sin.

This is not to suggest that all personal illness is a direct result of that individual's sin. When the disciples asked Jesus whether it was personal or parental sin that caused the man to be born blind, Jesus assured them that it was neither, and that God was going to get glory in healing him (see John 9:3).

Much sickness is merely the result of sin working in the human race. The most devout Christians are still members of the human race that lives under the curse of sin. Even when our faith is strong, we are subject to the workings of decay. Unless the Lord's return is very soon, we will all experience death.

I feel that it is foolish for any Christian to reject all healing that has its source outside of divine healing. We should rejoice in every provision God has made to restore us to healthy living, even when God uses other means in furnishing healing, as He did when He instructed Isaiah to put a lump of figs on King Hezekiah to heal him (see 2 Kings 20:7). It is certain that God did not need the figs, but perhaps Hezekiah's weak faith needed something outward to cause him to believe God's word.

Divine Healing

In His mercy, God has provided a repair department for the human body. It is likely that when God expelled Adam from the garden, Adam discovered leaves, roots, berries, and even animals that could alleviate wounds and sickness. He probably learned something of the curative power of the rays of the sun and the cleansing power of running water. Since his teacher was God the Creator, it is likely that Adam was well taught.

Through the centuries these discoveries have increased until today's medical science seems almost god-like. All these properties are God's gifts to suffering men and women. But beyond medicine, surgery, manipulation, and our latest curative machines, God has also provided a realm of healing commonly called divine healing. Admittedly religious charlatans have exploited people with false claims of possessing healing powers, but so did the medicine shows and so do many advertisements on modern television. Counterfeit never disproves the real.

We do believe, based on Bible passages that seem irrefutable, that God has made provision to heal a human body by direct intervention of His will through His Holy Spirit. The Bible not only promises to heal, but it gives graphic pictures of divine healing at work.

In his poetic and prophetic vision of the crucifixion of Jesus, Isaiah declared: "But he was wounded for our transgressions, he was bruised for our iniquities: the chastisement of our peace was upon him; and *with his stripes we are healed*" (Isaiah 53:5, emphasis added). Nearly 800 years later James wrote: "Is any among you afflicted? let him pray. Is any merry? let him sing psalms. Is any sick among you? let him call for the elders of the church; and let them pray over him, anointing him with oil in the name of the Lord: And the prayer of faith shall save the sick, and the Lord shall raise him up; and if he have committed sins, they shall be forgiven him" (James 5:13-15).

Both the Old and the New Testaments abound in demonstrations of this healing grace God has promised. In both Testaments, God's provision of healing for the entire person can be viewed in three categories:

1. Healing by covenant
2. Healing by the Word
3. Healing by identification

Healing by Covenant

Although Adam made a covenant with death through his disobedience, Jesus made a covenant of life by His complete obedience. The same verses that blame Adam for sickness and death in the human race credit Jesus with the antidote — life: "For since by man came death, *by man came also the resurrection of the dead*. For as in Adam all die, even so *in Christ shall all be made alive*" (1 Corinthians 15:21-22, the emphasis added).

This covenant with life was in the original plan of God, and although the price of that covenant was Christ's death on the cross, the product of the covenant became available before God carved the Law with His finger on tables of stone at Mt. Sinai.

God showed the power of this covenant of divine health to the Israelites very soon after their deliverance from Egypt. Standing at the far edge of the Red Sea through which they had just walked, these Hebrews watched in awe as the sea closed so quickly that none of the pursuing army of Egypt escaped drowning.

The whole experience of coming out of Egypt and seeing their enemies forever destroyed was so overwhelming to these Hebrews that they danced, sang, shouted, and played tambourines in wild abandonment. Some commentators say that this continued for three or more days. This expressed exuberance in the desert sands dehydrated their bodies, but there was no fresh water available to quench their thirst. Moses dispatched scouts to go and search for water, and they returned with the report of a large pool of water at Marah.

Once the people heard this announcement, they departed more like a murmuring mob than a military machine. It was each person for himself or herself. When they arrived at Marah, they found the waters bitter to the taste, but they quickly quenched their thirst and filled their water skins anyway. They soon discovered that the waters of Marah produced severe diarrhea. Most of the campers expected to die: "And the people murmured against Moses, saying, What shall we drink?" (Exodus 15:24).

Moses cried out to God on their behalf. In response, God pointed out a tree growing at the edge of the pond and instructed Moses to cut it down and cast it into the pool of water. Moses obediently threw the felled tree into the water, and it healed and purified the waters. When the people could be convinced to take a second drink, the sweetened water healed them, too. God used this occasion to introduce His covenant of divine health to them. We read: "There he made for them a statute and an ordinance, and there he proved them, And said, If thou wilt diligently hearken to the voice of the LORD thy God, and wilt do that which is right in his sight, and wilt give ear to his commandments, and keep all his statutes, I will put none of these diseases upon thee, which I have brought upon the Egyptians: for I am the LORD that healeth thee" (Exodus 15:25- 26).

This was a covenant pledge to keep them in good health, and God sealed the covenant with His name — *Jehovah-Rapha*, here translated as, "I am the LORD that healeth thee". Some scholars of the Hebrew language say that *Jehovah-Rapha* should be translated, "I am a physician by nature. I cannot help myself". God ratified this covenant with His very nature, for all God's covenant names reveal another facet of His very being. The people were to ratify the covenant with obedience to the voice of God. As long as they were obedient, God preserved their health during their wilderness wanderings. When they murmured and disobeyed, God sent plagues among them. After they repented, He removed those plagues and healed the people.

This pledge of divine health preceded the Old Covenant, for it began before God gave the law to Moses, and it flows into the New Covenant. The tree that Moses cast into the bitter waters of Marah is a beautiful type of the work of Christ at Calvary. Paul wrote: "Christ hath redeemed us from the curse of the law, being made a curse for us: for it is written, Cursed is every one that hangeth on a tree" (Galatians 3:13).

The tree is a type or picture of the cross. God placed the curse of sin on Christ when He was crucified at Calvary. This personal divine involvement with the curse of sickness has purchased and provided a redemption from that curse for us. As we live in obedience to God's will, we can expect the covenant of divine health to apply to our lives. Since God sealed this covenant with His name *Jehovah-Rapha*, divine healing is more than a gift of health. It is a gift of God's very nature.

Healing by the Word

The beautiful Psalm that begins, "O give thanks unto the LORD, for he is good: for his mercy endureth for ever" (Psalm 107:1), goes on to recount four categories of life that have experienced the goodness of God. Each division ends with, "Oh that men would praise the LORD for his goodness, and for his wonderful works to the children of men!" (Psalm 107:8,15,21,31).

In the very center of this Psalm that extols the provision and protection of God is the statement: "He sent his word, and healed them, and delivered them from their destructions" (Psalm 107:20).

God's earliest covenant of healing was based on His name. Here He declares that He has opened an avenue of healing and deliverance based on the divine Word. This is not a lesser provision; it is an enlargement on the first, for we are told: "Thou hast magnified thy word above all thy name" (Psalm 138:2).

This could cause theological problems unless we remember that since God's name reveals God's nature, no word that God speaks can ever be a violation of that nature. He who is the truth can speak only the truth, and Jehovah-Rapha will speak words of healing.

We understand God through His self-revelation, and He has used His Word to reveal Himself. For our safety, God has chosen to give priority to honoring His Word, for that is our surest and safest revelation of God. Dreams and feelings come and go, "But the word of the Lord endureth for ever" (1 Peter 1:25). He has chosen to magnify that Word above His very names, and both His name and His Word promise us healing.

We do well to remind ourselves that God's Word is creative. God simply said "light" and there was light. Creative commands of God brought into existence all that we call nature. Surely, He who created with His Word, can also repair our bodies, restore our souls, and renew our spirits with a word from His mouth.

Matthew and Mark record a touching incident involving a man who had been isolated from society by leprosy. Mark tells the story this way: "There came a leper to him, beseeching him, and kneeling down to him, and saying unto him, If thou wilt, thou canst make me clean. And Jesus, moved with compassion, put forth his hand, and touched him, and saith unto him, I will; be thou clean" (Mark 1:40-41).

Leprosy was the incurable disease of that day, very much as AIDS is in our day. One statement from Jesus — "Be thou clean" — was all it took to cure this man. There is creative and curative power in the Word spoken by the triune God. Jesus spoke sight into blinded eyes, strength into lame legs, and life into corpses. A word from Jesus is always a positive answer to sickness, for it can even recreate what disease has destroyed.

The word of God is also directive, for sometimes God chooses to get us involved in an act of obedience before destroying sickness. Naaman discovered this. Captain of the Syrian army, Naaman was a leper. Through the testimony of a captive Hebrew girl, he learned that the God of Israel could cure leprosy. When his king sent him to Israel's king with a demand for a cure, the king of Israel was terrified; thinking it was a provocation for war. The prophet Elisha heard of the dilemma and sent for Naaman to come to him.

Upon his arrival, Elisha merely sent word to him telling Naaman what Jehovah had said. This lack of respect for his rank insulted and angered Naaman, but his servants finally persuaded him to obey the word that God spoke through Elisha. When he dipped seven times in the Jordan River, as God had directed, God healed him. It was not the muddy water, but the obeyed Word of God that made this Syrian whole.

In the ministry of Jesus, He directed the lame man at the pool of Bethesda to take up his bed and walk. He sent a blind man to the pool of Siloam, directed a dead boy to get out of his casket, and commanded the dead Lazarus to come out of the tomb. None could do what was commanded before the word of direction came, but when they obeyed the direction, Christ gave them life, sight, or healing.

I have observed over the years that when people, for whom prayer had been offered, responded obediently to what they were told to do, the healing they desired was given to them. Often the commands seem impossible to obey, as when a person is commanded to step out of a wheel chair and walk, or a blind person is told to read a sign on the wall. The step of obedience releases inner faith. Some persons have so accommodated their infirmity that they need to take drastic measures to step out of their unbelief.

Sickness in any form can become captivating, but Jesus came to set the captive free. He testified in his home town synagogue, "The Spirit of the Lord is upon me, because he hath anointed me to preach the gospel to the poor; he hath sent me to heal the brokenhearted, to preach deliverance to the captives, and recovering of sight to the blind, *to set at liberty them that are bruised*" (Luke 4:18, quoted from Isaiah 61:1, emphasis added).

The word of God is equally imperative. When God speaks, there is no room for delay. During the days when God dwelt among us in the person of Jesus, His word was obeyed instantly. Water congealed under His feet. Food multiplied from a boy's lunch to a banquet for thousands. Diseases departed immediately, and infirmities fled at the command of His voice. The deaf heard His voice when He spoke. The dumb could repeat His words after Jesus spoke to them. The lame leaped for joy, and businessmen forsook their businesses to follow Him. He spoke with creative and directive authority, and those words had an imperative in them that caused immediate response.

When Jesus speaks a word against sickness in human experience, it doesn't take a lengthy convalescent period to be restored to health. When He says, "I will. Be thou clean" (Mark 1:41), the action is instant.

God has so many ways to produce healing in human experience that we cannot categorize His actions. God instructed Moses to raise a bronze serpent when Israel was dying from serpent bites. To look was to live. Elijah stretched his body over the body of the dead son and breathed life into his nostrils. Elisha sent Naaman to the Jordan River, but Isaiah put a plaster of figs on dying Hezekiah's boil. There didn't seem to be a healing ritual in the Old Testament.

Jesus was equally varied in the way He healed people. Once He formed clay balls and put them into the empty eye sockets of a blind man, and then sent him to wash in the pool. Another time He simply spoke the word to heal blind eyes. Although Jesus was the first person in the Bible to heal blindness, and the New Testament records more incidents of Him doing this than any other miracle, He never healed two blind persons the same way.

The New Testament is as void of a healing formula as was the Old Testament. Although James tells us to anoint with oil and pray the prayer of faith, Peter's shadow healed sick persons laid on pallets on the roadside. The ill and infirmed sought access to Paul's handkerchiefs and aprons, for merely touching them released healing power.

Perhaps God wants us to realize that formulas and rituals are always empty without His nature and creative, directive, and imperative word. When He is present, methods are quite unimportant and where He is absent, the methods are useless. He sealed His covenant of health with His name, and He has set His Word higher than His name.

Healing by Identification

When John wrote the prologue to His gospel he said: "In the beginning was the Word, and the Word was with God, and the Word was God ... And the Word was made flesh, and dwelt among us, and we beheld his glory, the glory as of the only begotten of the Father, full of grace and truth" (John 1:1,14).

Jehovah-Rapha of the Old Testament and Jesus Christ of the New Testament are the same person. In the Old Covenant, He was the spoken and written Word of God, but in the New Testament, He became the Living Word of God. In the book of Revelation, Jesus is pictured as: "Clothed with a vesture dipped in blood: and his name is called The Word of God" (Revelation 19:13). The Word of God is His eternal name, and "He dwelt among us." He tasted of our lifestyle with all its limitations.

In becoming human flesh and living with us, Christ identified completely with us. The Bible assures us: "For he hath made him to be sin for us, who knew no sin; that we might be made the righteousness of God in him" (2 Corinthians 5:21). In taking our sins in His own body, Jesus felt what we feel (see 1 Peter 2:24). Jesus saw what sickness does to human bodies. The testimony of the disciples was: "How God anointed Jesus of Nazareth with the Holy Ghost and with power: who went about doing good, and healing all that were oppressed of the devil; for God was with him" (Acts 10:38).

Through the blood of His cross, Jesus has made a life-giving identification with us. The seven wounds of Calvary (head, hands, back, feet, and side) inflicted by thorns, whip, nails, and spear all brought Him into identification with our sicknesses. Peter assured us: "Who his own self bare our sins in his own body on the tree, that we, being dead to sins, should live unto righteousness: by whose stripes ye were healed" (1 Peter 2:24).

At Calvary, we can identify more fully with the finished work of God through Jesus Christ. It is a great mystery that only divine wisdom could solve, but God did solve it and brought to us the sprinkled blood of Calvary which not only cleanses from sin, but offers us physical healing as part of the package.

Healing By Grace

Some groups of Christians have made divine healing a sacrament of the church. Others declare it to be in the atonement the same way salvation is in that atonement. In either of these scenarios, we declare that it will always work. That has not been my personal experience. I was raised in a family that believed and practiced divine healing. My father prayed for the sick long before I was born. I have prayed for the sick since my boyhood days. I have never seen 100% success no matter who did the praying.

I must admit that what I do not know about divine healing far exceeds what I do know. I have watched saints go to their deaths unhealed in spite of many prayers of righteous persons. Conversely, I have seen sinners healed instantly the first time they were anointed with oil and prayed over. I do not understand this, and it certainly is not the way I would administer healing if the results were within my power. But they aren't. God is the healer; I am not. He is sovereign and His ways are past our discovery.

I can attest that every time I have made a doctrine out of Divine healing, it has hindered the flow of this grace of God. It was when I got the sick individual into the presence of a healing God that marvelous things took place. I have discovered that God refuses to allow us to completely codify divine healing, for He dislikes being placed in a doctrinal box or being asked to conform to our concepts. Jehovah is a God of infinite variety who seems to delight in doing things in different ways.

He can cause three feet of snow to fall on an area of land without duplicating a single snowflake. Similarly, God likes to personalize His intervention in the physical needs of those who love Him.

I have come to accept that every work of divine healing is an active work of God's grace extended to needy persons. We do not deserve this grace, and we certainly cannot command it. We can, however, ask for it, and that is what I do every time a person requests a healing prayer.

"But aren't you holding out false hope to sick persons?" you may ask.

Absolutely not! We offer a provision, but we make no guarantees. We are willing to do what the Bible tells us to do; believing that this opens a channel that allows God to flow His healing grace. However, if He does not flow healing into the person, he or she is no worse off than before we prayed.

Some persons sidestep praying for the sick and say: "What if God doesn't heal them?" My attitude is, "What if God does heal them?" If we ask God and He says "No", that in itself is an answer. But we'll never know until we ask.

When Jesus was on this earth, He said: "The thief cometh not, but for to steal, and to kill, and to destroy: I am come that they might have life, and that they might have it more abundantly" (John 10:10). Our spiritual enemy wants to steal our health, kill our soundness, and destroy our bodies. Jesus came to undo everything the devil tried to do. He came to give us the antidote for all the poison of the enemy. Jesus gives us the gift of Himself and He is life. The prologue of John's gospel says: "In him was life; and the life was the light of men" (John 1:4).

Healing, then, is an impartation of the very life of God into the sick body of the person God is healing. The method used to achieve this impartation is greatly varied and actually quite unimportant. It is the results that matter.

Healing in the Gifts of the Spirit

In listing the nine gifts or charismas of the Spirit, the Apostle Paul included "gifts of healing" (1 Corinthians 12:9). This is one of the three gifts of supernatural power: faith, gifts of healing, and working of miracles. Some persons mistakenly believe that these are resident gifts in special believers, but the Bible declares, "Now there are diversities of gifts, but the same Spirit" (1 Corinthians 12:4). It would seem that the gifts remain resident in the Holy Spirit, and He is resident in believers. The "gifts" remain His as surely as the fruit is always the fruit of the Spirit in the believer, not the fruit of the believer in the world.

While the other gifts of the Spirit are given in the singular, this wonderful flow of power that produces healing in the human body, soul, and spirit is listed as plural; "gifts". I have heard this interpreted that the Spirit imparts the gift of healing cancer to one, the gift of healing faulty eyesight to another, and so forth. This speculation is usually undergirded with personal examples, but we do not look to experience to illuminate the Word. We go from the word to experience.

There is no Bible basis for believing healing is divided into categories. Jesus, Paul, Peter, and others healed all forms of sickness and disease. They were not specialists in one or two types of human suffering.

It is far more likely that presenting the gifts of healing in plural form indicates that the sick person got the gift, not the person doing the praying. Every healing is a work of Christ's Spirit; it is a special gift of God's grace flowing through the Spirit. Often that flow is through the person praying for the sick, but not always. In healing the sick, God is not limited in His Word to the availability of a human channel.

It is wise to sidestep the title of "healer" when God uses us in alleviating suffering in others. That is a title that belongs exclusively to the Lord Jesus Christ. One of the quickest ways to get into trouble with God is to apply His titles to ourselves.

If He gives us a gift of healing for another, we should pass it on, but never take credit for it. It is His gift, not ours.

Divine Healing Requires Faith

Although divine healing is not "faith healing" (Jesus, not "faith", is the Healer), the operation of faith is essential for divine healing to flow. Matthew said that when Jesus visited His hometown and preached in the synagogue that people would not believe, "And he did not many mighty works there because of their unbelief" (Matthew 13:58). Still, Jesus did not always demand that faith come from the sick person. There were at least five channels of faith that produced healing miracles in the days of Jesus:

1. The faith of Jesus Himself.
2. The faith of the sick person.
3. The faith of the persons who brought the sick.
4. The faith of the disciples who helped minister to the sick.
5. The faith of God — the gift of faith that makes it possible for anyone present to believe.

God responds to faith. He isn't too particular whose faith touches Him. All He wants is the channel of faith through which He can flow a measure of His nature to the afflicted person.

Just as the channels for faith were varied, the way faith was released or the point of faith's release, were equally varied. There are five or more ways illustrated in the New Testament.

1. Confession — a declaration to Christ that they did, indeed, believe.
2. Desperation — as illustrated by the woman who rushed up behind Jesus to touch the hem of His garment and received healing.

3. Obedience — as when Jesus told the cripple at the pool to take up his bed and walk. It was when he obeyed that he released his faith.
4. Anticipation — as when the people placed the sick in the streets anticipating the passing of Peter's shadow.
5. Association — as when the sick asked for articles that had been close to Paul's body.

In this thumb nail sketch of divine healing, I have simply stressed that God is the Healer, faith is the channel, and that there are many different ways this healing is effected in sick people. The real diversity is not in the healing, but in the method used for touching the nature of God for that healing. That will be as varied as the nature of the sick person or the manner that is comfortable to the person who ministers God's healing grace. Who cares how it came? We just rejoice that it did.

Chapter 9

The Basics of Our Enemy

Jesus, who shares His life with and in us, faced a powerful rebellious angel in the wilderness. It was obvious that this high ranking created being had put himself in a position of enmity with God. All through the life-span of Jesus, satan warred against Jesus seeking to prevent Jesus from fulfilling His plan of redemption. Satan lost; Jesus won! Satan, although the loser, was not destroyed. He still rants against the kingdom of God and those who have become heirs of this kingdom. He was the chief enemy of Jesus and he is our second greatest enemy. It is likely that we are our own greatest enemy.

The New Testament says: "For we wrestle not against flesh and blood, but against principalities, against powers, against the rulers of the darkness of this world, against spiritual wickedness in high places" (Ephesians 6:12). People are not our enemies; principalities and powers are. There is a spiritual realm composed of demons, fallen angels, and satan that consistently makes war on the Church and seeks to hinder the development of a holy life in Christians. They often use people as unwitting tools in the course of their activities, but it is this dark spiritual force that has arrayed itself against every manifestation of the kingdom of God.

I cannot deal with this entire kingdom in a single chapter, so I will concentrate on satan, the ruler of the powers of darkness.

Peter wrote in his first letter to believers: "Be sober, be vigilant; because your adversary the devil, as a roaring lion, walketh about, seeking whom he may devour" (1 Peter 5:8). He clearly defined our enemy as the devil or satan. His name was Lucifer in heaven, but after being cast out, he was called by his nick names:

1. Accuser (Revelation 12:10).
2. Dragon (Revelation 12:7).
3. Serpent (Revelation 12:9).
4. Devil (Matthew 4:1).
5. Satan (Mark 8:33).

For the sake of this writing we will consistently call him satan, and out of complete disrespect to him, I refuse to capitalize his name unless it is the first word in a sentence.

The Reality of satan

It is a shame that in our era that is experiencing a greater display of satanic power and influence than in past generations, there is a general disbelief in satan. He is presented as a figment of our imaginations or the personification of evil, but far too few persons actually admit that he is a real person with conferred power and an unchanged goal. The longer he can hide his personality, the easier it is for him to work in the hearts and minds of people.

The Bible presents satan as a very real person. It speaks of him having a heart, pride, speech, knowledge, power, desires, lusts, soul passions, and spirit faculties. Here is a list of a dozen Bible pictures that present satan as a real person:

1. Jesus taught that satan was a real person (Luke 10:18).
2. Jesus dealt with him as He would a person (Matt. 4:1-11).
3. Jesus waged war on him as a person (Luke 13:16).
4. The apostles fought with him as a person (Eph. 6:10-18).
5. The apostles warned against a personal devil (James 4:7).
6. Personal singular pronouns are used of him (Matt 4:7-11).

7. Personal statements are made to him (Isa. 14:12-15).
8. Personal descriptions are given of him (Ez. 28:11-19).
9. Personal names and titles are given to him (Isa. 14:12).
10. Personal acts are ascribed to him (Matt. 4:5).
11. He is an angel with a body, soul, and spirit (Ez. 28:14).
12. He has been seen with a body (Matt. 4:1-11).

There is not a single book in the Bible that would even hint at satan merely being a thought in the mind or an influence in the world. From Genesis to Revelation, the Bible acknowledges satan to be a person as real as Gabriel or Michael. While he is not a person with a human body, he possesses the spiritual body of an angel which makes him invisible to persons unless he desires to displace himself to them. This is a tremendous asset to his undercover work here on the earth.

The oldest book of the Bible, Job, presents satan as joining the "sons of God" [an Old Testament title for angels] to report his activities to Jehovah. Satan made accusations against Job and was granted permission to test Job's faith in the Almighty. He is seen as a person as real as these other angels. He and Jehovah conversed as person to person.

In the temptation of Jesus, satan was a person as real as Jesus. Satan tempted; Jesus resisted. They conversed, disagreed, and parted company for a season. Jesus was not having problems with His mind. A real person had confronted Him.

Satan is mentioned 55 times in 49 separate verses, and in each of these he is viewed as a person. Under his title of "devil" he is mentioned 61 times in 57 verses, and again he is seen as a living person who could talk, function, and create real havoc in humans.

Our enemy is not a political power, an economic control, or an individual. Our enemy is a spirit person who is often behind these forces that seek to dominate and control our lives. We must learn to contest the devil if we want to walk a life of victory.

The Rank of satan in Heaven

There can be little doubt that satan is one of the highest species of God's creation. Evangelical Bible scholars see Ezekiel 28:12-19 as a description of satan in his glory before he sinned. His title, work, and sphere of influence are quite clearly listed. He is called "the anointed cherub that covereth" (Ezekiel 28:14). We know from Exodus 25:20 that Cherubs attend the holiness of God; they guarded the mercy seat in the Holy of Holies. The Hebrew word for "anointed" here is *mimshach*, which has the significance of outspreading, as of wings. Interestingly, this is the only time it is used in the Bible. This verse in Ezekiel could read: "Thou wast the *overspreading* cherub that covereth." Likely, this was one of the highest offices in the realm of angels, if not the absolute highest. No other angel is ever mentioned as having such a title. Even in his fallen state, satan is still intellectually the greatest and keenest personality ever created by God.

Michael, designated the archangel, is a person of great power and position, but he must have been beneath satan, for he refused to rebuke satan in the dispute over Moses' body (see Jude 1:9).

Satan must have been a most gorgeous creature. We read, "Thou wast perfect in thy ways from the day that thou wast created, till iniquity was found in thee" (Ezekiel 28:15). His headquarters was a beautiful mineral kingdom and he was "covered" with the most costly of stones (Ezekiel 28:13). This prophet also suggests that satan was the first created being with musical ability, for he wrote: "The workmanship of thy tabrets and of thy pipes was prepared in thee in the day that thou wast created" (Ezekiel 28:13). Very likely the praise of music was satan's specific duty. This may account for satan's tremendous use of music today in directing human souls with lyrics and rhythms that focus minds on physical sensations rather than on God.

Satan is spoken of as "walking up and down in the midst of the stones of fire" (Ezekiel 28:14,16). Stones are a strong type of Christ (*viz.* the Ebenezer stone of Samuel, Daniel's stone cut with a divine finger, the "chief cornerstone", and the confession of Peter to Christ's divinity was called a rock).

Similarly, fire is often used to speak of the presence of Jehovah as seen in the burning bush at the call of Moses, the pillar of fire over Israel, the supplied fire for the Tabernacle worship, and the clear statement "Our God is a consuming fire" (Hebrews 12:29).

The combination, then, of "Stones of fire" indicates a place for the overspreading cherub that was nearest the throne of God. It was a place of high honor.

It is likely that satan was over the angels of heaven. He may have been the connecting link between God and the angels because of his close positioning to the throne of God. He probably received the divine energy needed to execute the will of God and dispensed it to the angels of God's bidding. Few will deny that prior to his expulsion from Heaven, satan was second only to God Himself. He was exalted, glorious, resplendent in beauty, and highly favored.

The Revolt of satan

That one so glorious would revolt against God is almost unbelievable. We read, however, "By the multitude of thy merchandise they have filled the midst of thee with violence, and thou hast sinned: therefore I will cast thee as profane out of the mountain of God: and I will destroy thee, O covering cherub, from the midst of the stones of fire. Thine heart was lifted up because of thy beauty, thou hast corrupted thy wisdom by reason of thy brightness: I will cast thee to the ground, I will lay thee before kings, that they may behold thee" (Ezekiel 28:16- 17).

It seems that satan first fell through pride in his own beauty. It also appears that "physical things" began to supplant his spiritual service. His physical beauty, the beauty of his personal "Eden", and the multitude of possessions lifted his heart in pride. These have been his major tools in tempting persons into sin ever since. If these things could produce iniquity in the "cherub that covereth", how easy for them to produce iniquity in sinful flesh like ours!

Satan's revolt expressed itself in trying to exalt himself above God. The prophet Isaiah says that satan expressed his self-will five times. He writes: "How art thou fallen from heaven, O Lucifer, son of the morning! how art thou cut down to the ground, which didst weaken the nations! For thou hast said in thine heart, I *will* ascend into heaven, I *will* exalt my throne above the stars of God: I *will* sit also upon the mount of the congregation, in the sides of the north: I *will* ascend above the heights of the clouds; I *will* be like the most High" (Isaiah 14:12-14, I've emphasized his expressed will using italics).

Not content to be the most beautiful, intelligent creature of God's creation and the highest order of angels, satan aspired to a position of equality with God. He was the first associate pastor to try to take over the senior pastor's position, but certainly he was not the last.

From our position on the earth, we cannot imagine the confusion this created in heaven. Until this moment there had been but one will in all of creation — the will of Almighty God. Satan's action introduced a second will. Now with two wills, choice was forced upon the angels. The glorious unity of heaven was disrupted as angels were divided in their allegiance. It seems that at least one third of the angels eventually sided with satan and were cast out of heaven with him.

Satan, as so many of us since him, was not content to be what God had created him to be. He wanted the top position. He wanted to replace God. The curse of our generation is this same desire to replace the will of God with our own wills. Isaiah said that this was the heart of sin: "All we like sheep have gone astray; we have turned every one to his own way; and the LORD hath laid on him the iniquity of us all" (Isaiah 53:6). It is this exertion of our "own way" that necessitated Christ's substitutionary death at Calvary. Satan may have taught us to rebel, but he fails to show us what rebellion cost him.

The Removal of satan

That God put up with the rebellious will of satan four times before He did anything about it is indication of how greatly His grace and mercy affect His actions. Perhaps God sought to subdue satan's will and bring him back to his pristine nature. Maybe God was seeking to renew the allegiance of the angels who had chosen to side with satan. We do not know God's reasons. We only know His actions.

For whatever span of aeons satan continued to exert his will in five progressive stages, there came a time when God's patience was exhausted. He called for the glorious arch-angel, Michael, and commissioned him to expel satan from heaven. The account is given to us as: "There was war in heaven: Michael and his angels fought against the dragon; and the dragon fought and his angels, And prevailed not; neither was their place found any more in heaven. And the great dragon was cast out, that old serpent, called the Devil, and Satan, which deceiveth the whole world: he was cast out into the earth, and his angels were cast out with him" (Revelation 12:7-9).

It was not a war of thunderbolts or hand-to-hand fighting. It was a forensic battle — a battle of words. Satan expressed his will, but Michael had the Word of Almighty God, and God's Word always prevails. When Michael informed Lucifer (his name in heaven) that the Father said to leave heaven, there was no basis for argument. A thousand wills may exalt themselves against God, but the will of the Almighty always prevails. Satan was cast out of heaven conclusively. Everything that was connected with him joined in his expulsion.

It is valuable for us to realize that this conflict was not directly between God and the devil. It was between two angels of unequaled rank. Although satan has repeatedly challenged God to a direct confrontation, God seems to have viewed this as an unfair fight — the Creator against the created. In heaven, an angel of lower stature was successful in casting Lucifer out of heaven when he had the Word of the Father as

His weapon. Even the humble saints on earth have authority over the devil's kingdom when they, too, possess the living Word of the Father. Satan is not big enough to take on God directly. He can't even win a battle against those who are lower than himself.

When the seventy disciples, who Jesus sent out two by two to minister in the cities He planned to visit, returned with great excitement over their ability to cast out demons, Jesus told them: "I beheld Satan as lightning fall from heaven" (Luke 10:18). He undoubtedly referred to satan's expulsion from heaven. He wanted them to know that not only have demons been reduced to obeying Christians, but that satan himself had been demoted from his exalted position.

Satan's eviction from heaven caused him to relocate here on earth. We can only speculate as to why he came here, but it takes no supposition to realize we were not blessed by having him in our community. His expulsion from heaven did not temper his revolt against God; it intensified it. While he does not seem to have direct access to God now, he has forged an access to those who are special and precious to the heart of God. His anger against men and women is so great that he would have destroyed us long ago if God had not limited satan's nature, restricted his power, and delineated his sphere of operation.

The Restrictions on satan

It is true that in heaven satan was second only to God, but there was a great distance between number one and number two. Satan had access to God's presence, but he could not duplicate His person. That was the reason for the rebellion. Whatever part of God's divine nature satan may have been allowed to participate in, it was taken from him at his expulsion.

It is unfortunate that many Christians do not seem to understand this. They have an infinite devil and a finite God. This may be their mental impressions, but it is the reverse of Bible truth. The Scriptures declare God to be sovereign and infinite, but the devil is subordinate and subservient to God. He even had to have permission to give Job boils.

Satan possesses none of the essential nature of God. God is *omnipotent* — all powerful. Satan operates with limited conferred power. God is *omnipresent* — everywhere present at all times. Satan is not. He can be in but one place at a time. What seems to be an omnipresence is merely the way he operates his kingdom of fallen angels and demons who are scattered throughout the world. They represent him, but they are far beneath him. God alone is *omniscient* — all knowing. While satan's knowledge may exceed ours, in comparison to what God knows, he is like a kindergarten student trying to take a class at Yale or Harvard. The only part of God's essential nature satan possesses is being *eternal*, but then God has shared that with all born-again Christians.

Neither does satan share any of God's moral nature. The Bible declares that God is love, light, holy, righteous, a consuming fire, and just. None of these designations fit satan. He is hatred rather than love. He is darkness rather than light. His very nature is unholy, unrighteous, and unjust, and the only fire he will experience will be the lake of fire of God's punishment.

No, satan is not God gone bad. He is an angel gone bad. He has the qualities and character of an angel, but that has always been far beneath the Almighty God. He boasts about what he can do, but his ability never matches his ambitions. He can express his will — he did that in heaven — but he cannot execute that will without the express permission of God.

The concept of satan's equality with God comes from ancient Greek mythology, not from the Word of God. Poets, philosophers, and artists have often glamorized the role of satan, but the Bible consistently unmasks this lie.

Just as satan's nature is far beneath God's, so his power is amazingly inferior to the power of God. Satan's power is conferred power, and conferred power can be withdrawn without prior notice. Before His ascension, Jesus said: "All power is given unto me in heaven and in earth" (Matthew 28:18). If

Jesus has all power then there is no power left to the devil except what our Lord chooses to allot him.

Similarly, satan's sphere of operation is as controlled as is his power. Our enemy may be formidable, but he is not divine. He pretends, but he cannot produce half of what he boasts. He roars like a lion, but he is not a lion; Jesus is the "Lion of the tribe of Judah" (Revelation 5:5).

Satan cannot function against Christ's Church or even against individual Christians without the permission of Jesus. Satan is always inferior to God the Father, God the Son, and God the Spirit. His "kingdom" is vastly inferior to the kingdom of God, and its boundaries are imposed by God, not determined by satan himself.

The Reign of satan

That satan was a leader in heaven is obvious. When he was banished from heaven "His angels were cast out with him" (Revelation 12:9). Since the fourth verse of this chapter tells us, "His tail drew the third part of the stars of heaven, and did cast them to the earth", most Bible scholars teach that Lucifer brought a third of heaven's angels with him.

This would be consistent with the concept of the early Christian church that since only three angels are named — *Michael, Gabriel, and Lucifer* — all three were archangels with one third of heaven under their control.

Lucifer was a leader in heaven, and he remains a leader on earth. He had angels under his jurisdiction in heaven, and he has them under his command on earth. In addition to these, he has gained control over the demonic realm here on the earth. We know nothing of the origin of demons, and none of the speculations I have read have any scriptural foundation to them. Whoever they are, they have become active agents for satan.

Satan has organized and arranged his kingdom on earth the way God has His kingdom ordered in heaven. Why not? After all, everything he knows he learned in heaven. There is no scriptural indication that satan has creative powers or original thoughts. He is preprogrammed.

In his letter to the Colossian Christians, Paul described the progressive order of God's kingdom as being five-fold: "For by (1) him were all things created, that are in heaven, and that are in earth, visible and invisible, whether they be (2) thrones, or (3) dominions, or (4) principalities, or (5) powers: all things were created by him, and for him" (Colossians 1:16) (I have added the parenthetical numbers)].

With Almighty God at the head, His kingdom has five levels. It is interesting that when Paul warned the Ephesian Christians about satan's kingdom, he also listed four levels beneath the devil. He wrote: "For we wrestle not against flesh and blood, but against (1) principalities, against (2) powers, against the (3) rulers of the darkness of this world, against (4) spiritual wickedness in high places" (Ephesians 6:12) (I have added the parenthetical numbers).

Satan is not everywhere present, but he has agents of his angelic beings and demonic world working for him throughout the entire world. Although they are not equal in authority or ability, the ultimate responsibility for their actions is charged to satan. He operates much as the head of a world-wide corporation. It is a serious mistake to call every level of this kingdom "the devil". If we express our commands to satan while in spiritual warfare against demons, we miss the mark. Perhaps some of the opposition we believers experience is the work of satan, but most of it is not satan personified. It is satan portrayed by a lower level of his kingdom.

When we scathingly denounce the shipping clerk in the name of the president of the corporation, we not only make ourselves look ridiculous; we are totally ineffective in producing results. Similarly when we rebuke satan when we are actually dealing with a demon, we will be incompetent in our work.

Not only does satan work through his angels and demons, he exerts an amazingly strong influence upon world rulers to do his bidding. Some he completely controls, while many others he merely persuades on specific issues.

Satan may have organized his earthy kingdom after the pattern of God's kingdom in heaven, but it is a copy in miniature. Through persuasion, threat, intimidation, and broad lies satan has formed a powerful kingdom organized here on earth, but it is exceedingly trivial when compared to the majestic kingdom of God that is both on earth and in heaven. God's angels greatly outnumber satan's angels, and God's saints are far more numerous than satan's demons. God's organizational skills are infinite compared to satan's finite skills. Satan may roar while God whispers, but the final results are not determined by the volume of the voice. It is ability, not amplitude, that determines the winner, and God's abilities are absolute.

The Relationship of satan to Jesus

Although satan was number two to God in Heaven, Jesus was always number two in the Godhead. That this was a point of contention in the mind of satan is illustrated on earth in satan's attempt to match the titles, names, and power of Jesus. Rather than match, satan always comes out the loser. When he claims, "I came in second", he fails to tell us there were only two in the contest. He didn't come in second; he came in last! Look at some of the contrasts and comparisons the Bible makes between these two.

Satan is pictured as the fallen one, while Jesus is consistently viewed as the exalted one. Satan likes to present himself as the angel of light. Paul wrote: "Satan himself is transformed into an angel of light" (2 Corinthians 11:14). Jesus presented Himself as the light of the world when He said: "I am the light of the world: he that followeth me shall not walk in darkness, but shall have the light of life" (John 8:12).

Twice Jesus called satan "The prince of this world" (John 12:31; 16:11). The world has acclaimed satan as its prince, but God has declared Jesus to be the "prince of *peace*" (Isaiah 9:6) and the "*King of kings and Lord of lords*" (Revelation 19:16).

All Christians have come to know the accuracy of Peter's statement that the devil is our adversary (see 1 Peter 5:8), but we have also come to know that Jesus is our advocate, for John wrote: "My little children, these things write I unto you, that ye sin not. And if any man sin, we have an advocate with the Father, Jesus Christ the righteous" (1 John 2:1).

Satan is a tempter, but Jesus is our succorer. We are assured: "There hath no temptation taken you but such as is common to man: but God is faithful, who will not suffer you to be tempted above that ye are able; but will with the temptation also make a way to escape, that ye may be able to bear it" (1 Corinthians 10:13). Nothing that satan can bring against us can overwhelm God's ability within us to stand in faith.

Satan is called the deceiver, while Jesus is called the revealer. Satan is called a hinderer in 1 Thessalonians 2:18, but Jesus is consistently called the helper (see Hebrews 4:16). Jesus called satan a murderer (John 8:44), but He declared Himself the giver of life when He said: "The thief cometh not, but for to steal, and to kill, and to destroy: I am come that they might have life, and that they might have it more abundantly" (John 10:10). Similarly Jesus called satan a liar when He told the Jews, "Ye are of your father the devil, and the lusts of your father ye will do. He was a murderer from the beginning, and abode not in the truth, because there is no truth in him. When he speaketh a lie, he speaketh of his own: for he is a liar, and the father of it" (John 8:44). In contrast to this Jesus said: "I am the truth" (John 14:6).

In the rejoicing in Heaven at the fall of satan, our enemy is called an accuser: "For the accuser of our brethren is cast down, which accused them before our God day and night" (Revelation 12:10). In contrast to this, Jesus is called our intercessor: "Wherefore he is able also to save them to the uttermost that come unto God by him, seeing he ever liveth to make intercession for them" (Hebrews 7:25). Although satan's charges presented before God the Father, the "judge of the whole earth" (Psalm 94:2) seem severe, we can take refuge in the knowledge that our lawyer (intercessor) is the Son of the judge. We are assured of an acquittal. Hallelujah!

There are other contrasts between Jesus and satan that could be presented, but these are sufficient to remind us that Jesus is always superior, and He successfully undoes whatever satan has done. John testified of Jesus, "For this purpose the Son of God was manifested, that he might destroy the works of the devil" (1 John 3:8). The Greek word we've translated "destroy" is *luo*. It is used in the book of Acts to describe the breaking up of a ship. It literally means "to cause to come unglued". No matter what satan seeks to do in the world of believers, Jesus causes the cohesive force to lose its grip, and everything falls apart. It is like sewing with no thread in the bobbin of the sewing machine or laying bricks with no cement in the mortar.

The Ruin of satan

The ultimate defeat of satan was at Calvary. Satan thought he had won a conclusive victory when from the cross, "Jesus ... cried with a loud voice, ... Father, into thy hands I commend my spirit: and having said thus, he gave up the ghost" (Luke 23:46). Satan may well have bragged that God had made a serious tactical error in sending His Son to become a man who could die, but while the hosts of satan rejoiced over their destruction of Jesus, Heaven had a celebration party. Heaven knew that satan had been unable to do one thing outside the perfect will of God for His Son and their plan of redemption.

On the day of Pentecost, Peter preached: "Him, being delivered by the determinate counsel and foreknowledge of God, ye have taken, and by wicked hands have crucified and slain" (Acts 2:23). Every step in the arrest, trial, and crucifixion of Jesus was predetermined by God, and satan was forced, whether knowingly or unknowingly, to follow that plan.

When Jesus cried from the cross: "It is finished" (John 19:30), satan's insurrection against God was over. The war was over. All that remained was to sign the terms of surrender.

When Jesus came forth from the grave, even satan's demons knew that it was over. The entire kingdom of satan lost it all at Calvary, and at the resurrection their arch enemy arose to enforce the terms of surrender. Jesus enlarged the ministry He had demonstrated while He was on earth, and this ministry has been destructive to both the satanic and demonic kingdoms. Through individual believers in general and the Church on earth specifically, Jesus continues to bring light into the world to destroy darkness. He brings in love to destroy satanic inspired hate, and divine harmony to undo the discord the devil loves to sow among brethren.

Talk about undoing the works of the devil, Jesus offers true happiness to dispel the sorrow sin induces; faith to replace doubt, and divine health to undo demoniacal induced sickness. Little wonder, then, that the Apostle John exclaimed: "Ye are of God, little children, and have overcome them: because greater is he that is in you, than he that is in the world" (1 John 4:4). This verse is all the more remarkable when we realize that in the preceding verse John was talking about false spirits and the spirit of the antichrist. The Spirit of Christ dwelling in believers is far greater that the highest spirit in satan's world.

At Christ's ascension, He paused at satan's headquarters to strip him of all rank, position, authority, and power. Paul declares this in writing: "And having spoiled principalities and powers, he made a shew of them openly, triumphing over them in it" (Colossians 2:15). The Greek word we have here translated as "spoiled" is *apekduomai* which means "to divest wholly; to despoil". It is a military term used nowhere else in the Bible, but Paul, familiar with the ways of the Roman army, chose this word with full knowledge of its meaning and implication.

Apekduomai refers to a conqueror stripping from the defeated general all insignias, medals, badges, and other symbols of position and authority that pertained to his position of

177

leadership. When every symbol of power, position, rank, and honor had been forcibly ripped from the uniform, the Roman general would announce, "Now all of these are mine by right of conquest. The titles you held, I now hold. Your armies will now obey me, and your nation will forever be subject to the rule of Rome."

It was with full understanding of this ceremony that Paul declared that Jesus divested satan of every position of authority and every vestige of power that God had ever given him before the expulsion from heaven. Jesus also stripped the devil of every position or title that men and women had given to him.

Every member of satan's kingdom knows that Jesus divested their leader of all power and authority. Every angel in heaven knows that satan has been completely plundered. Both heaven and hell know that satan is merely a figurehead, a puppet, an exile. He functions in conferred but limited power.

It is only men and women who seem unaware that the "roaring lion" (1 Peter 5:8) has had his teeth pulled and is on a leash to the "Lion of the tribe of Judah" (Revelation 5:5). The only power left to him is the power of persuasion, but this was all he needed in the Garden of Eden to con Adam and Eve into departing from God's control.

The Reduction of satan

As if the humiliation of the defeat at Calvary and the complete stripping at the ascension were not enough, Jesus told His disciples just before He ascended into Heaven: "These signs shall follow them that believe; In my name shall they cast out devils" (Mark 16:17). Jesus had given this power and authority to His disciples when He sent them out on teaching missions, but now He offers it to all who will believe. The weakest Christian has authority over the strongest demon.

This effectively puts Christian believers in a position above the demonic realm of satan's kingdom and greatly frustrates satan, for he cannot be everywhere present. He needs his demon hoards to do his bidding. When Jesus made satan's servants subject to the servants of Jesus, satan was hopelessly handicapped.

Ever since Calvary, the working force of the satanic realm has been subject to Christians. The book of Acts illustrates the complete authority believers have against the demonic. Modern experience provides current illustrations. Satan's kingdom has been so reduced in its power and authority that Christians can: "Submit yourselves therefore to God. Resist the devil, and he will flee from you" (James 4:7). Instead of watching persons flee from his armies, satan now is forced to watch as his demon forces flee from the presence of those who submit their lives to God. What a come down for him; what a come up for us! Jesus wins, and we share in His victory over satan.

To some it appears that it is "business as usual" for satan, but this is not the truth. He has been conquered. His business is subject to Christ and the Church. He cannot do one thing beyond the permissive will of God.

It reminds me of the book of Esther where King Ahasuerus was tricked by Haman to order the slaughter of the Jews. When Queen Esther successfully prevailed on the king to reverse this order, he explained that such edicts were not reversible, but he gave Esther and her uncle, Mordecai, permission to write and distribute a counter decree granting the Jews permission to fight back. This ruined the plan of Haman, for the Jews won on every front.

God has issued a decree that Christians can fight back against satan's forces, and with that decree God conferred power to make the Christians victorious on every front. Satan can roar, rant, and resist, but he cannot win. He has been reduced to a loser both in Heaven and on earth.

How frustrating it must be to satan and his followers to know that no matter how thoroughly they plan, how completely they prepare, or how sacrificially they battle, they are predestined to lose.

In a Sunday morning service at my home church in Phoenix, Arizona, a visiting warlock and a leader of a satan worshiping church, was soundly converted. When I asked him if the satanists believe that these are the "last days", he told me that the satanists see themselves up to bat in the bottom of the ninth inning. They do not know how many strikes remain, but they know that they lose! Satan knows that his time has come, and his serious followers know it too.

The Restriction of satan

Since satan signed the surrender at Calvary, he knows that his worst is yet to come. After the return of Jesus, God is going to give the world a thousand years without the interference of satan. During this period of peace, satan will be incarcerated in a bottomless pit. John the revelator tells it like this: "I saw an angel come down from heaven, having the key of the bottomless pit and a great chain in his hand. And he laid hold on the dragon, that old serpent, which is the Devil, and Satan, and bound him a thousand years, And cast him into the bottomless pit, and shut him up, and set a seal upon him, that he should deceive the nations no more, till the thousand years should be fulfilled: and after that he must be loosed a little season" (Revelation 20:1-3).

Satan's fall started when he was cast out of heaven, continued when he was repositioned at Calvary, and will continue though this thousand year period. He tried so hard to exalt himself, but he has been falling ever since.

John says that satan must be loosed from this pit for a season. During this season he again uses his amazing powers of persuasion to amass a huge army of men to make war with God in heaven. Satan has never abandoned his desire to replace God. In this final attempt to overthrow God, satan's armies are destroyed by fire. John tells it: "And they went up on the breadth of the earth, and compassed the camp of the saints about, and the beloved city: and fire came down from God out of heaven, and devoured them. And the devil that deceived them was cast into the lake of fire and brimstone, where the beast and the false prophet [are], and shall be tormented day and night for ever and ever" (Revelation 20:9-10).

That is the final end of satan — the Lake of Fire. He will never again be released from God's prison. God has no further use for him, and he will have no further power to contend either with God or with men.

We look forward to the final disposal of satan. He has been a formidable force against God, the Church, and individuals. How close we are to the coming of Christ and the bottomless pit is anyone's guess. It is certain that we are closer to it now than when John saw this happening in vision form.

By faith we can now live in this promised victory. God has promised it, Christ has purchased it, and the Holy Spirit will provide it for all of us. While we cannot live in the future victory, we can live victoriously in the victory of Calvary. Sin and satan have no power over the lives of the blood-bought saints of God. Long before John ever had the vision of the end times, he wrote: "For whatsoever is born of God overcometh the world: and this is the victory that overcometh the world, even our faith" (1 John 5:4).

By faith we can apply the conquest Christ made at Calvary. We can exercise our conferred authority over demons. By this same faith we can look to the coming of Christ and the final restrictions that will be put on satan. Whether we look back to the cross or forward to the bottomless pit and the lake of fire, we know that we have been set free from satan's power. Jesus said: "If the Son therefore shall make you free, ye shall be free indeed" (John 8:36). That settles it!

Chapter 10

The Basics of Righteousness

The wise man observed, "Righteousness exalteth a nation: but sin is a reproach to any people" (Proverbs 14:34). He also observed, "When the righteous are in authority, the people rejoice: but when the wicked beareth rule, the people mourn" (Proverbs 29:2). We need not pick up a history book to validate these declarations. Our daily newspapers and news telecasts proclaim this same message day after day.

The foundations of morality and righteousness have just about been destroyed in the modern society. It is becoming extremely difficult to tell the difference between the pagan and the Christian nations. Centuries ago David wisely asked the question, "If the foundations be destroyed, what can the righteous do?" (Psalm 11:3). Righteousness is the foundation for the moral fiber of any society from the home to the national government.

Our Western society offers little guidance in moral living or social behavior. Most restraints have been removed in the name of liberty; leaving each individual to determine what is right for him or her. This is causing a disintegration of society as we once knew it, for God did not create us to make our own moral rules. We were formed to be led by the rules of God's Word as applied by His indwelling Spirit. Where these are disregarded, we are as lost as the confused hiker who threw away his compass because he did not recognize his surroundings.

While I am grateful for the cleansing power of the blood of Jesus and the saving power of the Spirit of Christ, I am increasingly aware that each of us needs to: "*Receive* the blessing from the LORD, and *righteousness* from the *God* of his salvation" (Psalm 24:5 emphasis added).

Salvation is more than an experience that spares us from going to hell. It is an entering into a new way of living. It is God's provision of a new code of ethics to govern our behavior, both in our relationships with God and with other persons.

The Bible frequently speaks about righteousness. The word righteous appears 238 times in 225 verses, while the word righteousness occurs an additional 302 times in 285 verses. Anything mentioned that repeatedly in God's Word needs to be looked at seriously. It not only defines and pictures the righteousness of God, it declares that God shares His righteousness with us.

God declared through the prophets: "I will bring them, and they shall dwell in the midst of Jerusalem: and they shall be my people, and I will be their God, in truth and in righteousness" (Zechariah 8:8), and, "Fear thou not; for I am with thee: be not dismayed; for I am thy God: I will strengthen thee; yea, I will help thee; yea, I will uphold thee with the right hand of my righteousness" (Isaiah 41:10). In each verse, God defines His nature as righteous and pledges that righteous nature to the lives of His people.

A Righteous God

Modern Christians need an introduction to the righteousness of God and its availability to us in our every day living. Lacking a workable standard in society, we need to turn to the Bible and see God's standard of righteousness and embrace this as our standard for daily behavior; both in our relationships with God and with one another.

God's righteousness and His holiness are interconnected. The Bible declares Jehovah to be both holy and righteous. Perhaps we should see the holiness of God as a part of His inherent nature while the righteousness of God is the demonstration or manifestation of that holy nature in His relationship with His people.

The Hebrew word for righteousness is *tsaddik* which means *just, innocent,* or *virtue.* When the Bible speaks of the righteousness of God, it refers to the absolute, uncompromising justice of God, through which His plans, promises, and purposes are executed without deviation or partiality. God's righteousness assures us of divine consistency. Because God is just, we can always count on God to function according to His own laws and rules. The Bible does not present God as an autocratic Being who is ruled by emotion or changed by flattery, nor should we. We are introduced to "A just God and a Savior" (Isaiah 45:21) of whom Isaiah further testified, "The LORD of hosts shall be exalted in judgment, and God who is holy shall be hallowed in righteousness" (Isaiah 5:16).

Perhaps the best known passage of Scripture is the Twenty-Third Psalm. In this beautiful analogy of God as our shepherd, David stated: "He leads me in the paths of righteousness for His name's sake" (Psalm 23:3), thereby connecting righteousness with the nature of God — "For His name's sake." The statement is so simple that it is often overlooked, and yet it is so profound that it takes the help of the Holy Spirit to comprehend its vastness. For His own sake and purposes, God has promised to lead us into righteousness like the righteousness of the divine nature.

In this simple sentence, David extols a righteous God, His righteous paths, and His righteous purpose. The Spirit's emphasis upon the personal pronoun "He" shows that God, the leader, is Himself righteous or else how could He lead us into righteousness? The surrounding nations at the time this Psalm was written certainly did not view their idol gods as righteous. Neither were the devotees concerned with uprightness in the way they worshiped their deities. Most idol worship involved gross immorality, ritual prostitution, and human sacrifices. In stark contrast to the perceived nature of heathen gods, "the righteous God" (Psalm 7:9) of Israel, Jehovah, leads His people righteously and leads them into His righteousness. David consistently viewed this as a positive action. He declared, "My mouth shall sing aloud of Your righteousness".

(Psalm 51:14), and, "My tongue shall speak of Your righteousness and of Your praise all the day long" (Psalm 35:28). God's righteousness did not terrorize David. It was an obvious cause for his rejoicing.

Just before his death, Moses sang: "He is the Rock, His work is perfect; for all His ways are justice, a God of truth and without injustice; righteous and upright is He" (Deuteronomy 32:4). The stated reason Moses wrote the song was to give Israel a musical remembrance of God and His ways with people. David said almost the same thing when he wrote, "The LORD is righteous in all His ways, and holy in all His works" (Psalm 145:17).

The righteousness of God is a declaration of Scripture that is never open for debate. He is upright in all His relationships, honest in all His dealings, and faithful in all His promises. He is unvarying in His nature, unmovable in His attitude, and unchanging in His action. His thoughts toward us are pure, His purposes are permanent, and His love is constant. His righteousness is never subject to situation ethics. "Righteous are You, O LORD, and upright are Your judgments. Your testimonies, which You have commanded are righteous and very faithful" (Psalm 119:137-138), the psalmist wrote. One would expect the saints to sing this theme in a major key with full instrumentation.

This righteous nature of God was a constant source of rejoicing for David. He instructed the Chief Musician to sing to the accompaniment of stringed instruments; "Let the peoples praise You, O God; let all the peoples praise You. Oh, let the nations be glad and sing for joy! For You shall judge the people righteously, and govern the nations on earth. Selah" (Psalm 67:3-4). On another occasion, he wrote, "Let the heavens rejoice, and let the earth be glad; let the sea roar, and all its fullness; let the field be joyful, and all that is in it. Then all the trees of the woods will rejoice before the LORD. For He is coming, for He is coming to judge the earth. He shall judge the world with righteousness, and the peoples with His truth" (Psalm 96:11-13). David's joy was not merely that God would judge the world, but that He would execute righteous judgment with all the peoples of the earth. The constancy of God's nature was what delighted him, for he recognized that God would act in equity, justice, and faithfulness, because God is righteous by nature.

A Righteous Kingdom

Matthew said, "Jesus went about all Galilee, teaching in their synagogues, and preaching the gospel of the kingdom" (Matthew 4:23). Young John Mark summarized the ministry of Jesus in writing, "Jesus came into Galilee, preaching the gospel of the kingdom of God, And saying, The time is fulfilled, and the kingdom of God is at hand: repent ye, and believe the gospel" (Mark 1:14-15). The kingdom of heaven was not a sub-theme for Jesus. It was His main theme. He mentions this kingdom fifty-five times in the Gospel of Matthew alone. The four gospels speak of the kingdom more than 125 times. Even after His resurrection, Jesus spent forty days with His disciples, "Speaking of the things pertaining to the kingdom of God" (Acts 1:3).

Jesus consistently considered the kingdom as His. He embraced His legal rights to every facet of the kingdom, and He invited men and women to turn from unrighteousness and enter that kingdom with Him. Jesus never projected the kingdom of God as future. He saw it as a present reality. When the convict who was crucified at Christ's side asked to be remembered when Jesus entered His kingdom, Jesus told this repentant thief, "Verily I say unto thee, *To day* shalt thou be with me in paradise" (Luke 23:43, emphasis added).

After Jesus ascended into heaven, the Apostle Paul became an outspoken advocate of the kingdom of God. When he sought to define Christ's kingdom on earth, he said: "For the kingdom of God is not meat and drink; but righteousness, and peace, and joy in the Holy Ghost" (Romans 14:17).

It is inconceivable to imagine a kingdom without a king or governing laws. Jesus is the proclaimed king, and the Bible are the governing laws in His kingdom. God is a God of law, and His kingdom is built upon righteous law. All creation manifests this. There is the *law of conscience*, where God has impressed His principles in the subconscious mind of man. There is the *law of nature*, where God has set processes in motion; the *law of His Word*, in which He has revealed Himself to us; and there is the *law of His Spirit*, through which God implements His processes in the affairs of mankind.

No matter which branch of law you look at, it is God's law, and He is the ultimate judge of that law. Only He can hand down the sentence that law imposes, but he can and will do so. Therefore, both life and death originate in Him. God's law is irrefutable, irreversible, and irrevocable. If God decrees it, that settles it!

In God's kingdom laws, higher law overrides lower law. For instance, in the law of man's conscience, the rule of cleansing overrides the law of defilement. In the law of the Word, the ordinance of repentance overrides the decree of retribution. In the law of the Spirit, "The law of the Spirit of life in Christ Jesus has made me free from the law of sin and death" (Romans 8:2).

Just as a naturalized citizen of the United States or England is no longer subject to the laws of the country of his origin, but is now completely subject to the laws of his new country, so men and women who have, by faith, entered the kingdom of God have traded the jurisdiction of his or her spirit from the kingdom of death to the kingdom of life. The old laws no longer apply, and the new ones are rigidly enforced.

Paul seemed to be very much aware of this, for he wrote, "I see another law in my members, warring against the law of my mind, and bringing me into captivity to the law of sin which is in my members. O wretched man that I am! Who will deliver me from this body of death?" And then he answered his own question with the declaration, "I thank God — through Jesus Christ our Lord!" (Romans 7:23-25). Trapped in the dominion of sin, he was convinced that Jesus Christ could deliver him!

How can it be done? By the application of a higher law than the law of death. The "Spirit of life" can free us from the law of sin and death.

Compare the law of sin to the law of gravity, and the law of the Spirit of life to the principle of aerodynamics. In the law of flight, there are four forces at work: *force*, the engine; *lift*, the flow of air over the wings; *drag*, the resistance the control surfaces make on the lift; and *pull*, the tug of gravity. When these four forces are correctly balanced, the plane rises above the earth in seeming defiance of the law of gravity, but if the passenger steps outside the plane, he quickly discovers that the law of gravity is very much operative — it has only been superseded by the higher law of flight. As long as he remains in the plane, however, he need not fear falling from the sky.

Christ is like that plane. The power of God that raised Him from the dead is still resident within Him. This power, when exercised, can lift a passenger load far above the "gravitational" pull of sin and death, and in a completely controlled flight bring those passengers to the predetermined destination. As long as believers will remain in Him, the law of sin and death is superseded in their lives, "for the law of the Spirit of life in Christ Jesus has made me free from the law of sin and death" (Romans 8:2).

There is law and there is higher law. We live involuntarily in the lower law — it is the controlling force of our lives — but we enter into the superseding higher law by option. The person who refuses to enter an airplane and submit to the law of flight will forever remain bound to the law of gravity. Similarly, the person who refuses to enter into the righteous life of the Spirit and submit to His rule and authority will forever remain under the control of the law of sin and death.

It is far too common to hear Christians declare that they cannot help themselves — "My father was like this," they say. They have, obviously, elected to remain under the bondage of the laws of heredity, completely forgetting that at conversion, they received an entirely new heredity through Father God.

Other Christians testify that some habit is far too strong for them to break, and so they condemn themselves to live forever under the law of controlling habits or passions. They reject participation in the higher law that would release them from the law of their flesh.

Paul told the church at Rome, "We have been delivered from the law, having died to what we were held by, so that we should serve in the newness of the Spirit and not in the old-ness of the letter" (Romans 7:6). We have been delivered, but the option to live in that deliverance rests with us. We can enter into the new and higher law, or we can remain forever bound under the lesser, but controlling principle. We can live in the Spirit or walk in the flesh. We can be dominated by sin or we can have dominion over sin. God has chosen for us to live in the righteousness of Jesus Christ as residents of His righteous kingdom.

Righteous Paths

King David knew that any paths God would lead him into would be righteous paths because of God's righteous nature. His use of the word *path* in the Twenty-Third Psalm is his poetic expression for a way of life. He had said, "Teach me Thy way, O LORD, and lead me in a plain path, because of my enemies" (Psalm 27:11), and, "Thou wilt show me the path of life; in Thy presence is fullness of joy; at Thy right hand are pleasures forevermore" (Psalm 16:11). The Good Shepherd will lead us into a way of life that involves integrity, honesty, and righteousness.

This is, of course, consistent with the Pauline teaching of the New Testament. He told his spiritual son, Titus: "The grace of God that brings salvation has appeared to all men, teaching us that, denying ungodliness and worldly lusts, we should live soberly, righteously, and godly in the present age" (Titus 2:11-12).

These "paths of righteousness" that our "righteous God" chooses to lead us into, run north, south, east, and west in our lives. One path deals with upright living in relationship to God, and the other path involves righteous behavior in our day-to-day dealings with one another. Divine righteousness will involve a right relationship with God, and it will produce a just relationship with people, but self-righteousness offers only a sham pretense of uprightness either with God or man.

Righteousness between us and God will also produce righteousness with one another, for righteousness has both a vertical and a horizontal flow. The two lines intercept, forming a cross in our lives. Unless both beams of this cross are seen in a person, he or she will not be viewed as a righteous person in the sight of God. King Saul observed this in the life of David. After David had mercifully spared Saul's life when he entered David's cave, the king, "said to David: 'Thou art more righteous than I; for thou hast rewarded me with good, whereas I have rewarded you with evil'" (1 Samuel 24:17).

David dealt righteously with Saul, but he also dealt righteously with God, for he could honestly write, "The LORD rewarded me according to my righteousness; according to the cleanness of my hands He has recompensed me. For I have kept the ways of the LORD, and have not wickedly departed from my God. For all His judgments were before me, and I did not put away His statues from me. I was also blameless before Him, and I kept myself from my iniquity. Therefore the LORD has recompensed me according to my righteousness, according to the cleanness of my hands in His sight" (Psalm 18:20-24).

The Good Shepherd does not drive us into righteous paths; He leads us into them. Neither does He carry us on the paths of righteousness; we walk in them standing erect with our shoulders squared. "He leadeth me" leaves a free choice for us, for righteousness is more behavioral than belief.

Righteousness is an action of the life expressing the attitude of the heart. Progression in righteousness is the result of walking rather than talking. The lips may say righteous platitudes, but God is looking for upright lives. Being led into righteousness shows that righteousness is learned more by doing than by studying.

Since the Hebrew word used for righteousness means "just or innocent", the prophets used it to describe the person who conformed to a standard. The person was righteous because he or she lived undeviatingly according to predetermined rules. We need to be led into righteous paths, for we are incapable of either compiling those rules or conforming to them.

In the Bible's genealogy of Noah, the first thing we read is: "Noah was a just man" (Genesis 6:9). The Hebrew word that is translated here as "just" is *tsaddik*. This word is more commonly translated "righteousness". Noah dared to conform to God's standard in a time of depravity, debauchery, and departure from God, and God declared him to be a just man.

Noah lived at a time when the sinful line of Cain overshadowed the Godly line of Seth. Sin, which is the exercise of self-will against the known will of God, always erodes righteousness. The Bible singles out the days of Noah as positive proof that sin causes degeneration and disintegration. Yet, although righteousness was very unpopular in his time, by an act of his will, Noah conformed to the known will of God, and God declared him to be a righteous man. He did not conform to the pattern of the world. He had set his heart to pattern after the will of God.

Believers should not concern themselves too much with the standards of the society in which they live. God has a standard for His people, and to live according to that standard is the route to righteousness. Since God has established the criterion for righteousness — both in relationship to Himself and to others — He is best qualified to lead us into and through these paths of righteousness.

Righteous Purposes

Not only is God a righteous God who leads us in righteous paths, but He has righteous purposes for our lives. Good parents take the time to train their children in proper behavior and manners so they will neither embarrass the parents nor themselves. Similarly, God, who has acknowledged us as His children by putting His name upon us, wants to teach us to "Live Godly in Christ Jesus" (2 Timothy 3:12).

Training in polite behavior begins with a powerful example, for children are far more apt to do what they see their parents do than what their parents say. Our Father, who instructs us in righteous behavior, is Himself, a righteous God. He leads us in righteous paths by walking with His children in those paths. His first line of teaching is "do what I do". We need to be good observers, followers, and learners.

David wanted continuity for his kingdom, and God gave it to him. This favored king of Israel knew well that "God is with the generation of the righteous" (Psalm 14:5). In his sermon at Antioch, Paul testified that, "David ... served his own generation by the will of God" (Acts 13:36), but this Godly king wanted to do something outstanding enough to cause people of coming generations to worship Jehovah with the love that he himself experienced. He proposed building a temple unto God, but Jehovah told him through Nathan the prophet that this would be unacceptable because of the great bloodshed for which David had been responsible. But God added, "Your house and your kingdom shall be established forever before you. Your throne shall be established forever" (2 Samuel 7:16).

Many generations later, another prophet, this time one who was in prison because of what he preached, heard God say, "For thus says the LORD: 'David shall never lack a man to sit on the throne of the house of Israel'" (Jeremiah 33:17). While this is divine confirmation, it is also completion, for Jeremiah in the final words of the preceding verse had just declared: *"'The LORD our righteousness' — Jehovah-Tsidkenu"* (Jeremiah 33:16).

The context of Jeremiah's message is gloomy. Many Hebrews had already been carried into Babylon, and now the army of Nebuchadnezzar had an impenetrable siege against Jerusalem. Jeremiah had repeatedly prophesied that the city would fall to these Chaldeans, and God continued to remind the remaining citizens of their sins and iniquities. He reviewed how they had violated their covenants with the True and

Living God when they began worshiping the false gods of the nations around them.

In this portion of Jeremiah's prophecy, God reaffirmed His covenant with them and assured them that no amount of unrighteousness on their part could change His righteous relationship with them. He declared that His name was *Jehovah-Tsidkenu*: *"The LORD our righteousness"*. His is a nature so righteous that nothing we do can change it, but that righteousness can gloriously change us. We can never defile God, but He can, and will, make us holy.

There comes a time in each of our lives when our righteousness fails us. Human frailty and often personal rebellion turn our hearts away from God's paths to walk our own way, but that is not the end for any of us. Jehovah is our righteousness. We may fail, but He cannot. We may sin, but He has become our Savior.

It is an inviolate principle of Scripture that what God demands from us in one passage of Scripture, He offers to us in another portion of the Bible. God does demand righteousness of us. God also knows we cannot produce the righteousness that He requires. Therefore God shares His perfect righteousness with us. In contrast to this, the prophet admitted: "We are all like an unclean thing, and all our righteousnesses are like filthy rags" (Isaiah 64:6). This is as true in our day as it was in his. This defiled self-righteousness, of course, is totally unacceptable to God, so He became our righteousness. The best we can do is polluted in His sight. We cannot manufacture righteousness; we can but receive it and release it.

David seemed to understand this, for he wrote, "Hear me when I call, O God of my righteousness!" (Psalm 4:1). God, who desires to lead us into paths of righteousness for the sake of His own name, has willingly become the source of our righteousness.

Righteous Provisions

Out of his own personal experience Paul was able to declare: "You are in Christ Jesus, who became for us wisdom from God — and righteousness and sanctification and redemption — that, as it is written, 'He who glories, let him glory in the LORD'" (1 Corinthians 1:30-31).

Jesus Christ has become our uprightness before God and man, "for His name's sake". All glorying must be in the LORD, for He is the source of our right standing before God. By His action, we have been justified and declared righteous in His sight. As David pled, "Oh, continue Your lovingkindness to those who know You, and Your righteousness to the upright in heart" (Psalm 36:10). Christ's righteousness that He gives to those who know and love God is progressive; not perfect. God brings us into one realm of righteousness at a time. We mature in righteousness toward God and toward one another. God declares us righteous; we never deserve it. Nothing we can ever do will become divine righteousness, but God has affirmed us righteous even while we are in the process of becoming upright in our walk before others. Furthermore, we are made righteous from the divine viewpoint rather than the human. Long after God declares His loving children to be righteous, there are observers who dispute God's claim, but if God says that we are righteous, we are! What we received came as a gift. It is inherited, but it is not inherent. We can, and must, learn to live in this new realm of righteousness in Christ Jesus, for He has sent His Spirit to dwell in us "Teaching us that, denying ungodliness and worldly lusts, we should live soberly, righteously, and godly, in this present world" (Titus 2:12).

As his Psalms indicate, when David found himself in gross unrighteousness, he praised the LORD, his righteousness. He cooled his spirit to the dew point until the righteous God distilled upon him as the dew of the morning. David sinned, but he refused to live as a sinner. He had learned how to secure the righteousness of God through praise. He knew what we must learn: it is one thing to fail and still another thing to live in failure. Through praise and worship of God, David learned to live victoriously, uprightly, and righteously both before God and his fellow beings.

This loving gift of righteousness from the hand of a righteous God reassured David that God was, indeed, a living God. He found Jehovah to be less exacting than He was giving. Although Jehovah demanded that His people observe a standard of behavior that conformed to the righteous Law of God, the giver of the Law graciously shared His intrinsic righteousness with His worshipers. It is rare for any of us to approach worship without introspectively remembering unrighteous behavior. Our consciences may remind us of yelling at our husband or wife, or slamming the door, or discourteous driving on the highway. This didn't bother us much until we began to approach the Righteous God. His Presence acts like a full length mirror that allows us to see our unrighteous imperfections in all their hideous realities. Usually, this awareness causes us to withdraw from worship with feelings that we are too unworthy to worship such a righteous God.

God has never revealed any aspect of His nature to hinder our worship. He wants us to know that He is available to us. When we are made aware of our unrighteousness, He invites us to approach the Throne of Grace in His righteousness. Paul affirmed, "You are in Christ Jesus, who became for us wisdom from God — and righteousness and sanctification and redemption — that, as it is written, 'He who glories, let him glory in the LORD'" (1 Corinthians 1:30-31).

When we cannot come to God *in* righteousness, we should come to Him *for* righteousness. He is a living God easily moved by our inadequacies. Everything we need to approach Him in worship has been made available in Himself.

Righteousness is by Faith

That righteousness comes by faith is a dominant theme of the book of Romans. Paul says: "Even the righteousness of God which is by faith of Jesus Christ unto all and upon all them that believe" (Romans 3:22); "For what saith the scripture? Abraham believed God, and it was counted unto him for righteousness" (Romans 4:3); "But to him that worketh not, but believeth on him that justifieth the ungodly, his faith is counted for righteousness" (Romans 4:5). This apostle had to admit, "The Gentiles, which followed not after righteousness, have attained to righteousness, even the righteousness which is of faith" (Romans 9:30).

So true righteousness, the sharing of the righteous nature of Christ, comes by believing God's provision, not by playing copy cat. One of the most dangerous things a Christian can do is to try to emulate or copy the righteousness of God. The Christian life is far more than a code to be followed; it is a life to be lived. God puts a grace within us that He expects us to release in daily occupation. Until it has been received, it can never be released. This change of inner nature will be seen in our outer behavior. The life of faith does not eliminate the harsh facts of life. Faith simply enables a person to reach into the provision of God's nature to face these facts victoriously. Faith is extreme action; not inaction.

When God led His chosen people out of Egypt toward the Land of Promise to make of them a great and mighty nation, He had them pause at Mt. Sinai where He introduced Himself to them with great physical demonstrations and by speaking to them out of the fire that burned on the top of Mr. Sinai. He then gave them the Law amidst the blaring of a loud trumpet. In the hearing of all Israel, God spoke the Ten Commandments as a code of behavior and then carved them into tables of stone. The first four commands concerned Israel's relationship with God, and the final six governed their relationship to one another. Look at them.

Righteous relationships with God were shown as:

1. Have no other Gods before Him.
2. Make no graven images of God.
3. Not to take God's name in vain.
4. Keep the sabbath day holy.

Righteous relationships with others was defined as:

5. Honor thy father and mother.
6. Don't kill.
7. Don't commit adultery.
8. Don't steal.
9. Don't lie.
10. Don't covet.

(The full list of these commandments is in Exodus 20:1-17). These commandments are basic, but they form the foundation for civilization. Wherever a society has abandoned this code of righteous living, chaos has replaced culture.

In His teaching in the New Testament, Jesus not only endorsed the Ten Commandments, He amplified them making them extremely practical for our everyday living. Furthermore, in the Sermon on the Mount (Matthew 5:1-12), He dealt with proper attitudes for kingdom believers. We call them the beatitudes. He said:

1. Happy (or "blessed) are the poor in spirit.
2. Happy are they that mourn.
3. Happy are the meek.
4. Happy are those who hunger and thirst after righteousness.
5. Happy are the merciful.
6. Happy are the pure in heart.
7. Happy are the persecuted for righteousness sake.
8. Happy are men who are reviled falsely for His sake.

Then Jesus encapsulated it all by saying, "Rejoice, and be exceeding glad: for great is your reward in heaven."

As He continued to develop His discourse, Jesus called for us to be salt and light in this world (Matthew 5:13-14). He spoke of unresolved anger (Matthew 5:22) and hypocrisy in worship (Matthew 5:23-24). He enlarged the commandment against adultery to include even inner lustings that don't become outward acts (Matthew 5:28). The whole of this discourse cuts against the grain of selfishness and greed. Jesus wanted His people to know that there was a higher plane of life where righteousness brings its own rewards.

One reason Jesus was so unpopular with the religious leaders of His day is that Jesus was so very practical in His teachings. He dealt with principles of righteousness that affected the lifestyle of covenant people. Jesus taught that entering the kingdom of God changed the standard of behavior. It is as true today as it was when Jesus walked the shores of Galilee.

Righteousness is Practical

When Paul sought to broaden the concept of the Roman Christians who lived in the decadence of Rome's immoral society, he told them: "For the kingdom of God is not meat and drink; but righteousness, and peace, and joy in the Holy Ghost" (Romans 14:17). In saying this, Paul merely elaborated on the teaching of Jesus that entering the kingdom changed the inner attitudes of kingdom dwellers; bringing them into positive living in the present.

Born-again Christians have been changed inwardly. Past sin has been forgiven and sin's power over the individual life has been broken. New principles of living have been instilled. Paul explained it this way: "The law of the Spirit of life in Christ Jesus hath made me free from the law of sin and death" (Romans 8:2). New principles [laws] supplant old principles. We can expect, then, that since the life is governed by new standards, it will have fresh, Christ-honoring ethics and morality. Righteousness should reign over unrighteousness in the lives of the redeemed.

Some persons have said that the Ten Commandments, especially as they are amplified and applied by Jesus in the New Testament, take all the fun out of living. Nothing could be further from the truth. God's revealed code of righteousness is the manufacturer's instructions given to insure pleasurable service. In our natural life, we've learned that if we follow the manufacturer's instructions, we will have the best service out of his product. We are not compelled to follow them; we are but told what is best. For instance, it is not a violation of the law to refuse to change the oil in your car, but the manufacturer recommends it at specified intervals. If you ignore those instructions, you will wear out your automobile far too rapidly, and you may have to rebuild the engine.

Similarly, we can ignore God's code of righteousness, but we will suffer the consequences later on. God is not trying to make life difficult or miserable by calling for righteous living. He is merely saying that this is good maintenance for the life He created in us.

If following God's rules for life squeeze all the enjoyment of living out, why does God call His kingdom "righteousness, peace, and joy in the Holy Ghost?" It is unfortunate that religious persons have given us a picture of doom and gloom when the indwelling life of Jesus offers us destiny and the bloom of life.

I guess that some religious persons are so heavenly minded that they are of no earthly use. Their goal seems to be to escape life, but Jesus came to bring the maximum participation in the life in the present as well as to prepare us for the future life.

Jesus said: "I am come that they might have life, and that they might have it more abundantly" (John 10:10). He came to bring life, abundant life, and more abundant life. That sounds like living life to the max and it is! The entire work of Jesus Christ at the cross of Calvary was intended to raise our level of life. He did not come to take away anything but our sins. He did provide, however, to reintroduce to our lives higher ethics and standards of morality that would increase and enhance our enjoyment of life here and now.

The person who does not steal, need not worry about being pursued. The person who consistently tells the truth doesn't have to remember just what he or she said to different persons. The man or woman who averts adultery does not have the destructive force of guilt to contend with in his or her marriage. Righteous living is relaxed living. Righteous living is rewarding living.

Righteousness affects every area of our lives. The person living in the righteousness of Christ will be faithful in handling money. He or she will have embraced the exhortation of the Bible: "Let your conversation [literally "manner of living"] be without covetousness; and be content with such things as ye have: for he hath said, I will never leave thee, nor forsake thee" (Hebrews 13:5).

Being free from deep lusting for things unobtainable makes it possible to enjoy what we now have. The Bible calls this an escape from corruption: "Whereby are given unto us exceeding great and precious promises: that by these ye might be partakers of the divine nature, having escaped the corruption that is in the world through lust" (2 Peter 1:4). It also declares that most of the things that people lust after are very transient and perishable: "The world passeth away, and the lust thereof: but he that doeth the will of God abideth for ever" (1 John 2:17).

Twentieth century Christians living in a decaying society need to join David in praying: "Lead me, O LORD, in thy righteousness because of mine enemies; make thy way straight before my face" (Psalm 5:8).

Chapter 11

The Basics of Peace

When Paul characterized the kingdom of God, his second descriptive word was peace. He wrote: "For the kingdom of God is not meat and drink; but righteousness, and peace, and joy in the Holy Ghost" (Romans 14:17). God's kingdom is a peaceful kingdom. In contrast, satan's kingdom is characterized by anxiety, strife, fear, and contention.

Not only is the kingdom of God, or kingdom of heaven as it is sometimes called, a peaceful realm, but its ruler, Christ Jesus, bears the title: "The Prince of Peace" (Isaiah 9:6). David understood Christ's peaceful reign for he sang: "I will both lay me down in peace, and sleep: for thou, LORD, only makest me dwell in safety ... The LORD will give strength unto his people; the LORD will bless his people with peace ... But the meek shall inherit the earth; and shall delight themselves in the abundance of peace" (Psalms 4:8, 29:11, 37:11).

Sometimes peace is described as non-activity, but peace is not a vacuum; it is not even the absence of disturbing factors. Peace is a gift from God. It is a grace God grants to those who enter into His kingdom through repentance. Peace is always a positive factor; not the absence of negative influences.

We are probably never more aware of peace, or at least the word peace, than during the Christmas season, for then the carols declare it, the cards herald it, and the media repeats it endlessly: "Peace on earth, good will toward men." It is the message of Christmas. It is the mood of Christmas. Good will and tranquility are the accepted attitudes of the Christmas season; frenzied throngs of shoppers notwithstanding.

During this season, personal guilt is sublimated, anger is repressed, and retribution is postponed. It is the season of peace and goodwill to all men. All this religious hoopla is based on the angelic message given to the shepherds on the Judean hillside. Or is it?

The Luke account of the birth of Jesus records this angelic message as being: "Glory to God in the highest, and on earth peace, good will toward men" (Luke 2:14). This is one of those statements recorded in Scripture that is difficult to accept literally when viewed in the light of either history or current events. "Peace on earth?" Surely the angels could not have actually meant this. Perhaps this is excited exaggeration for which we mortals are famous. Maybe it was angelic aspiration or possibly it may simply be a worshipful euphemism.

"Peace on earth." Is this a prediction? Could it simply be a promise, or, at most, a possibility? It is written as an announcement, but it doesn't lend itself to actualization. It may have been a proclamation, but it has not become perceivable. If this is, indeed, a decree, then we need to know what the angels were talking about, for, as we generally view it, it has not come to pass even after two thousand years.

I have preached God's Word long enough to know that we dare not go from the newspaper to the Bible to understand what God says. We must consistently go from the Bible to current events in order to understand what God is now doing in our world. Still, this prophetic song of the angels still seems to be out of step with life as we live it.

Perhaps we need to examine the what, where, whom, and how of this proclamation before we completely reject the angelic declaration.

Peace On Earth — *What*?

What were the angels talking about when they declared "peace on earth?" If they spoke in the language of the Old Testament, they would have used the Hebrew word *shalom*, which fundamentally means *peace, perfection, compensation,* or *recompense.* In his book, *Old Testament Synonyms*, Robert Baker Girdlestone says that *shalom* "always implies a bringing of some difficulty to a conclusion, a finishing off of some work, a clearing away of some charge". Certainly the coming of Christ was intended to do just this for all believing mankind, for Christ came to settle sin once and for all. The promise of God's Word is: "Therefore being justified by faith, we have peace with God through our Lord Jesus Christ" (Romans 5:1).

As beautiful as the Hebrew word *shalom* is, it is, nonetheless, highly unlikely that the angels would use the religious language of the scribes and priests when talking to common shepherds who spoke Aramaic and understood the trade language of Greek. It is far more reasonable that the angels spoke the Greek language to these keepers of the sacrificial lambs for the Temple.

If this is true, the angels would have used the Greek word *eirene* that refers to the harmonized relationships between God and man plus the sense of rest and contentment that flows from this relationship. Peter put it: "Grace and peace be multiplied unto you through the knowledge of God, and of Jesus our Lord" (2 Peter 1:2). Peter felt that knowing God the Father, God the Son, and God the Spirit multiplied both grace and peace to the student.

Eirene also suggests the bringing of this harmony into our other relationships in life. When Paul described the spiritual armor to be worn by Christ's followers he said: "And your feet shod with the preparation of the gospel of peace" (Ephesians 6:15). He seemed to feel that everywhere our feet walked should bring peace. Our movement through life is on the well built and padded shoes of peace.

Eirene is a strong word which appears in every New Testament book except 1 John. Adam Clarke, the great English expositor of a previous generation, defines this word as: "quiet and comfort in the conscience", which is pretty much what Paul told the church in Philippi when he wrote: "And the peace of God, which passeth all understanding, shall keep your hearts and minds through Christ Jesus" (Philippians 4:7).

It is interesting that after His resurrection, Jesus greeted His disciples differently than He saluted others. To most people, Christ's first words consistently were: "Be not afraid." Jesus was handling their negative emotion of fear. But when Christ confronted His disciples, His words of greeting were: "Peace be to you." We see this in Luke when Jesus appeared in the Upper Room just as the two disciples from Emmaus reported having walked and talked with the risen Lord. Dr Luke reports: "And as they thus spake, Jesus himself stood in the midst of them, and saith unto them, Peace be unto you" (Luke 24:36). Jesus more than dispelled the fear of His disciples; He imparted peace to them, for He had promised them before His crucifixion: "Peace I leave with you, my peace I give unto you: not as the world giveth, give I unto you. Let not your heart be troubled, neither let it be afraid" (John 14:27).

Christ has a higher goal for our lives than merely dispelling our fears. He wants to impart His positive and dynamic peace that prevents the occurrence of fear. He says to us, as He said to His disciples: "These things I have spoken unto you, that in me ye might have peace. In the world ye shall have tribulation: but be of good cheer; I have overcome the world" (John 16:33). His peace in us is far more powerful than the pressure, persecution, and privation in the world.

Six or more times the New Testament calls God "the God of peace" (Romans 15:33, Romans 16:20, 2 Corinthians 13:11, Philippians 4:9, 1 Thessalonians 5:23, and Hebrews 13:20). He is also declared to be the author of peace (see 1 Corinthians 14:33).

Paul declares that when we relate prayerfully to God instead of anxiously to life, we will live in peace. He wrote: "Be careful [anxious] for nothing; but in every thing by prayer and supplication with thanksgiving let your requests be made known unto God. And the peace of God, which passeth all understanding, shall keep your hearts and minds through Christ Jesus" (Philippians 4:6-7).

God's peace may be incomprehensible, but it is gloriously comforting. It sets a guard to protect our hearts and minds from the disturbing thoughts the enemy loves to project to us. Also, God's peace is our protection from life's pressures. It is not what happens to us that disturbs us as much as how we react to that happening. When God's peace rules and guards the inner thoughts and emotions, outside forces cannot enter the inner sanctum of life.

Peace On Earth — *Where*?

If the angels actually declared that the coming of Christ Jesus brought a harmonized relationship between God and man as well as between man and man, where is it happening? Certainly it is not seen in the political world. Rome did not evacuate her occupied territories at the birth of Christ. Actually, Roman oppression became increasingly severe, culminating in the destruction of Jerusalem. Eventually that Roman empire itself was captured and destroyed.

There have been wars and rumors of wars from the birth of Jesus until the present time. Rather than experiencing harmonious relationships, men have sought to impose their will upon others through force and subjugation. Throughout the earth today, Third World nations are locked in civil war or war with neighboring countries. All sides are being conveniently supplied with war materials from the super powers, and terrorism is shaking these supplying world powers. We seem to lack a statesman leader in the western world.

We've recently watched the fall of Communism in Russia with the subsequent disintegration of the Soviet Union. Instead of these "liberated persons" enjoying their freedom, there has been continual infighting, civil strife, and, in many countries, a replacement of Russia's government's arm with the mafia. Extreme crime has replaced extreme repression. There is no peace in the political world today.

Neither is there peace — harmonious relationships — in the economic world. Most western nations are on the verge of bankruptcy. The national debt is astronomical and increasing yearly. Unemployment is still high in the major nations of the world, and labor and management seem to be locked in conflict regularly. Many of America's largest employers are laying off workers by the multiple thousands, causing unemployment figures to continue to rise. More and more people are working longer hours for smaller wages, while our college graduates desperately take jobs at the minimum wage.

Fires, crime, earthquakes, tornadoes, and floods have swept across our nation for months while imposing financial ruin upon thousands. None of this seems to be very peaceful.

In spite of amazing progress over the past decade, there is little peace in the social world of America. Blacks and Hispanics still cry "discrimination". Homosexuals and lesbians continue to demand rights equal to heterosexual marriages, and AIDS is climbing to an epidemic level in our nation.

In spite of some protesting by consumers, violence and sex fill our television screens. Much of the music sung today is anti-establishment and wildly revolutionary at best. Murder by gunshot is worst now than in the wild west period of our history, and most of it is done by young people and children, and we continue to kill thousands of our unborn infants every month through abortion. To a society quite like our own, God twice warned: "There is no peace, saith the LORD, unto the wicked" (Isaiah 48:22; 57:21).

In spite of a governmental war against drugs, the drug problem in America is larger now than when that war began. Drugs and guns have made many of our schools places of terror and fear. Sociologists continue to warn us that inner city unrest is a lurking danger far more real than a third world war. "Peace on earth?" — certainly not in the social world.

Nor is there much peace to be found in the religious world. Even a cursory reading of Church history will remind us of the inquisitions, persecutions, and Holy Wars where acts of gross inhumanity were committed in the name of God. Historians tell us that there have been more martyrs in the past fifty years than in the entire history of the world. That doesn't sound too peaceful to me.

Even currently it is difficult to find peace in the religious world when competition outstrips completion in the Body of Christ, and faction rises against faction in the church here on earth. There is more religious civil war that pits brother against brother than there is peace. In the past ten years, there have been myriads of church splits all across our nation. In many places pastors have been fired by congregations or church boards over very small issues, while in other places, congregations have been deeply wounded by revelation of immorality in their pastors.

In addition to all of this, most religion is based on fear, not on faith, and on law rather than on grace. Hence it knows anxiety, but it does not know peace. Perhaps American Christians should heed the pleading of the psalmist of old: "Pray for the peace of Jerusalem" (Psalm 122:6).

Even in our marital world we have lost our peace. Our great prosperity and unexcelled educational opportunities have failed to bring us into family tranquility. Quite the opposite; it seems to have helped to disintegrate the home more than it has brought peace to it. American families are full of stress. Even Christian homes are crumbling at an alarming rate. Divorce, fornication, adultery, wife and child abuse, and incest are far too evident for us to declare that America's homes, even the Christian homes, are filled with peace. A survey revealed that the most dreaded musical sound in America was the wedding march.

Sociologists are now blaming the mass murders and gang wars we are experiencing on the disintegration of the American home. Membership in a gang has replaced membership in the family because family life has become non-existent in so many marriages. We find ourselves economically unable to build prisons as fast as the courts fill them, but incarcerating persons doesn't seem to be bringing peace to our society.

America's politicians, criminologists, psychologists, and pastors can't seem to find a way to bring peace to our nation. Since it is difficult, if not impossible, to find true peace in our economic, social, religious, and marital worlds, where on earth is this peace to be found?

Peace on Earth — to *Whom*?

The coming of Christ to an individual's life is no panacea, nor is it a guarantee of peace, not even to Christians. Being "saved" is not insurance for peace, for many believers lack peace — real peace — in every area of their lives. They rely on tranquilizers and various forms of chemicals to just cope with day-to-day living. They refer to their lives as a "rat race", just as their unconverted neighbors do. Perhaps these believers have accepted conversion as an experience rather than as a different way of living. They must have forgotten the cry of God's heart: "Look unto me, and be ye saved, all the ends of the earth: for I am God, and there is none else" (Isaiah 45:22). What a shame to seek peace where the world has continually been unable to find it, when an upward look at our God will fill our hearts with inexpressible peace.

The angelic announcement of Christ's birth was qualified and very specific. The literal Greek is "peace ... to the men of His good pleasure". Various translators have handled this Greek phrase differently. The *Revised Standard Version* reads, "peace ... among men with whom he is pleased". The *New English Bible* puts it, "And on earth his peace for men on whom his favour rests". John Knox translated it, "... and peace on earth to men that are God's friends". Montgomery says, "peace among men who please him".

There is an obvious cause/effect relationship between pleasing God and living in the peace of God. It is not by accident that the verse that forms the center text of the Bible declares: "Mercy and truth are met together; righteousness and peace have kissed each other" (Psalm 85:10). Righteousness is consistently coupled with peace in the Bible.

Righteousness is right harmony with God and a right relationship with people. It forms a cross in our lives as the vertical and horizontal compatibilities work in unison. How can we expect to have peace with God if we are out of tune with Him and His ways? Similarly, we are unable to live peaceably with others — even our brothers and sisters in Christ — if our dealings with them are not rooted in righteousness.

The angelic messengers brought God's bulletin to far more than the lowly shepherds. God said to proclaim: "Peace on earth to men that are God's friends ... and on earth peace among men in whom he finds pleasure." Who are God's friends? Who gives Him pleasure?

God's friends are the persons who consistently believe God and unhesitatingly obey Him. The Bible says of Abraham: "Abraham believed God, and it was imputed unto him for righteousness: and he was called the Friend of God" (James 2:23). This same pattern can be seen in these shepherds. They heard what was said, they believed what they were told, they obeyed their instructions, and they saw Christ. Little wonder, then, that their hearts were overwhelmed with the peace of God.

Frequently when counseling with distraught Christians, I shock them by asking, "What has God told you that you have refused to obey?" To them my question seems far off the subject, but more often than not, it is the heart of their problem. God's peace abides with those who listen to His voice and obey His commands.

The Apostle Paul told his converts in Philippi, "Those things, which ye have both learned, and received, and heard, and seen in me, do: and the God of peace shall be with you" (Philippians 4:9). Faith and obedience are consistently the foundation for peace.

Twice during the ministry of Jesus there came, "A voice from heaven, saying, This is my beloved Son, in whom I am well pleased" (Matthew 3:17). The first time was when Jesus was baptized in the river Jordan by John the Baptist, and the second time was on the Mount of Transfiguration. Jesus had submitted to the known will of God on both occasions. The Father was extremely pleased with the obedience of His Son, and Jesus lived a life filled with the peace of God because He pleased the "God of peace" (Romans 16:20).

We read in the closing words of the great book of Hebrews: "Now the God of peace, that brought again from the dead our Lord Jesus, that great shepherd of the sheep, through the blood of the everlasting covenant, make you perfect in every good work to do his will, working in you that which is well-pleasing in his sight, through Jesus Christ; to whom be glory for ever and ever. Amen" (Hebrews 13:20-21 emphasis added). Could anything be plainer?

Yes, there is "peace on earth", but it is not universal. It is shared with those who will trust and obey.

Peace On Earth — *How*?

Paul places peace in great company in two separate lists. When teaching on the fruit of the Spirit, Paul said that peace was in the first group to ripen: "But the fruit of the Spirit is *love, joy, peace*, longsuffering, gentleness, goodness, faith, meekness, temperance: against such there is no law" (Galatians 5:22-23 emphasis added). Love and joy lead into peace. Love produces obedience, joy is the response to obedience, and peace is the fruit of that obedience. God's peace comes as a work of the Holy Spirit in the lives of believers.

Similarly, when Paul was listing the characteristics of God's great kingdom here on earth as well as up in heaven, he said: "For the kingdom of God is not meat and drink; but righteousness, and peace, and joy in the Holy Ghost" (Romans 14:17). He was assured that where righteousness reigned, peace would follow and joy would result. Being an active participant in God's kingdom is to experience "The peace of God, which passeth all understanding, that shall keep your hearts and minds through Christ Jesus" (Philippians 4:7).

This peace is not promised to all men who are on earth. God's peace was wrapped up and sent to men in the package of Jesus Christ our Lord. Our obedient relationship to Him determines the measure of peace we will experience in our lives.

Peace comes out of relationship, not out of religion. Jesus promised, "My peace I give unto you" (John 14:27), and thirteen times in the New Testament we read of "peace from God the Father". Observance of religious codes will create more conflict than it will produce peace, but an intimate relationship with God will bring increasing peace to the human heart. It is closeness to God, not codes and ethics, that is the source of our peace.

Peace is not a concept; it is a condition. It is far more than a feeling; it is a fact. God's peace is independent of circumstances, but is completely dependent upon relationship. Actually, peace is received, not achieved. It is a gift that affects relationships.

When we receive the "Prince of peace" (Isaiah 9:6), we receive the peace of the Prince. Additionally, peace is not necessarily permanent, but it is progressive. Peace, imparted, wears thin when it is separated from the Person who imparted that peace. As surely as Peter began to sink beneath the waves when he took his eyes off Jesus, we begin to sink into the morass of life's problems when we look down instead of up.

Furthermore, peace in circumstance "A" may not mean peace in circumstance "B". Some may have great peace in trusting God for finances, but are void of peace when facing sickness. We need the presence of Christ in all circumstances to have the inner tranquility, trust, confidence, and calm assurance that His peace brings to His sons and daughters.

Let the public address systems repeatedly play, "Peace on earth, good will toward men: Christ is born in Bethlehem." It creates a mental attitude that is positive and conducive to Christmas shopping. But the historic fact does not bring peace. Only the Christ of history brings that peace. The warmer the relationship with Him, the stronger His peace will be in our lives.

Did the angels exaggerate in their proclamation? No! A thousand times no! Christ Jesus brought peace that has infected and affected the lives of countless thousands of people from that day until this. While not all men now know peace, those men and women who please God know a peace that is unearthly in quality — it is divine! There is, indeed, "Peace on earth to men who are God's friends" (Knox).

Peace Is Relational

To whom, then, was this peace proclaimed? Perhaps we need to remind ourselves that this angelic announcement was highly qualified. The declaration that peace had come was preceded by the statement, "For unto you is born this day in the city of David a Saviour, which is Christ the Lord" (Luke 2:11). The proclamation was far more affirmation that a *Person* had come than that *peace* had come. Peace was the outgrowth of His coming. Christ was the product; peace was the by-product.

Three titles were given to this Person by the angels. He was called:

1. Savior
2. Christ
3. Lord

The first qualification to the announcement of peace was the declaration that a Savior had come. To Joseph, the angel Gabriel had affirmed, "Thou shalt call his name JESUS: for He shall save His people from their sins" (Matthew 1:21). Coming into peace with God and knowing the peace of God starts by meeting Jesus as Savior. Peace does not come at a bargaining table. It begins at Calvary's cross. It is rooted in an acknowledgment that we are unable to save ourselves, and that we need someone to save us.

Becoming a son of God is an act of faith made possible by grace. Christ came not merely to make us sons, but to release sons of God from the captivity of sin. As our Savior from sin, Christ Jesus brought us the peace of release. When sin is removed, we not only come back to peace with God; we find peace with ourselves.

The second qualification to the pronouncement of peace was the declaration that *Christ* had come. This was the promised Messiah, the Anointed One of God. This term as used in the

214

epistles of the New Testament refers to the second Person of the Godhead. It is the title of the divine side of the God-man. Christ came as the intermediary between God and man and became the reconciler of men to God. As such, He brought us the *peace of restored relationship*. Our fear of God becomes faith in God, and instead of running from Him, we run to Him. The feud is over, for man was reconciled to God through Christ Jesus our Lord.

The third qualification to the declaration of peace was the announcement that the *Lord* had come. This was the Old Testament name for the God-head. The scribes viewed the name of God as too sacred to write, so they generally substituted the term "Lord" for the sacred and secret name of God. This term speaks of authority, dominion, and position.

Modern evangelism tends to assert that confession of sin and subsequent forgiveness make us sons of God, but Paul declared that it is confession of the Lordship of Jesus that brings us into sonship. For the record he said, "That if thou shalt confess with thy mouth the Lord Jesus, and shalt believe in thine heart that God hath raised him from the dead, thou shalt be saved. For with the heart man believeth unto righteousness; and with the mouth confession is made unto salvation" (Romans 10:9-10). It begins by confessing the Lordship of Jesus.

The One who was born in the manger in Bethlehem of Judaea was far more than a Savior — He was Christ the Lord. He is God who is in charge of our lives. As the Lord, He brought us the *peace of submission*. We are no longer in charge of our lives; He is in charge, and this removes the pressure of decision from our lives. When sin no longer has dominion over us, we have the peace of release. When we embrace the Christ of God, we have the peace of restored relationships, and as we surrender to the Lordship of Jesus, we enter the peace of submission. It is then that we can understand the cry of the prophet: "Ye shall go out with joy, and be led forth with peace: the mountains and the hills shall break forth before you into singing, and all the trees of the field shall clap their hands" (Isaiah 55:12).

The promise of "peace" was inexorably wrapped up in the Person whom the angels called Savior, Christ, and Lord. He came to bring us into the peace: "Now the Lord of peace himself give you peace always by all means. The Lord be with you all" (2 Thessalonians 3:16).

Unfortunately, however, it is not automatic. If this peace is, indeed, in a Person then the measure of peace we possess will be in proportion to our relationship with this Person. If we do not walk with God, we will have no peace. Probably the greatest battle in any Christian's life is the battle over self-pleasure and learning to honestly say, "Nevertheless, not my will, but Thine, be done" (Luke 22:42). Those who can say it with meaning live in a peace that others know nothing about.

Peace rules the day when Christ rules the mind. "For he is our peace, who hath made both one" (Ephesians 2:14), so: "Let the peace of God rule in your hearts, to the which also ye are called in one body; and be ye thankful" (Colossians 3:15).

Peace is such a priceless possession that one could be content with this while lacking everything else, but God has coupled peace and joy together. Peace leads to joy. It is the foundation of true joy.

Chapter 12

The Basics of Joy

The man Christ Jesus blazed the trail into life that has joy at its center. It differs from happiness in that it is not dependent upon circumstances. It differs from pleasure in that it is lasting rather than momentary. Christ came to impart a deep, lasting joy to mankind. One would naturally expect, then, that when worshipers of Jesus gather at church, it would be a very joyful occasion. Not necessarily so!

Because the church represents a sovereign God who is awesome, and the ministries of that church grapple with sin, sorrow, and death, it is understandable that many persons approach church services in a very somber mood. Some are actually fearful.

Sometimes pastors unwittingly contribute to this solemn attitude by so emphasizing negative circumstances in our society that we fail to lift our congregation into joyful praise.

On the day the earthquake caused such extensive damage in Los Angeles in 1994, the news media concentrated on the point of the great devastation; telling over and over again of the billions of dollars worth of damage that five seconds of quaking earth could cause. The mayor was passed from one camera crew to another to answer the same questions for different networks. At one point, he stared directly into the lens of the camera and said, "We ought to realize that while many have suffered, most of Los Angeles is in excellent condition."

Disaster is news worthy; normalcy is not. Too many Christians so focus on their little "disaster" areas of life that they fail to realize they are enjoying peace, provision, and pleasure most of their life. Often the difference between living in misery or living in joy is simply the focus of the life.

The Bible speaks of joy over 165 times in 155 separate verses, while it mentions sorrow only 70 times in 65 verses. If God's Word to us speaks of joy two and a half times more frequently than it speaks of sorrow, shouldn't our responses to God be twice more joyful than sorrowful?

In *The Bible Reader's Encyclopedia and Concordance*, Rev. W.M. Clow writes:

> *In no other religion and in no other literature is joy so conspicuous as in Christianity and in the Bible. Physically and psychologically speaking, it is the criterion of health whereby all the powers and affections are enriched and harmonized. So in religion it denotes the satisfaction of the soul at attaining its desire; and Christianity stands firm so long as men who have it are invested with joy".*

(Collins' Press, England © 1962)

The reasons given for attending church are varied. Some worshipers come out of habit; others attend out of fear of retribution if they stayed away. A great number of suppliants come to have their needs met, while other attendants admit they attend for social reasons. Wouldn't it be wonderful if we came together to receive, release, and respond to "the joy of the Lord"? (Nehemiah 8:10).

Shouting or Sighing?

The psalmist sang: "Oh come, let us sing unto the LORD! Let us shout joyfully to the Rock of our salvation. Let us come before His presence with thanksgiving; *Let us shout joyfully to Him* with Psalms" (Psalm 95:1-2, italics added). "Shout joyfully to the LORD!" While it sounds so irreligious, it does sound inviting. It is usually pleasurable to be among "the happy worshipers".

Happy worshiper? That's far too weak. Joyful worshipers is more accurate. Happiness is usually a response to happenings where pleasant experiences produce pleasant responses. "Happy worship" is usually inconsistent and vacillating. It rises and falls with the change of circumstances. God's Word tells us: "Many sorrows shall be to the wicked: but he that trusteth in the LORD, mercy shall compass him about. Be glad in the LORD, and rejoice, ye righteous: and shout for joy, all ye that are upright in heart" (Psalms 32:10-11).

In contrast to happiness, which is a response to circumstances, joy is the expression of a deep, settled relationship with God. It is less a response to outside stimuli than it is a release of a deep, inner emotion.

David was certainly invested with joy — true joy. His was not a giggling laughter, but something that came from the depths of his inner being. He did not need a court jester to bring him a humorous release from tension, for he had found joy as a glorious by-product of his submission to the LORD. God, who was the object of his joy, was also the origin of it. After confessing his sin of adultery, David pled with God, "Make me to hear joy and gladness ... Restore to me the joy of Your salvation" (Psalm 51:8,12).

Once a person has sampled the joy of God's salvation, all other pleasures seem flat and unappetizing. Having tasted the best, David ignored the rest, for he was king, and he was used to having the finest of everything.

Back in 1924, the People's Publication Society of Chicago published *The People's Bible Encyclopedia* in which the editor, Charles Randal Barnes, AM, DD, wrote:

> *Joy is a delight of the mind arising from the consideration of a present, or assured possession of a future good. When moderate it is called gladness; raised suddenly to the highest degree it is exultation or transport; when the desires are limited by our possessions it is contentment; high desires accomplished bring satisfaction; vanquished opposition we call triumph; when joy has so long possessed the mind that it has settled into a*

> *temper, we call it cheerfulness. This is natural joy.*
> *There is a moral joy ... this kind of joy is called peace,*
> *or serenity of conscience; if the action be honorable,*
> *and the joy rise high, it may be called glory.*

Quite obviously, Dr Barnes has thought his subject through most thoroughly. There are degrees of joy, and differing causes for joy as well as various methods of expressing that joy, but in our society, joy is usually seen as the antithesis to sadness or sorrow. Unfortunately, however, sorrow and grief are such powerful emotions that they usually dominate a person's emotions while destroying all sense of joy and well being.

Shouting releases happy pent up emotions. When we consider the goodness of God to our lives and count up the blessings that have accrued since we received Him as our Lord, how could we help but shout occasionally? The Psalmist declared, "The LORD hath done great things for us; whereof we are glad" (Psalm 126:3). In our public gatherings we need to spend more time reflecting on the goodness of the Lord than on the need of the worshipers. We need something to shout about. Where life does not provide it, the Gospel of Christ will.

Joy versus Sorrow

Still, all lives are subject to some tragedy, confusion, and disappointment. We have all known our share of hurts, pain, and sorrow, but we also know our God. As we mature in Christ Jesus, we don't expect Jehovah to insulate us from the harsh realities of life, but we do allow God to turn those sorrows into joy. Sorrow turns to joy in the Lord when we "look away to Jesus".

Jesus told His disciples and us, "These things have I spoken unto you, that my joy might remain in you, and that your joy might be full" (John 15:11). Christ offers us at least a double measure of joy:

1. God's joy in us
2. Our joy fulfilled

The Christian is not removed from joy; he has twice more joy than anyone else.

We have heard many testimonies of persons who experienced their deepest joy while in the midst of their greatest trials and disappointments. Their attention was turned from their sorrow to their God, and they found a deep, settled peace in His presence. They have been able to join David in singing: "O LORD my God, I cried out to You, And You have healed me. O LORD, You have brought my soul up from the grave; You have kept me alive, that I should not go down to the pit ... Weeping may endure for a night, But joy comes in the morning" (Psalm 30:3,5).

The Apostle Paul wrote, "We know that all things work together for good to those who love God, to those who are called according to His purpose" (Romans 8:28). It is wonderful to know this experientially; not just mentally. Our relationship with God can be so strong that even in struggling with sorrow, we can expect God to make good to come of it.

We cannot always respond with happiness, but we can respond with joy. We can honestly share the ballad of the psalmist: "You have turned for me my mourning into dancing; You have put off my sackcloth and clothed me with gladness, To the end that my glory may sing praise to You and not be silent. O LORD my God, I will give thanks to You forever" (Psalm 30:11-12).

We dare not pretend that we have had no grief or sorrow; that is dangerous denial. But when we see beyond the physical and emotional changes that these pressures produce in us, and look up to God, we realize that God is completely unchanged. Since God is the source as well as the subject of our joy, we can worship God jubilantly in the darkest hours of gloom. We can rejoice in the LORD just because the LORD is present. God does not need to do anything to produce a rejoicing spirit in our hearts, for it is the person of God that fills our beings with joy.

It has well been said that joy is more divine than sorrow, for joy is bread and sorrow is medicine. While sorrow may correct some things in our lives, it is joy that becomes the mainstay of our existence. Remove joy and life is not worth living.

Jesus well understood this. When He was giving His final teaching to the disciples in the Garden and retelling them that He must be crucified and return to the Father, He said: "Ye now therefore have sorrow: but I will see you again, and your heart shall rejoice, and your joy no man taketh from you" (John 16:22). He realized that His impending arrest, trial, and crucifixion would induce such fear, pain, and sorrow as to throw their lives into an emotional tail spin, so He guaranteed them a rejoicing joy and challenged them to let their inner joy become so secure that nothing another person could do or say could diminish it. If Jesus could go to the cross because of an offered joy, certainly the disciples should be able to survive this pain with a remaining joy.

Divine joy is God's provision for His children. The psalmists knew this, for they wrote: "He brought out His people with joy, His chosen ones with gladness" (Psalm 105:43). What difficulties the Israelites would have had if their exodus had not been a joyous event. They were leaving the only way of life they had ever known, carrying on their backs the few possessions they could salvage. If their hearts had been filled with sorrow and dread, the burden of leaving Egypt would have been overwhelming.

Instead, God filled their hearts with joy. They were a minor type of Jesus of whom it is written: "Who for the joy that was set before him endured the cross, despising the shame, and is set down at the right hand of the throne of God" (Hebrews 12:2).

Joy is a marvelous motivator. We are willing to endure hardships and suffering when we know that we will have a joyful end. Jesus knew this. He said: "Verily, verily, I say unto you, That ye shall weep and lament, but the world shall rejoice: and ye shall be sorrowful, but your sorrow shall be turned into joy. A woman when she is in travail hath sorrow, because her hour is come: but as soon as she is delivered of the child, she remembereth no more the anguish, for joy that a man is born into the world" (John 16:20-21).

We Christians dare not lose the motivation of divine joy. We must keep it before us as the young lady keeps her engagement ring in close view. While we experience joy right now, the joy that is yet to come is far greater than anything we have yet experienced in this life. Religion tends to make us sad, but God makes us glad. As the psalmist said, "For You, Lord, have made me glad through Your work" (Psalm 92:4).

Joy in Relationship

Steve Sampson in his recent book, *Enjoying God*, observes: "God is misunderstood. Few people understand that God wants us to enjoy Him and He wants to enjoy us. Deceived, we have protected ourselves from getting too intimate with Him, thinking He is going to make life rough on us" (page 89; © 1985 by the author). This may well have been the attitude of the children of Israel at Mount Sinai when God introduced Himself from heaven and offered them an intimate relationship with Him. Terrorized by the display of the divine Almightiness, they pled with Moses to tell God not to speak to them again. They said that if God would tell Moses what He wanted done, they would do it, for they were professional slaves who were trained to take orders.

In this one action, they traded relationship with God for law from God. They exchanged the joy of relationship for a job based on regulations, and there is little scriptural evidence of joy from that point on. Again and again, we read of Israel's murmuring, complaining, and insurrecting, but do we hear of them rejoicing with the song and dance after passing through the Red Sea?

One of the psalmists sang out, "Oh, send out Your light and Your truth! Let them lead me; Let them bring me to Your holy hill And to Your tabernacle. Then I will go to the altar of God, *To God my exceeding joy*; And on the harp I will praise You, O God, my God" (Psalm 43:3-4; the emphasis added). When God is our "exceeding joy", our responses to Him will be joyful responses. Perhaps outward singing, shouting, leaping, and dancing will again release our inner joy as we worship the One who has lifted us from the darkness and weight of sin into the light and joy of His own countenance. David cried, "But let all those rejoice who put their trust in You; Let them ever shout for joy, because You defend them; Let those also who love Your name be joyful in You" (Psalm 5:11). We don't trust God grudgingly or desperately. We trust Him joyfully. Our intimate relationship with Him gives us a relaxed confidence that all is well.

How can any of us be active participants in the kingdom of God and lack an inner joy? The very definition of God's kingdom is: "The kingdom of God is not meat and drink; but righteousness, and peace, and joy in the Holy Ghost" (Romans 14:17). Right relationship with God and one another plus the peace of God are joy producing. Something is out of order if we have true righteousness and peace, but lack the "joy in the Holy Ghost".

This joy of the Spirit is listed as the second fruit of the Spirit to ripen in the hearts of believers. Paul said: "The fruit of the Spirit is love, joy, peace ..." (Galatians 5:22). The only part of the divine nature that comes into our lives ahead of holy joy is God's love. We need not produce our joy; it is inherent in the indwelling Spirit of God. Maintaining a vital relationship with God the Father, Jesus the Son, and the Holy Spirit is a guarantee of indwelling joy.

My sister, Iverna Tompkins, gave me an engraved picture of *The Laughing Jesus*. I have it hanging on my office door. I have had trouble with the somber, joyless artistic renditions of Jesus that are popular. I believe Jesus enjoyed life to the fullest. I know He was living in the slums compared to the heavenly glory He had left, and I recognize that He was constantly surrounded with human misery and suffering. Still, he knew the full plan of the Heavenly Father and realized that He was here as an exhibition of God and His love.

I don't understand how men, women, youth, and children were so attracted to Jesus if he was colorless, joyless, and religiously sober. The Gospels present Him as vibrant, forceful, and charismatic in His person. I can visualize Him seeing the funny side of life, and even telling jokes to the disciples.

If this offends you, please forgive me, but I believe the gospels bear me out. Scholars of the Greek New Testament love to point out how cleverly Jesus used Jewish humor to teach divine principles. This humor must have been the natural outgrowth of His inner joy, for if joy is the produce of relationship with God, the joy of Jesus must have been the greatest in the world, for He had the greatest relationship with God than any of us.

We need to embrace the statement of Charles Spurgeon: "There is more in God to cheer you than in your circumstances to depress you." An active joy in the Lord and a rejoicing in the Spirit is indicative of a vital contact with Christ Jesus. Such a saint is daily "renewed in the spirit of his mind" (see Ephesians 4:23).

A good way to determine your spiritual condition is to take a reading of the inner pressure of joy, and to count the pulse of your outer rejoicing. Despair, despondency, depression, and gloom reveal a serious spiritual condition. In contrast, rejoicing, happiness, joy, and gladness are good indications of spiritual healthiness.

In speaking to a rebellious people, God said, "Behold, My servants shall sing for joy of heart, But you shall cry for sorrow of heart, and wail for grief of spirit" (Isaiah 65:14). The difference lies in the relationship of the individuals to God. Self-will brings sorrow, while submission to God's will brings songs of joy. Those who are trying to "live their lives for Jesus" usually have more sighs than songs, but those who allow Jesus to live in their lives have shouts of joy that must be expressed.

Joy's Source

The object of our joy is God Himself. Joy does not come because Jesus was born in Bethlehem, but because He has been born within our lives. He came into the world to come into our lives. This is joy-producing. It is the visitation of God Himself to the individual that induces such great joy.

As the fountain of all our mercies, God must be the center of all our joys. To come to God for mercy, and then go to the world for joy is what inhabitants of the land of Israel did when: "They feared the LORD, and served their own gods, after the manner of the nations whom they carried away from thence." (2 Kings 17:33). All we will ever need can be found in Jesus.

God takes pleasure in the joy of His people. Our songs of gladness are more pleasing to His ears than any sighs or sadness can possibly be. He has paid such a great price to make joy available to us that He is pleased to see us rejoicing. Just as the father who has sacrificed to buy his son a bicycle loves to hear the joyful noise of his son riding the bike, so God delights in hearing His happy people. He must merely endure His melancholy sons.

Paul's favorite worship expression was *rejoice*! He wrote: "Rejoice in the Lord alway: and again I say, Rejoice" (Philippians 4:4). To rejoice in the Lord is to be joyful:

1. In His name
2. In His work
3. In His Word
4. In His kingdom
5. In His church

Being joyful in the Lord is one of the most aggressive of all spiritual forces. This joy is power, because it is the evidence of a life happily adjusted to the perfect will of God. This joy is also our strength, for the promise is: "The joy of the LORD is your strength" (Nehemiah 8:10). This strength is needed to overcome the world, the flesh, and the devil in our day by day living.

Joy in Worship

Through the pages of church history, those who have embraced religious rules and regulations as their security have displayed little joy. Occasionally, even singing was banned from worship sessions. Religion — with its rites, rituals, ceremonies, and sacred persons — has a way of wringing all joy from the hearts of worshipers, for joy is never the result of performance; it is always the expression of a relationship with God. The more distant that relationship is, the less joy will be released in worship. Surprisingly, the Mosaic Tabernacle in the Wilderness was not a place of expressed joy. It was a place of bloody sacrifices, confession of sins, ceremonial cleansing, and repeated rituals. While it was a sacred and hallowed place with outward demonstrations of God's Presence, it was equally a solemn and hierarchical place that was approached with fear and dread.

They did not hear singers or see dancers in the outer court; they heard confessions of sin and they saw death all around them.

All of these divine provisions were intended to bring God and man closer together, but usually the priesthood had to be a substitute for the people's approach to God. The congregation did not enter into an adequate relationship with God in order to enjoy Him sufficiently to want to approach Him. Consequently, their worship lacked joy.

In contrast to this, David pitched a tent to protect the ark of the covenant when it was brought to Jerusalem, and God was worshiped joyfully before it. The procession that brought the ark into Jerusalem was one of singing, shouting, waving of banners and dancing. David made it a day of national celebration, for he visualized God returning to His Holy City.

Once the ark was established in its new home, David appointed singers and instrumentalists to minister musically unto the LORD twenty-four hours a day. David wanted his people to enjoy God, and he coveted an atmosphere where God could enjoy His people.

On the day that the ark was first placed in this tabernacle, "David first delivered this psalm into the hand of Asaph and his brethren, to thank the LORD: 'Oh, give thanks to the LORD! ... Sing to Him, sing psalms to Him; ... Glory in His holy name; Let the hearts of those rejoice who seek the LORD! ... Let the heavens rejoice, and let the earth be glad; And let them say among the nations, "The LORD reigns." Let the sea roar, and all its fullness; Let the field rejoice, and all that is in it. Then the trees of the woods shall rejoice before the LORD, for He is coming to judge the earth'" (1 Chronicles 16:7-10; 31-33).

Joy is a privilege of worship, and it should be a natural consequence of an individual's fellowship with God. We must challenge people to joyfully worship. Each of us needs to approach worship with the expectancy that, "You will show me the path of life; In Your presence is fullness of joy; At Your right hand are pleasures forevermore" (Psalm 16:11). Where there is joy there is hope, strength, and peace.

Solomon, must have learned something about joy from his father, for he wrote, "He who is of a merry heart has a continual feast", and, "A merry heart makes a cheerful countenance, But by sorrow of the heart the spirit is broken", and, "A merry heart does good, like medicine, But a broken spirit dries out the bones" (Proverbs 15:15,13; 17:22).

Israel in the wilderness had the ritualistic worship of the Tabernacle in the Wilderness. While becoming a kingdom, they had the Tabernacle of David, and while enjoying the established kingdom, they had the Temple of Solomon. In the days of the Apostles, while seeking to settle a dispute of whether or not the Gentiles needed to be circumcised according to the custom of Moses, James declared, "It is written: 'After this I will return And will rebuild the tabernacle of David which has fallen down. I will rebuild its ruins, And I will set it up, So that the rest of mankind may seek the LORD, Even all the Gentiles who are called by My name, says the LORD who does all these things'" (Acts 15:15-17).

228

It was not the Mosaic Tabernacle in the Wilderness or Solomon's Temple that would be rebuilt to allow the Gentiles to enter into the worship of Jehovah — it was the Tabernacle of David — that humble tent with no other piece of furniture than the Ark of the Covenant.

God is bringing the Gentiles into a place of worship where solemnity gives place to psalms, and where ritualistic ceremony and endless sacrifices have been replaced with rejoicing shouts and ceaseless singing. Christ Jesus became the final blood sacrifice, but in that same action, He became the blessed One — "... whom having not seen you love. Though now you do not see Him, yet believing, you rejoice with joy inexpressible and full of glory, receiving the end of your faith — the salvation of your souls" (1 Peter 1:8-9).

The priestly garments have been put away. The furniture of the Temple no longer exists. The rituals of Mosaic worship have, for the most part, been forgotten or set aside, but the rejoicing of the Tabernacle of David will live on forever. Let others search for the Ark of the Covenant. We have met the Living God. Ritual has been replaced with rejoicing, and joy, not sacrifice, is the order of the day.

If Bible reading, preaching, public worship, or private meditation do not induce joy to the life, it is probably because we are looking inward at our failures rather than upward to our unfailing God.

When Ezra opened the Word of God and read and explained it to the Hebrews who had returned from captivity: "All the people wept, when they heard the words of the Law. Then he said to them, 'Go your way, eat the fat, drink the sweet, and send portions to those for whom nothing has been prepared: for this day is holy to our LORD. Do not sorrow, for the joy of the LORD is your strength ... And all the people went their way to eat and drink, to send portions and rejoice greatly, because they understood the words that were declared to them" (Nehemiah 8:9-12).

Even under the Old Covenant, God wanted the worship of His people to be filled with joy. How much more does He desire this from the New Testament saints.

When we observe worship in heaven, as unveiled for us in the book of Revelation, we are overwhelmed to see singing, shouting, waving of palm branches, and loud declarations of jubilation and excitement. Heaven's worship is not mournful; it is joyful!

This praise-filled, jubilant, rejoicing worship has been the by-product of every new revelation of God to people. Fresh faith induces fresh joy, and this is as it should be. Mirth is never good without God. Christians need to rejoice so they can rejoice over their rejoicing. David did, the apostles did, as well as the living creatures and the twenty-four elders in heaven do. Let's be renewed in the spirit of joy so we, too, can live, work, and worship joyfully.

Chapter 13

The Basics of Prayer

In much of the Old Testament, the expression "I pray you" is used to gain permission much as we say, "I ask you." The New Testament writers used the word *pray* as an imperative command! Jesus said: "Watch ye and pray, lest ye enter into temptation" (Mark 14:38). He also said, "But when ye pray ..." [not *if* you pray] (Matthew 6:7).

Paul, who was both a great man of prayer and a man of great prayers, commanded believers to pray. He wrote: "Pray without ceasing" (1 Thessalonians 5:17), and, "Pray for us" (1 Thessalonians 5:25). He taught Timothy, "I will therefore that men pray every where, lifting up holy hands, without wrath and doubting" (1 Timothy 2:8).

The Apostle James also commanded the believers to pray, especially when they had a personal need. He said, "Is any among you afflicted? Let him pray" (James 5:13). The writer to the Hebrews pled, "Pray for us" (Hebrews 13:18).

Prayer as the New Testament teaches it, is not optional; it is obligatory. God says to do it, and we live in disobedience to that command unless we do pray. Prayer is a blessing, prayer meets a need, and prayer changes people and things. Even if there were no direct benefits to prayer, it is a divine command for every believer.

Over the years I have discovered that announcing "Prayer" as my sermon title produces an almost immediate sense of guilt. All Christians believe in prayer, but few Christians regularly pray, and because of this, they live in a state of self-imposed shame.

It is not because we lack information on the subject, for when we visit a Christian bookstore, we find shelves filled with books about prayer. Perhaps we know that we should pray, but we do not know how to pray. Even the disciples of Jesus ask Him, "Lord, teach us to pray, as John also taught his disciples" (Luke 11:1).

Earlier generations learned to pray by association with their parents as they prayed. When prayer is a regular part of the home atmosphere, we learn it as easily as young children assimilate language. But if Christians grow up without being surrounded by prayer, whether in the home or in the church, they know very little about the dynamics or the mechanics of praying.

During the years that I pastored congregations, I taught them to pray not merely by lectures and sermons on praying, but by inviting them to be with me while I prayed. I invited them to say what I said and do what I did until they felt comfortable to function on their own. We discovered together that prayer was a learned response. It could be taught and understood. We also learned that prayer was more than a mental exercise. It was communication between two persons — one here on earth, the other in Heaven.

I had the advantage of praying parents who taught their five children the secret of personal prayer. After I left home, I found that I could strengthen my praying by taking the great prayers of the Bible and read them to God as though those thoughts had originated in my own spirit. David and I became very close as I prayed his prayers and then added, "Me, too, Lord!"

I've often read the prayers of Paul and made them mine by praying them. Paul's prayers have an extraordinary depth to them that forced me to mature spiritually to be able to pray them in faith. Some of Paul's prayers adjusted my theology, for he prayed as one who knew God as a person.

The Bible contains many great invocations of men and women who knew how to contact God in this intimate relationship we call prayer. The Holy Spirit wrote and preserved them for our edification, instruction, and pattern. We can use them as models for our own prayers.

Today's generation of Christians needs to return to the fundamentals of praying, for if the foundation of prayer is wrong, the expression of prayer can hardly be right. There are five basics to prayer we need to examine.

Prayer is Getting Alone with God

The ministry of Jesus required His close involvement with people. When He was not teaching the multitudes, healing the sick, or delivering persons from demonic powers, He was instructing His disciples in the principles of the kingdom of God. To balance this ministry to people, we read: "When he had sent the multitudes away, he went up into a mountain apart to pray: and when the evening was come, he was there alone" (Matthew 14:23). Jesus deliberately took time to get away from the multitudes and His disciples in order to have nights of communion and fellowship with God.

We can suggest that Jesus felt a depletion of divine energy after public ministry and He knew that this energy (*virtue*) could be replenished by spending time with God in prayer. While this is probably true, isn't it far more likely that Jesus deeply felt the isolation from His Father? Being enclosed in a human body interrupted the harmony, closeness, union, and fellowship He had known from eternity. Prayer released His spirit from its fleshly tomb and allowed it to reach into eternity to fellowship and enjoy Father God.

If Jesus felt the urgency to creatively find time to get alone with His Father, shouldn't we? A prime purpose of prayer is privacy with God. While it is true that He is our Redeemer and we have become His servants [slaves], the Scriptures also reveal that He is our Father and we are His sons and daughters. He wants more than service out of us. He wants intimate relationship with us. He likes to spend time with His children in loving, even playful ways.

It seems easy to limit prayer to petitioning God to meet our needs, but a much higher form of prayer is enjoying the presence of God. Prayer is not so much getting something from God as it is getting to God. Prayer releases the human spirit to contact the divine Spirit of God in fellowship and communion. It brings God and persons together in such beautiful harmony that bonds are strengthened between them.

Praying "on the run" or praying scared emergency prayers do not bring us into this confidential closeness. There are "business" prayers that are almost like inter-office communications, but these are very impersonal. True prayer is far greater than a brief memo sent to God by fax. Prayer is two loving persons meeting undisturbed in a face-to-face conversation. Such prayer will, of course, flow facts between the person and his God, but it will equally flow feelings.

David knew the value of private times of communication with God. He wrote: "Unto thee will I cry, O LORD my rock; be not silent to me: lest, if thou be silent to me, I become like them that go down into the pit ... Blessed be the LORD, because he hath heard the voice of my supplications. The LORD is my strength and my shield; my heart trusted in him, and I am helped: therefore my heart greatly rejoiceth; and with my song will I praise him" (Psalm 28:1,6-7). He approached God in trouble and left the divine presence in rejoicing. He had learned that fellowship with God in time of prayer brought release to his inner tensions and returned the song to his spirit.

Prayer is, indeed, getting alone with God, but this is a discipline of life. Our fastpaced generation does not allow for many periods of being along with anyone, much less being alone with God. Few persons even want to be alone with their own thoughts. They keep a radio on or carry a portable recorder with them. They do not know the inner peace that comes from withdrawing from all the outer stimuli of life to reach beyond their circumstances, worries, anxieties, and fears to have a little talk with Jesus. Consequently, they know little or nothing about inner peace or the joy of God's presence.

Jesus told His disciples, "Come ye yourselves apart into a desert place, and rest a while: for there were many coming and going, and they had no leisure so much as to eat" (Mark 6:31). This principle of getting away from the pressures of daily activities — even of ministry — needs to be applied to our lives. The "desert place" was simply an uninhabited place. Jesus spoke of this as a *closet* when He told His disciples, "But thou, when thou prayest, enter into thy closet, and when thou hast shut thy door, pray to thy Father which is in secret; and thy Father which seeth in secret shall reward thee openly" (Matthew 6:6).

The psalmist said this much earlier when he wrote: "He that dwelleth in the secret place of the most High shall abide under the shadow of the Almighty" (Psalm 91:1). The person who consistently stays in the public place will never know this divine shadow of God's presence. We must "come apart", "enter our closet", or come to "the secret place" to be alone with God.

It is true that God is everywhere present. It is also true that He dwells within us by His Spirit. But developing a God consciousness — an awareness of the presence of God — requires a sense of aloneness with God. The world needs to be pushed from the conscious mind. All other relationships in life must be neutralized, and all the energies of our souls and spirits must concentrate on God. This is when prayer begins to take on meaning.

While there is a great place for public praying, it can never satisfactorily replace coming into God's presence in a one-on-one confrontation. Saying the "amen" to the pastor's prayer Sunday morning cannot be compared to talking with God personally.

It is amazing that God has made such fellowship with Him available to us. In the Old Testament, Moses went before God and spoke for the people. Repeatedly the prophets told others that they would communicate with God on their behalf. In contrast to this, the New Covenant invites us to come into God's presence as individuals. The blood has cleansed us from sin. We have entered a new covenant that declares us to be kings and priests unto our God (see Revelation 1:6; 5:10). The Bible encourages us, "Having therefore, brethren, boldness to enter into the holiest by the blood of Jesus ... Let us draw near with a true heart in full assurance of faith, having our hearts sprinkled from an evil conscience, and our bodies washed with pure water" (Hebrews 10:19, 22).

We need to get alone with God. God has invited us to come into His presence to enjoy a time alone with Him. When we do this, it enables us to get alone with God.

Prayer is Getting Along with God

Far too many Christians view their salvation as an impersonal route of escape from the fires of hell. They treat it as a legal maneuver in which they confessed and Christ forgave their sins. The New Testament puts our salvation on a much higher plane than this. Paul wrote: "According as *he hath chosen us* in him before the foundation of the world, *that we should be* holy and without blame *before him in love:* Having predestinated us unto the adoption of children by Jesus Christ to himself, according to the good pleasure of his will, To the praise of the glory of his grace, wherein *he hath made us accepted in the beloved*" (Ephesians 1:4-6, emphasis added). Salvation from sin is but the beginning step in bringing us back into a loving fellowship with our Creator.

Each of the ten major Bible divisions compare our relationship with God to a husband and wife or a bride and bridegroom. It is a loving, on-going relationship that requires many adjustments as time goes on.

God spoke through Ezekiel in story form to tell Israel that their relationship with God began when He discovered them as an abandoned newborn child in the desert. He speaks of cleansing this daughter, clothing her, rearing her, and when she came to maturity marrying her. Read this parable in Ezekiel 16.

Similarly, God accepts us in extreme immaturity and helplessness. He is first our deliverer, then He becomes our need supplier and teacher. If we continue to grow to maturity, He desires to present us to Himself as His special bride; chosen from the foundation of the world.

A married couple starts learning how to get along with each other early in the bonded relationship. Agreement is not automatic. Personality conflicts become apparent, and different ways of doing things make compromise necessary. Unless the couple can communicate honestly and without penalty, the marriage will disintegrate.

Is this any less true of our relationship with God? Through the prophet, God let us know how our ways are so diverse from His. He said: "For my thoughts are not your thoughts, neither are your ways my ways, saith the LORD. For as the heavens are higher than the earth, so are my ways higher than your ways, and my thoughts than your thoughts" (Isaiah 55:8-9). With such great distances between us, we need to communicate privately and passionately to preserve this love relationship. We need to learn to get along with God, and prayer is the vehicle that enables us to develop this harmonious relationship.

We desperately need to talk things over with our Lord so we don't become confused, resentful, or rebellious. Jonah is a good example of this. He clearly understood God's command to go to Ninevah and warn them of impending divine judgment, but this violated his nationalistic spirit. These Assyrians were mortal enemies of the Jews. Jonah could not understand why God would give them a warning. He just wanted Jehovah to wipe them out completely. It wasn't until Jonah cried out to God from the belly of the whale that he was willing to go to Ninevah, but it took further communication with God about the withered vine before Jonah understood the mercy of God upon innocent people.

Similarly, we do not understand the greatness of our God. We expect Him to feel as we feel and to do what we instruct Him to do. When He remains sovereign and unbending to our will, it often creates barriers between us and God. If we would take the time to get alone with Him in prayer, He could help us to understand His heart, or at least cause us to accept His will.

The book of Acts includes the story of Simon who, though converted, could see good merchandising in laying hands on people to be filled with the Spirit. The story goes, "When Simon saw that through laying on of the apostles' hands the Holy Ghost was given, he offered them money, saying, Give me also this power, that on whomsoever I lay hands, he may receive the Holy Ghost. But Peter said unto him, Thy money perish with thee, because thou hast thought that the gift of God may be purchased with money. Thou hast neither part nor lot in this matter: for thy heart is not right in the sight of God. Repent therefore of this thy wickedness, and pray God, if perhaps the thought of thine heart may be forgiven thee" (Acts 8:18-22). Peter warned Simon that his attitudes were wrong, but he told him that if he would repent and pray, God could forgive and adjust him. Similarly, we must pray to get adjustment to our motives and selfish desires, or we will not successfully get along with God who judges motives as though they were actions.

The person who does not regularly pray usually has a difficult time getting along with God. They see the will of God expressed in the Bible, but they don't understand the heart of God in that issue. God is not an autocrat who delights in issuing commands just because He is superior. He is a Father who is trying to bring us into maturity in increment steps of behavior. He is willing to discuss this with us, but prayer is the channel in which this discussion occurs. If we won't talk things over with God, we are reduced to blind obedience or wilful disobedience. Neither of these helps very much in our spiritual development.

We meet Saul of Tarsus in the ninth chapter of Acts. He was a learned theologian very zealous for the law. His great devotion to the principles of Judaism spurred him to become the outstanding persecuting zealot of his day. He imprisoned and murdered Christians because they did not relate to God as he did. When God arrested him on the road to Damascus and talked with him, it completely changed Saul. God not only changed his name to Paul, but He changed Paul's mission from murderer to missionary, and he who had been the persecutor became the persecuted all the way to a martyr's death.

Paul had to learn how to get along with God. He found the prayer channel his source of understanding the will and ways of God. He became so dependent upon the inner voice of the Spirit of God that no matter how logical a situation seemed, he waited until there came confirmation or contradiction from God's Spirit. He did not even want to be in a community outside the will of God, and he was content to spend years in prison in the will of God.

Paul had learned to verify the will of God through communication with God, and so can we. Most of us have hearts that are basically submitted to the will of God. We just don't know His will sufficiently to step out in obedient action. If we would talk to Him more frequently, we would understand more than His commands; we would begin to understand His reasons and feel His heart of compassion and mercy.

We need to embrace the principle that God is uncompromising and unchanging to get along well with God. He clearly told us, "I am the LORD, I change not" (Malachi 3:6). This is a positive affirmation that enables us to count on past revelations and promises of God to be current. It is also a clear statement that none of our whining, nagging, or threatening prayers will change God. He is the only "constant" in life. We cannot manipulate or exploit God. Where there is confrontation between natures, it is our nature that must change. Where there is conflict between wills, we must follow the example of Jesus Who prayed in Gethsemane: "Nevertheless not my will, but thine, be done" (Luke 22:42). Such praying will enable us to get along with God and become adjusted to life.

Prayer is Getting Adjusted to Life

For years I have had a beautiful plaque hanging over my desk. It reads simply, *Prayer Changes Things*. I interpreted

239

this in the earlier days of my ministry to mean "Prayer Changes God." I have now lived long enough to realize that this is not true. Prayer changes *me*, and it often changes my relationship to "things".

We come into this life knowing nothing. Everything must be learned, and often we are poorly instructed. Much of what we learn in life is by trial and error, and some errors are fatal. Other things we learn need to be unlearned and relearned as we mature or as our world changes.

In a most wonderful way, prayer enables us to make consistent adjustments in and to life. It is like having a private tutor Who has lived this life before us. There is no problem, temptation, or situation we will face in life that Jesus does not understand. The Bible promises us, "There hath no temptation taken you but such as is common to man: but God is faithful, who will not suffer you to be tempted above that ye are able; but will with the temptation also make a way to escape, that ye may be able to bear it" (1 Corinthians 10:13).

How are we going to find that way of escape if we don't talk to God in prayer? It is His escape plan. Our tempter doesn't know what it is and neither do we. Admittedly, we don't feel like praying when temptation is enticing us, but we need to pray then more than any other time. We can escape much pain and damage if we pray before we fail.

How many parents of grown children have regretted having to bail their children out of financial trouble when they could have guided them to avoid the problem in the first place if the children had just talked with them before making these financial commitments. It must be similar with God. He wants to be in on the decision making, not just salvaging the pieces after the explosion. Some Christians don't seem to realize that God offers guidance in our natural lives. He's a great financial planner. He understands parenting. He is an expert in every kind of work imaginable. After all, He made this world and everything in it, so His knowledge must go beyond what we call "spiritual" things. There is nothing in our lives that goes unnoticed by God. He even assured us that He takes notice of the death of wild birds (see Matthew 10:29). How much more, then, does He notice His living children who are seeking to adjust to a new lifestyle as Christians?

We need to talk to God about the things in life that matter to us. He promised, "Call unto me, and I will answer thee, and shew thee great and mighty things, which thou knowest not" (Jeremiah 33:3). The order is: (1) you call, and (2) I'll answer and show you great things. God answers our prayers in verbal communication, but He often answers them in demonstration. He shows us far beyond what we were capable of asking.

It is not unusual for God to answer our prayers for guidance through circumstances or through other persons. This is God's willingness to adapt His communication to us in ways we can understand. He is a great teacher Who realizes that He has not taught until we have learned, so He adapts His teaching to our learning skills.

Even if a college student can pay his entire tuition in advance, he will learn little or nothing unless he attends classes. Just living on campus and participating in extra curricular activities cannot furnish him with an academic education. Similarly, being a Christian with a paid up church membership will not make a mature Christian out of anyone. Even vigorous activities in church programs may fail to mature him or her. There are classes to attend, and prayer is the major class for divine instruction. It needs to be balanced with Bible reading, for prayer is fundamentally our speaking to God, while the Bible is God speaking to us.

No matter what subject we bring to God in our times of prayer, God uses this time of fellowship and communication to help adjust us to life. We saw this in the story of Jonah. He felt so righteous in being obedient to God, but when he began to talk with God, he became aware of his lack of mercy and compassion. It was the same with Saul. When he began to talk to God in the prayer channel, he learned that God felt very differently about the Christians who Saul hated with a passion.

Prayer does change things, but the first "thing" it changes is the praying person. How can we come into the presence of Almighty God and leave unchanged? The dynamic of His person is sufficient to melt the hardest heart and adjust the most selfish mind. The expanse of His knowledge and ability is so great that none of our questions or petty problems need go unanswered or unresolved.

Prayer is Getting Answers from God

The most common impression of prayer is petition and provision. We ask; God supplies. This is a scriptural premise. Paul assured the Philippian Christians who had met God's conditions: "My God shall supply all your need according to his riches in glory by Christ Jesus" (Philippians 4:19). It is a timeless promise because we serve an eternal God. Jesus assures us: "Fear not, little flock; for it is your Father's good pleasure to give you the kingdom" (Luke 12:32), therefore, we do not have to overcome a reluctance in God. He is more anxious to give than we are to receive. The purpose of prayer is not to change God's mind, but to tap into His resources.

Jesus taught: "All things, whatsoever ye shall ask in prayer, believing, ye shall receive" (Matthew 21:22). The two qualifications Jesus listed were *ask* and *believe*. It is unfair to assume that God will provide our needs if we do not express those needs in prayer, but our prayer should not be a begging prayer. It needs to be a believing prayer. If God said He would do it, ask and believe that He will keep His Word. There is never a greater need to release faith than when praying. A prayer based on fear isn't worth much, but a faith-filled prayer produces results. If we cannot come to God with faith, we can come to Him for faith, and then release that faith back to Him in prayer.

One of Christ's most powerful teachings on prayer begins: "I say unto you, *Ask*, and it shall be given you; *seek*, and ye shall find; *knock*, and it shall be opened unto you" (Luke 11:9, emphasis added). The three levels of prayer — ask, seek, knock — probably do not refer to increased levels of petitioning God for our needs. *Ask* is simply stating a need for which provision has been made. It is like asking, "Please pass the potatoes" at a family meal. They are on the table, but you want some of them on your plate, so you ask for them.

Following this statement, Jesus says that when a son asks his earthly father for bread, the father will not give the son a stone. If he asks for a fish, he is not given a serpent. A request for an egg is not answered with a scorpion. Jesus concluded His analogy by saying that our heavenly Father responds with good gifts to His sons who ask. James reminded us, "Ye have not, because ye ask not" (James 4:2). We must continually remind ourselves that wishing is not praying. Praying is asking.

When Jesus told us to *seek*, He was surely aware that the Bible frequently associates this word with coming into God's presence. The psalmist instructed us, "Seek the LORD, and his strength: seek his face evermore" (Psalm 105:4). Prayer is not merely petitioning God for needs, it is pursuing the presence of God Himself. His availability to us is far more important than His allotments to us. We will find Him if we seek *Him*; not merely His things.

The encouragement to *knock* probably looks to the arena of service. It is concerned with the need for a door to open before we can move into further service. Paul testified, "For a great door and effectual is opened unto me, and there are many adversaries" (1 Corinthians 16:9). Demonic adversaries usually try to hinder opportunities in Christian service. Jesus taught us to *knock* and to *seek* divine permission to step beyond the adversaries and enter through the opening door. In Christian ministry, more can be accomplished through prayer than through pressure. When we petition God to open a door, we do not need to use human battering rams.

We should learn to *ask* specifically, *seek* diligently, and to *knock* enthusiastically. There is no place for the timid soul in any of these forms of petition. God's provision becomes the basis for our petitions. We come with assured rights, and we ask accordingly. God has promised us entrance to His presence, so we seek confidently, and the doors of service He has set before us cannot be closed by any power in hell. Christ said to the church in Philadelphia: "Behold, I have set before thee an open door, and no man can shut it: for thou hast a little strength, and hast kept my word, and hast not denied my name" (Revelation 3:8). He still promises this to the overcomer.

When we pray, we expect an answer from God. But sometimes we don't like the answer we get. We pray our prayers anticipating a positive response from God, but we need to be willing to accept a negative reply. "No!" is an answer. We petition from our viewpoint, but God answers from heaven's perspective. Just as we do not allow our children to nag or throw tantrums when we say "No" to their petitions, so we should accept God's answer with no further negative reactions on our part.

There are times when God says "later" to our prayers. While this is always threatening, for we never know how long "later" is, we do realize that He has said, "Yes, but not now." Often He wants us to mature further before granting our petitions. Other times He must work through the wills of other persons to give us the desire of our hearts. He will not violate those wills, but He will work on them until they submit to the divine will.

Perhaps the most frequent answer to prayer we Christians receive from God is, "I will if you will." That is, "When you meet the conditions, I will meet the promises." How prone we all are to read the promises of God as expressed in the Bible without noticing the conditions God has placed around that promise. Sometimes an act of our obedience is all that God requires to release what He has promised to do.

Christians throughout the world plead with God for a fresh visitation or revival. They forget that the divine order is: "If my people, which are called by my name, shall humble themselves, and pray, and seek my face, and turn from their wicked ways; then will I hear from heaven, and will forgive their sin, and will heal their land" (2 Chronicles 7:14). God's promise to *hear*, *forgive*, and *heal* are predicated upon humility, prayer, seeking God, and turning from wickedness. It is an "I will if you will" promise. The initiative for answered prayer often lies with us, not with God.

Still another way God answers our prayers is, "I have!" We often pray for God to do what He has already done. We need eyes of faith to see the finished work of God in our lives, in our homes, in our churches, and in our land. Frequently, we need but appropriate by faith instead of petition by prayer.

In whatever way God answers prayer, the Bible consistently teaches, demonstrates, and promises that prayer is getting answers from God. He probably will not give us the desires of our hearts if this is dangerous to us or damaging to our testimony. Still Jesus told us: "Verily, verily, I say unto you, Whatsoever ye shall ask the Father in my name, he will give it you. Hitherto have ye asked nothing in my name: ask, and ye shall receive, that your joy may be full" (John 16:23-24). God keeps our joy levels high by answering our prayers. This, if nothing else, should prompt us to give adoration to God.

Prayer is Giving Adoration to God

Adoration is the highest form of prayer available to humans. It is excessive love enthusiastically displayed. Although the words *adoration* and *adore* are not found in the King James Version of the Bible, they are frequently exemplified by men and women in the Bible. This attitude is expected of God's people, and prayer is the channel through which it is most frequently expressed.

Moses spoke adoringly of his God in the Old Testament. After the passage through the Red Sea, he said: "I will sing unto the LORD, for he hath triumphed gloriously ... Who is like unto thee, O LORD, among the gods? who is like thee, glorious in holiness, fearful in praises, doing wonders? ... The LORD shall reign for ever and ever" (Exodus 15:1,11,18).

David was also an ardent adorer of God. Sometimes he expressed his adoration in speaking of the greatness of God. He wrote: "Great is the LORD, and greatly to be praised in the city of our God, in the mountain of his holiness" (Psalm 48:1). He also said: "For the LORD is a great God, and a great King above all gods" (Psalm 95:3). He had a habit of keeping his gaze fixed on the greatness of God rather than the greatness of the enemy. Unlike many twentieth century Christians, he did not have a God who was too small and a devil who was too big. He regularly exalted the greatness of his God. When we, as he, see God as infinitely great, we will join David in greatly praising Jehovah.

In the New Testament, the story of Mary anointing Jesus with the spikenard is a beautiful picture of adoration (see John 12:1-7). She washed His feet with her tears of joy and anointed His head and feet with a very costly perfume. Although the disciples condemned her for this, Jesus accepted it as an act of deep love and devotion. She was demonstrating her inner joyful emotions for Jesus.

Sitting in my chair in the living room, I looked up from the book I was reading to see my dog sitting on the floor in front of me. He was staring intently at me as if to say, "If you need me, master, I'm here." While I gazed at him, the Holy Spirit spoke in my heart to say, "That's adoration." There must be times in our praying when we are basically looking at our Master with such love and devotion that we communicate an availability to Him for anything He might want from us.

Far too often we merely admire the Lord. We need to move from admiration to adoration and worship Him with everything there is within us because of everything there is within Him. It even moves beyond responding to His love and responds to His person.

Worship, at all levels, is often released in prayer. The Spirit within us begins to exalt the Lord our God. We find ourselves telling God what He has told us about Himself. We give expression to our love and often quote verses of Scripture about God to God. The prayer of worship is not the least bit concerned about personal needs or worldwide concerns. It is completely absorbed in the greatness and beauty of God the Father, God the Son, and God the Holy Spirit.

Many persons never reach this level of prayer, for they have not learned to vocalize their innermost feelings. They are the losers in this, for when we pour out our deepest adoration to God, we come into a far greater love relationship with Him.

Many persons, who have a built in mental censorship that edits out all expressions of deep feelings of adoration for God, have found a release in praying in the unknown tongue of the Spirit. Paul says that this praying bypasses the conscious mind and reaches from deep within our spirits to the throne of God (see 1 Corinthians 14:14). It can communicate emotion without creating self-consciousness in the person who is praying. This form of praying will always be according to the will of God, for it is God the Spirit Who is praying.

Three times the Bible calls for us to give to the Lord the glory that is due Him. First, it tells us: "Give unto the LORD the glory due unto his name: bring an offering, and come before him: worship the LORD in the beauty of holiness (1 Chronicles 16:29). Second, it says, "Give unto the LORD the glory due unto his name; worship the LORD in the beauty of holiness" (Psalm 29:2). The third time the psalmist says: "Give unto the LORD the glory due unto his name: bring an offering, and come into his courts (Psalms 96:8). It seems significant that two out of the three commands to give the Lord the glory due His name also add "bring an offering". We have a dual command: bring God the glory due Him and the gold that is due Him. Neither will substitute for the other. We can't worship and hoard. If we give God glory, we must also give Him the gifts He has required, for giving is an act of worship.

Chapter 14

The Basics of Giving

Most likely, the most memorized verse in the Bible is John 3:16: "For *God* so loved the world, that he *gave* his only begotten Son, that whosoever believeth in him should not perish, but have everlasting life" (emphasis added). We often call this verse "the heart of the Bible". This is true, but it also reveals the heart of God.

The *declaration* of the simple sentence in this verse is "God ... gave". God, by His essential nature, is a giver! He does not give out of our need; He gives out of His need to impart. If this verse of our childhood said nothing further than "God ... gave" we would at least know much about the moral nature of Jehovah. This blessed Trinity is compassionate and sharing. God is easily touched with the needs of others, and since He is the possessor of all things, He can match His giving nature with His gifts.

The *motivation* for God's giving is His love; "God so loved the world that he gave ..." *Love* best describes the moral nature of God. He is more love than all the rest of His nature. Love is not an emotion in God; it is a description of God. The New Testament announces: "God is love" (1 John 4:8, 16). The Bible repeatedly declares and demonstrates that it is this love motivation that inspires God to give.

The *manifestation* in this giving is Himself; "God ... gave ... his Son." Father, Son, and Spirit are one in the Trinity. God took an essential part of Himself out and birthed it into the world calling it "Jesus". While Jesus was here, He declared that He was a demonstration of the Father. He told Philip: "He that hath seen me hath seen the Father; and how sayest thou then, Shew us the Father?" (John 14:9).

Actually, God didn't merely give a gift — He gave Himself to us as a gift. It was not out of His abundance that He shared, but out of His very nature. It was not what He had, but Who He was that God shared in sending His Son Jesus into the world.

The *repercussion* of this giving is that the life of God impregnated those who lived under the curse of death. The verse says, "... that whosoever believeth in him should not perish but have everlasting life." In giving Himself to us, God gave us life, for God is life. John said of Jesus, "In him was life; and the life was the light of men" (John 1:4).

Had God not been a giving God, we would all live on death row awaiting execution. But, "God so loved ... he gave." He not only pardoned us from our sins, but He shared His inherent nature with us so that we, too, can be givers.

God gave us light when He gave Himself to us, for: "God is light, and in him is no darkness at all" (1 John 1:5). We who were creatures of darkness have become new creatures of light. Paul reminded us, "For ye were sometimes darkness, but now are ye light in the Lord: walk as children of light" (Ephesians 5:8). The apostle John put it, "The darkness is past, and the true light now shineth" (1 John 2:8). This indwelling light enables us to live in fellowship with God according to John who said: "But if we walk in the light, as he is in the light, we have fellowship one with another, and the blood of Jesus Christ his Son cleanseth us from all sin" (1 John 1:7).

The gift of God Himself also brought us love for, "God is love" (1 John 4:8). We may have known lust before we knew God, but we did not know love until God bestowed His love nature upon us in the gift of His nature. Paul's benediction was: "The grace of the Lord Jesus Christ, and the love of God, and the communion of the Holy Ghost, be with you all. Amen" (2 Corinthians 13:14).

Similarly, because "There is none holy as the LORD" (1 Samuel 2:2), when God gives Himself to us, He also shares His holy nature with us. We become a "Holy people unto the LORD thy God" (Deuteronomy 7:6). We cannot achieve holiness — it is God's essential nature. God sets us apart by giving a part of Himself to us. We live holy lives because of His holiness.

Since "Our God is a consuming fire" (Hebrews 12:29), we would expect this burning nature of God to be part of the gift of His nature to us. John the Baptist said, "I indeed baptize you with water unto repentance: but he that cometh after me is mightier than I, whose shoes I am not worthy to bear: he shall baptize you with the Holy Ghost, and with fire" (Matthew 3:11). This fire nature of God was visibly evident on the day of Pentecost when the Holy Spirit descended like a giant flame of fire very much like the pillar of fire that guided Israel through the wilderness in the days of Moses.

God's gift of Himself extended His entire nature to those who would receive it. God gave the ultimate gift — Himself.

Giving is Rational

When we receive God's donation of Himself, we become partakers of His divine nature. Peter assures us, "Whereby are given unto us exceeding great and precious promises: that by these ye might be partakers of the divine nature" (2 Peter 1:4). If we are actually "partakers of the divine nature", then we should desire to do what He does, and His nature is a giving nature.

The Bible clearly declares that we have the nature of God. The Holy Spirit spoke through Paul: "For in him we live, and move, and have our being; as certain also of your own poets have said, For we are also his offspring" (Acts 17:28). Later Paul wrote, "For we are his workmanship, created in Christ Jesus unto good works, which God hath before ordained that we should walk in them" (Ephesians 2:10). Being like God is not optional; it comes with being truly born-again. Therefore it is rational to act like God in giving.

The God-like person aspires, out of a love motivation, to allow Christ to, "Present it [the Church] to himself a glorious church, not having spot, or wrinkle, or any such thing; but that it should be holy and without blemish" (Ephesians 5:27). In his letter to the church in Colosse, Paul said that the reconciling work of Jesus was, "To present you holy and unblameable and unreproveable in his sight" (Colossians 1:22). Jehovah has made and redeemed us to become a present for God the Father, God the Son, and God the Holy Spirit. God created us "That we should be to the praise of his glory, who first trusted in Christ" (Ephesians 1:12). The prophet loudly declared that God's covenant people shall, "Be a crown of glory in the hand of the LORD, and a royal diadem in the hand of thy God" (Isaiah 62:3).

Our giving to God is reciprocal. We give back to God that which is similar in nature to what He has given to us. Much as "God so loved ... he gave *[Himself]*", we are motivated by love to give ourselves to God in whatever way He may want to use us; whether that be in ministry, work, play, or to stand-by in the reserves. We are a gift to God. We no longer belong to ourselves, but unto Him who gave Himself for us.

More specifically, God's gift of Himself to us gave us His inherent life. We did not know that we, "were dead in trespasses and sins" (Ephesians 2:1) until life came. Our return gift is to open our dead hearts and consciences and allow the life of God to enter every fiber of our being.

We didn't realize that we existed in a state of darkness, for we had never seen light until He came into our lives. When light entered our lives, our gift to God was to present all the dark places of our being to Him so He could illuminate them with the light of His presence.

Humanity existed on fondness, companionship, and lust until, "The love of God is shed abroad in our hearts by the Holy Ghost which is given unto us" (Romans 5:5). When God's love came in, we found it difficult to open ourselves to it, for life had sorely wounded us in areas of human relationships. Our gift to God is a willingness for His love to invade us in spirit, soul, and body.

252

We lacked a standard of holiness until a holy God entered our unholy world and made the commitment: "Be ye holy; for I am holy" (1 Peter 1:16). A major work of the coming of the Holy Spirit is to make us holy in thought, word, and deed. Our gift to God in the arena of holiness is to hand Him the keys to all the doors of our inner being. When He opens the doors, He will introduce His holiness to our unholy lives.

Similarly, God gives His fire nature to us, but it will soon go out unless we allow it to burn in our hearts and lives to reduce everything to ashes and dust that is not God-like. God's fire does not come simply to warm a cold nature. It comes to consume the wood, hay, and stubble in our lives (see 1 Corinthians 3:12-13). It is one of God's ways of removing qualities that are not His. Our gift back to God's fire is to respond positively to this burning presence of God.

In light of this, we must admit that it is both rational and reciprocal to give ourselves to God completely. He has given Himself to us, and we must give ourselves to Him. As we saw in the concluding words of the preceding chapter, the Bible urges us: "Give unto the LORD the glory due unto his name: bring an offering, and come before him: worship the LORD in the beauty of holiness" (1 Chronicles 16:29).

In the Old Testament's economy, it was impossible to worship God without bringing an offering. The prescribed approach to God was the sacrificial principle, and God did not provide the sacrifices; the worshipers did. The first step in individual worship, then, was presenting to the priest the sacrifice to be slain, the meal to be baked, or the wine to be poured out before the Lord in the Holy Place.

God did not intend for the sacrificial system to be unduly costly to the worshiper. He provided for the impoverished to trap a turtle dove and bring it before the Lord as an acceptable offering. The purpose of the sacrifice was not to penalize the worshiper, but to bring the worshiper into a relationship of fellowship with God. Each animal sacrifice was a picture, or a type, of the coming death of Jesus on the cross at Calvary. Every sacrifice was an active participation in substitutionary atonement. The animal died the death that the worshiper deserved.

This is why God instructed those who would approach Him to "bring an offering and come before Him". In the Old Testament, worship and giving were inseparable; they functioned as a team. It was one way of giving glory to the Lord. They are just as linked in the New Testament. We not only bring unto the Lord the glory due His name, we bring to Him the gold that is due Him.

Worship that costs us nothing is always suspect. When Araunah offered his threshing floor and oxen to David to offer a sacrifice unto the Lord for aborting His judgment over Israel, David replied, "Nay; but I will surely buy it of thee at a price: neither will I offer burnt offerings unto the LORD my God of that which doth cost me nothing. So David bought the threshing floor and the oxen for fifty shekels of silver" (2 Samuel 24:24).

God linked His provision for giving to the agricultural culture of the Hebrews. The shepherd could bring a lamb or a goat. The stockman could bring a bull, while the orchardist brought wine or olive oil. The gift required was the increase of the life and labor of the individual worshiper.

It is fitting, then, that Paul wrote: "I beseech you therefore, brethren, by the mercies of God, that ye present your bodies a living sacrifice, holy, acceptable unto God, which is your reasonable service" (Romans 12:1-2). This is not a requirement for everyone to enter full time ministry. In the agricultural economy of the Hebrews, the work of the farmer brought forth a crop or an increase in the herd of animals. When he brought a portion of this to the Lord, he was presenting his body.

To those of us who live in a monetary economy, we exchange the sweat of our brows or the product of our brains for money. Money is actually "you" in foldable form. It is you on deposit. When we bring that money as an offering to God, we are "presenting our bodies a living sacrifice". If we earn $10 an hour or ten pounds, each ten dollar bill or ten pound note we present to the Lord equals an hour of ourselves.

Paul, under the inspiration of the Holy Spirit, said that such presenting of ourselves was our "reasonable service". The Greek word here translated as "service" is *latreia* which means divine service or worship. Presenting our bodies is a rational or logical worship. Giving may be a prelude to worship or it can, in itself, be an act of worship. The Wise Men knew this, for once they arrived in Bethlehem, they presented gifts to the Christ child as an expression of their devotion and worship to Jesus.

Giving is Required

The phrase "Bring an offering" occurs 22 times in the Bible. It seems to me that anything mentioned that frequently is far more than a request; it is at command level.

Because God spared the firstborn of the Hebrews the night the plague of death killed the firstborn of the Egyptians, God considered all firstborn as His. He took the tribe of Levi as a substitute for these firstborn, but to be fair, He numbered Israel's firstborn and the members of the tribe of Levi. Since there were more firstborn in the eleven tribes than men in the tribe of Levi, God provided for these surplus firstborn to be redeemed by bringing a prescribed offering of five shekels. The instructions were: "Thou shalt give the money, wherewith the odd number of them is to be redeemed, unto Aaron and to his sons. And Moses took the redemption money of them that were over and above them that were redeemed by the Levites: Of the firstborn of the children of Israel took he the money ... And Moses gave the money of them that were redeemed unto Aaron and to his sons, according to the word of the LORD, as the LORD commanded Moses" (Numbers 3:48-51).

The lesson this teaches is that God chooses some persons to be in His full time service, but all who have been redeemed are expected to contribute toward this service. Some give their lives in ministry; others give their lives in offerings, but all contribute to the service of God.

God also required an offering when Israel took a census. God said:

> *When thou takest the sum of the children of Israel after their number, then shall they give every man a ransom for his soul unto the LORD, when thou numberest them; that there be no plague among them, when thou numberest them. This they shall give, every one that passeth among them that are numbered, half a shekel after the shekel of the sanctuary: (a shekel is twenty gerahs:) an half shekel shall be the offering of the LORD. Every one that passeth among them that are numbered, from twenty years old and above, shall give an offering unto the LORD. The rich shall not give more, and the poor shall not give less than half a shekel, when they give an offering unto the LORD, to make an atonement for your souls. And thou shalt take the atonement money of the children of Israel, and shalt appoint it for the service of the tabernacle of the congregation; that it may be a memorial unto the children of Israel before the LORD, to make an atonement for your souls.*
>
> *(Exodus 30:12-16)*

These two offerings were not requests; they were requirements. They acknowledged God's right of ownership of individuals, and bringing the required offering released these individuals to normal life in Israel. Their gift was their "income tax" paid to God.

When God instructed Moses to build the Tabernacle in the wilderness as a sanctuary for God's presence, He told Moses to invite the people to bring of the lavish gifts the Egyptians had pushed onto the Hebrews when they marched out of Egypt. "Moses spake unto all the congregation of the children of Israel, saying, This is the thing which the LORD commanded, saying, Take ye from among you an offering unto the LORD: whosoever is of a willing heart, let him bring it, an offering of the LORD" (Exodus 35:4-5). The people's response was so overwhelming that the workmen "Spake unto Moses, saying, The people bring much more than enough for the service of the work, which the LORD commanded to make. And Moses gave commandment, and they caused it to be proclaimed throughout the camp, saying, Let neither man nor woman make any more work for the offering of the sanctuary. So the people were restrained from bringing" (Exodus 36:5-6).

How exciting it would be for a pastor entering a building program to have to restrain his people from giving because of an overwhelming surplus. When hearts are willing and anxious to have the presence of the Lord in their midst, giving can be hilarious. No wonder Paul wrote, "Every man according as he purposeth in his heart, so let him give; not grudgingly, or of necessity: for God loveth a cheerful giver" (2 Corinthians 9:7). This type of freewill offering is an expression to God of our joy in His giving and in His Person. There is nothing sacrificial in it. It is a happy response. God delights in seeing His redeemed people respond with hilarity and joy to His command to bring Him an offering. No wonder Paul said, "To remember the words of the Lord Jesus, how he said, It is more blessed to give than to receive" (Acts 20:35). While getting is marvelous, being able to give is majestic.

Giving is Proportional

When God called Abraham and promised to make of him a mighty nation, He purposed to make this nation an example for all the world. Paul wrote concerning Israel: "Now all these things happened unto them for ensamples: and they are written for our admonition, upon whom the ends of the world are come" (1 Corinthians 10:11). After God delivered this mighty nation from the slavery of Egypt and enabled them to conquer the Promised Land, He divided the land among the people by tribes and families. He clearly told them: "The land shall not be sold for ever: for the land is mine; for ye are strangers and sojourners with me" (Leviticus 25:23). When we realize this premise of divine ownership of the land, God's rules of letting the land rest every seventh year and of returning all property to the original tenants every 50 years begins to make sense.

This also gives us insight into the principle of tithing. Since all the land was God's, all the increase of that land belonged to Jehovah. Those who worked the land were only share-croppers. Instead of claiming all the crop as His, or even that half the increase rightfully belonged to Him, God simply required 10% of all increase. The "rent" was based not on the size of the property holdings, but on the increase that property had produced. You can't get much more equitable than this.

Tithing is always proportional to the increase. Where there is no income, no tithe is due. God expected no Israelite to give if there had been no increase in what God had given to him.

Tithing, as a principle, antedates the law. Just as a knowledge that murder, adultery, and thievery preceded the law, so tithing was taught and practiced many generations before it was put into the divine code on Mt. Sinai. Adam and Eve understood the practice of tithing, for their sons brought a tithe offering unto God. Right along with the teaching of forgiveness of sin through the shedding of blood, there came the principles of devoting a tithe and the first fruits to God.

Abraham's giving of tithes to Melchizedek is the first actual mention of the consecration of a tithe to the service of God (see Genesis 14). The New Testament speaks of this in Hebrews 7:2,4,6,10. There can be no doubt that people practiced tithing before Abraham, and he lived more than 400 years before Moses received the law from God.

Jacob knew exactly what he should do to respond to the vision of the ladder from earth to heaven with the ascending and descending angels. He promised, "This stone, which I have set for a pillar, shall be God's house: and of all that thou shalt give me I will surely give the tenth unto thee" (Genesis 28:22). It is likely that Jacob's father taught him the principle of tithing, and he may have not obeyed. In the fearsome realization that he was in God's presence, he vowed to begin tithing. Many do similarly today. God's presence collects tithe better than any sermon can.

Tithing did not begin with the Hebrews. The Encyclopedia Britannica says: "The (tithe) custom was almost universal in antiquity. Greece, Rome, Babylon, Egypt, and many others practised tithing." There can be but one reason so many ancient nations had the tithing principle so deeply ingrained into their lives and culture. In the very beginning God taught the principle of tithing to mankind. The commandments, laws, and ordinances given to Moses by God on Mt. Sinai contained many new things. They also reaffirmed or restated certain moral principles that people knew and practiced long before God gave them the Law. This divine Law explicitly claimed God's tithe. The fruits of the land, tree, or plant were to be tithed. God said, "All the tithe of the land, whether of the seed of the land, or of the fruit of the tree, is the LORD'S: it is holy unto the LORD" (Leviticus 27:30).

Similarly, God required a tithe of the herds and flocks. The Law read, "And concerning the tithe of the herd, or of the flock, even of whatsoever passeth under the rod, the tenth shall be holy unto the LORD. He shall not search whether it be good or bad, neither shall he change it: and if he change it at all, then both it and the change thereof shall be holy; it shall not be redeemed" (Leviticus 27:32-33). "Passing under the rod" was a count. Every tenth animal to pass belonged to the Lord.

The tither threshed the grain, converted the fruit of the vineyard to wine and pressed their olives into oil before presenting it to the Lord (see Numbers 18:27). This basic tithe, (or heave offering as the Bible sometimes called it) was given annually to the Levites who had been denied any land acquisition. This is what this priestly tribe lived on through the year. These Levites, in turn, paid a tithe of what they received to Aaron and his sons for their maintenance (Numbers 18:26, 28).

Beyond this priestly tithe, the Hebrews paid a second tithe to provide for the sacrifices and feast observances, and then every third year a third tithe was assessed to provide for the poor and the oppressed. Considering the many taxes both religious and secular that the Jews had to pay, especially in post-

exile times, we have to admire their liberality and resourceful-
ness. If they faithfully paid three tithes, then they actually
gave God more than the 1/5 they had seen assessed upon the
Egyptians after the famine ended.

The law made a practical provision for paying tithes. Since
the tithe had to be paid in Jerusalem where God had set His
name, bringing cattle or sheep on feast days could be a problem, for some of these people came long distances to these
feasts. God said,

> *Thou shalt truly tithe all the increase of thy seed, that
> the field bringeth forth year by year. And thou shalt eat
> before the LORD thy God, in the place which he shall
> choose to place his name there, the tithe of thy corn, of
> thy wine, and of thine oil, and the firstlings of thy herds
> and of thy flocks; that thou mayest learn to fear the
> LORD thy God always. And if the way be too long for
> thee, so that thou art not able to carry it; or if the place
> be too far from thee, which the LORD thy God shall
> choose to set his name there, when the LORD thy God
> hath blessed thee: Then shalt thou turn it into money,
> and bind up the money in thine hand, and shalt go unto
> the place which the LORD thy God shall choose: And
> thou shalt bestow that money for whatsoever thy soul
> lusteth after, for oxen, or for sheep, or for wine, or for
> strong drink, or for whatsoever thy soul desireth: and
> thou shalt eat there before the LORD thy God, and thou
> shalt rejoice, thou, and thine household, And the Levite
> that is within thy gates; thou shalt not forsake him; for
> he hath no part nor inheritance with thee.*

> *(Deuteronomy 14:22-27)*

The Hebrews could exchange their tithe for money and then
bring that money to the feast to purchase "whatsoever thy soul
desireth" for observing the feast. This was God's way of providing for the people that came to the feasts. Although they
offered everything to the Lord, the Law gave the presiding

priests a portion and they returned the rest to the worshiper for a family picnic or barbecue, if you please.

This second tithe funded the three compulsory feasts held annually in Jerusalem. They were to be shared with the family and the Levites. Without them the visiting Israelites would have been an unbearable burden to the Hebrews who lived in Jerusalem. God never sets up freeloading. He provides for each to pay his or her fair share in the work of the Lord.

In much the same way, when we pay our tithes, we reap the benefits from them. We don't need to have buildings, pews, carpets, musical instruments, and lighting to worship God. Jesus had none of these during His ministry. However, we all admit that these amenities make our worship times together so much more comfortable. Our tithes and offerings make them possible. I guess it's a case of having what we are willing to pay for.

Some Christians rejoice in thinking that tithing ceased when Jesus came, but they are wrong in this assessment. Although Jesus did come to fulfil the law, tithing preceded the law and post-dates it as well. To say that Jesus mentioned tithing only twice, therefore it was unimportant to Him, ignores the fact that the entire Bible mentions the virgin birth of Jesus twice. Two was the number of witness under the law. Jesus taught persons who were steeped in the Law of Moses. They believed and practiced tithing religiously. He did not need to teach the principal of tithing to those who practiced it so carefully that they literally counted the seeds and leaves of their spices to give an accurate tenth to God (see Matthew 23:23).

Jesus did condemn the Pharisees for bragging about tithing and for overlooking mercy and faith when He said, "these ought ye to have done [tithe] and not leave the other undone [judgement, mercy, and faith] (Matthew 23:23; See also Luke 18:12). These words cannot be used as an excuse for not tithing. Jesus simply condemned using tithing as an excuse for an unholy life.

261

Tithing belongs to both the Old Covenant and the New Covenant. Tithing is a spiritual relationship that enables us to get closer to God. Tithing is a partner relationship that gives us a part in God's program. We are working the same farm. Tithing is a love relationship that tests our devotion to Christ. Tithing is also a life-filling association that places us in a position to share God's blessings. The challenge is: "Bring ye all the tithes into the storehouse, that there may be meat in mine house, and prove me now herewith, saith the LORD of hosts, if I will not open you the windows of heaven, and pour you out a blessing, that there shall not be room enough to receive it" (Malachi 3:10).

It is obvious that the way we handle God's money tests our maturity as Christians. Giving, to the tither, is a grace; not a disgrace. It is better to be a tither who is blessed than a distressed hoarder. Millions of persons have proved that nine tenths goes farther with God's blessing than ten tenths without it.

Tithing is the only church finance plan mentioned in the Bible. Those who love Christ will joyfully follow His plan rather than substitute their plan for His. This plan of tithing has been tested throughout Church history. It was reaffirmed in the Church councils of Ancyria (314 AD), Gangra (324 AD), Orleand (511 AD), Tuors (567 AD), Toledo (633 AD), Rouen (650 AD), Fimli (791 AD), and London (1425 AD). These councils of the church proclaimed that Christians were to pay tithes unto the Lord just as the Bible proclaims. It seems tragic that individual Christians today put their will (or their *won't*) against the wisdom of thousands of years of Church history.

In times of spiritual declension, it is often the tithe responsibility that is the first consecration to slip away. This was true of Jewish history. Whenever Israel's heart began to turn from God, the tithe ceased to come in. Time and time again, the Levites and priests had to forsake their duties to earn their living because the tithes were not being paid.

The treasurer of a local church can often tell the spiritual life of the church faster than the pastor. When coldness begins to set in, the payments of tithes and pledges begin to diminish. Usually they are not stopped at once. They are simply reduced gradually. It is amazing how tempting it is to use God's tithe for our needs when adversity, vacation, or special needs arrive.

When satan can keep the Christians from tithing, he so hobbles the work of the Lord as to nearly destroy the church. The suppers, sales, bazaars, bingo games, and card parties that churches have substituted for the tithe have brought the church of Jesus Christ into disrepute in the eyes of the world. We cheapen our gospel when we refuse to tithe.

Someone wisely said that a non-tithing Christian should never be elected to office in the church. If he will steal God's money, surely he would find no scruples against appropriating church finances. If he cannot keep his vows to God, he cannot keep his vows to the congregation.

Giving is a Response that becomes Reciprocal

Jesus did not remain silent on the subject of giving. He spoke about tithing and giving five times as often as on any other subject. Of His 38 major parables, 19 concern money, property, and our relationship to them. Someone counted and reported that in the New Testament, one verse in five refers to money, property, and their management.

Obviously, then, tithing is the floor of giving, not the ceiling. Paul quoted Jesus as saying, "It is more blessed to give than to receive" (Acts 20:35). Jesus taught that the measure of liberality is love, that will always go beyond the tithe.

Our Lord also assured us, "Give, and it shall be given unto you; good measure, pressed down, and shaken together, and running over, shall men give into your bosom. For with the same measure that ye mete withal it shall be measured to you again" (Luke 6:38). He assured us that giving would be reciprocal.

All that God has given is available to those who obey Him. Obedience to God's principle of tithing opens the way to

263

physical and spiritual blessings. It enables God to bless us, for He cannot and will not bless disobedience.

When Christians ask me to pray with them for financial help, I ask them if they are current in paying their tithe. When they say "No," I tell them, "That is your problem. You don't need prayer. You need to obey God's financial plan if you are to benefit in it."

Paul said, "Upon the first day of the week let every one of you lay by him in store, as God hath prospered him, that there be no gatherings when I come" (1 Corinthians 16:2). Paul here pleads for systematic, proportionate giving based on a commitment of love and not on any emotional plea he might make after he arrived. We give out of commitment, not out of mere concern.

Christ's promise to reward the tither is just as definite as His promise to save the sinner. We've trusted Him to save our souls, can't we trust Him to handle our money? A long term proverb among Jews is, "Pay tithes and be rich". The joy of true Christian living comes when we recognize that we are trustees of all God has given; both life and possessions.

It may sound like a cliché, but it is amazingly true. You can't out-give God. When you give Him a spoonful, He responds with a shovel-full. His resources are so much greater that ours that we can never equal His giving, much less exceed it.

"But," you may argue, "if His resources are so great, why does He need my money?" He doesn't need any of our giving, but we desperately need to give. Built into each of us is the inability to constantly be a receiver. We must give to release the deep sense of indebtedness. Since God is our creator, He, better than we, knows our psychological need to return favors just to get out from under a sense of obligation. Although God is always our benefactor, He offers to receive a proportional amount of our income to discharge this feeling of responsibility.

Three verses need to be memorized and put into practice:

1. "The Lord ... giveth thee power to get wealth" (Deuteronomy 8:18).
2. "Give an account of thy stewardship" (Luke 16:2).
3. "God loves a cheerful giver" (2 Corinthians 9:7).

Whether you choose to accept God's financial plan of tithing or not, these verses should undergird your giving.

God's giving is beyond our wildest imaginations. He has not only given His Son to be our Savior, He has given us godly persons especially endowed with spiritual gifts to prepare us for spiritual service.

Chapter 15

The Basics of Ministry

Seated on the front row of the church while I waited to speak to the congregation, I watched the pastor step to the pulpit to request: "Would all the ministers please stand so we may recognize you?"

Visiting pastors and evangelists stood, but instead of being recognized and welcomed, they heard the pastor say, "Please be seated."

Again the pastor asked, "Would all the ministers please stand?" Again pastors and full time Christian workers stood with a bewildered look on their faces.

Again the pastor said, "Please sit down."

"You must not be paying attention to what I am saying," the pastor said. "I have asked for all the ministers present to please stand. Doesn't the New Testament declare all of us to be ministers unto God? Now, will all the ministers present please stand?"

Catching on to what he meant, everyone in the auditorium stood. The pastor had made a dramatic point. We too often speak of the priesthood of the believer without realizing that this gives each believer a ministry. We may not all wear vestments, but God has vested us with spiritual ministry.

In religion there is diverse polarity in this idea. Some feel that only a person with a seminary degree is qualified to be called a minister, while others, especially when there is a fresh move of God, feel that anyone with an anointing of the Holy Spirit is a minister. Some declare an absolute equality of believers. Other Christians feel that God places His ministers in a hierarchical structure.

We would help ourselves get back to the basics of ministry if we would realize that although the word *minister* appears 100 times in 98 verses of the Bible, the Scriptures more frequently use the word as a verb than it does as a noun. The Old Testament consistently uses the word to denote activity of service. The New Testament uses the word about evenly between noun form and verb form.

To minister is to serve or to function for another. The New Testament abounds with this idea that to minister is to labor. It declares that we are co-laborers with God and with one another. It makes us fellow laborers, chosen laborers, anointed laborers, and directed laborers. The Bible affirms: "For we are labourers together with God" (1 Corinthians 3:9).

When the New Testament uses the noun form *minister*, it is but a reference to the person who is to function in the verb form — *to minister*. Too frequently we emphasize the person rather than the procedure. Some people yearn to be "a minister," without having developed "a ministry". Other persons seek the honor of the position without the hard work of the calling.

We need to understand the unction and the function of ministry. When this is working, we will not need to worry about the office of a minister. A ministry will always make room for itself.

There are at least seven basics to true ministry.

1. We minister unto the Lord.
2. We minister the Lord unto the family.
3. We minister *to* one another.
4. We minister *with* one another.
5. We minister by God's choice.
6. We minister by God's anointing.
7. We minister by God's direction.

We Minister unto the Lord

The first priority of any ministry is to direct it to the Lord. No sacrifice of the Old Testament could be used by the worshiper until he presented it to the Lord. We could hardly expect to do less in the wonderful New Testament season of grace. Why would we want to do less?

While we generally view the selection of the tribe of Levi as assistants to Aaron and his sons, the record shows: "At that time the LORD separated the tribe of Levi, to bear the ark of the covenant of the LORD, *to stand before the LORD to minister unto him,* and to bless in his name, unto this day" (Deuteronomy 10:8, emphasis added). The priests offered all the sacrifices, tended the fire, sprinkled the blood, and waved the grain offering as a ministry unto the Lord. This service greatly relieved Aaron and served the people religiously, but God declared that the work of the priesthood was unto Himself.

We dare not side-step this fundamental principle. Everything we do must be done unto the Lord. Paul instructed us, "Whether therefore ye eat, or drink, or whatsoever ye do, do all to the glory of God" (1 Corinthians 10:31).

This rule is violated far too frequently. Much public ministry plays to the grandstand. We often direct our ministry to people much as a stand-up comedian directs every gesture, tone of voice, and spoken piece of material to solicit a positive response from the audience. It is a performance perfectly polished to procure praise of the performer. Doesn't this fit much of what we see on our platforms on Sunday mornings?

If God chose the tribe of Levi to minister unto Himself, it is unlikely that He changed His rules when He selected us to be: "Kings and priests unto God and his Father" (Revelation 1:6). While much of our ministries will affect and benefit others, the main thrust should be unto God the Father.

A house rule for all our churches should be, "If it is not done unto the Lord, don't do it!" All our singing should be sung unto the Lord, but, unfortunately, most of the current choruses we sing are very self-centered in their messages and don't harmonize with being sung unto the Lord. Songs sung about the devil are actually sung to satan. Warfare songs never get out of the room that they are sung in, and the songs that are vocalized about ourselves never make it to the throne of God. Singing or playing musical instruments to draw attention to our talent and ability can never be interpreted as ministry unto God. Religion has its sacred artists whose sole purpose is to present a performance. That is acceptable as long as we do not call it a *ministry*, for true ministry is first done unto God.

Isn't this same principle applicable to the ministry of giving, preaching, praise, and worship? Some persons have received the "grace of giving", and faithfully support God's work as an act of worship. Other persons give only if they are in the spotlight, or if it puts them in a position to pull strings because of their gifts. Such giving may benefit a local church, but it is not ministry in the eyes of God.

The first thrust of any category of ministry must be upward. Prayer ministry must be unto the Lord. Similarly, all styles of ministering the Word must first be unto the Lord. Even the ministries of grace, mercy, compassion, and serving must be backed by an overriding motivation of a desire to minister unto the Lord by ministering to His people.

I do not mean to project that our only ministry is prayer, praise, and worship. These are vital and viable, and they must have first place in our priorities, but they are not exclusive. Christ commanded us to care for one another and to be compassionate for those less fortunate than ourselves. He said, in parable form, that ministry done to others can be received as ministry unto Himself. Having blessed them for giving a cup of cold water or sharing a coat, or tending the sick or visiting prisoners, the men in the parable denied having done any of this to Jesus. Christ replied, "Verily I say unto you, Inasmuch as ye have done it unto one of the least of these my brethren, ye have done it unto me (Matthew 25:40). God keeps good records of our motivations in everything we do in Christian service.

It is tragic to bypass this first step in ministry. If we have not ministered unto God, how can we minister God to the people? The person who has not prayed is deceitful in saying, "God spoke to me." Any person whose spirit cannot flow upward to God is an unlikely vessel for God's Spirit to flow downward through them.

A minister needs to know God's words before He can share them with another in need. If we do not regularly read God's Word as His message to our hearts, how can we dare preach it to others as a standard for their behavior?

The person who cannot or will not give to God will usually lack a motivation to give to others. Ministering unto the Lord is a prelude to ministering the Lord to others.

We Minister the Lord unto the Family

The desire to minister is almost inherent in born-again Christians, for giving and doing for others is inherent in the nature of God. There is, however, a wide discrepancy between desiring to minister and knowing how to minister. God has given us our personal families to learn how to unselfishly minister to another person.

It has amazed parents for centuries how their selfish, self-centered young children can become caring, loving, and giving persons after marriage — especially after children start to come to the home. Raising a family is God's process of teaching us to minister.

Learning to minister at home is so basic that when Paul listed the qualifications he felt should be in the lives of persons being seriously considered for church officers, he included: "One that ruleth well his own house, having his children in subjection with all gravity; (For if a man know not how to rule his own house, how shall he take care of the church of God?)" (1 Timothy 3:4-5). He added: "Even so must their wives be grave, not slanderers, sober, faithful in all things. Let the deacons be the husbands of one wife, ruling their children and their own houses well" (1 Timothy 3:11-12).

When we ignore these guidelines in the local church, we can expect to suffer, for ministry is not developed when an office is conferred. The office should be awarded after the ministry has developed, and God has provided for that ministry to develop in the local home where the results of that ministry stare the person in the face daily.

In God's economy, ministry in the home has priority over ministry outside the home. All too frequently we practice the reverse of this. How often have men and women had such a passion for ministering to others that they took little or no time to minister to their own family? God never intended His call to replace the commitment to a husband or a wife. The best of these two worlds is to involve the entire family in the ministry.

This was the philosophy of my father who entered the ministry when I was three years old. He and Mother reared five children in parsonages on the West Coast. All of us were involved in Dad's ministry. Dad was the same in the home as he was in the pulpit. He ministered God's grace to his family as certainly as he ministered it to God's church family. It is likely that this contributed to four of his five children entering the full time ministry.

I listened to the excited voice of a man in his mid-thirties after the service where I had shared about the call of God. "God has used you to confirm my missions call to Mexico," he said.

Something didn't ring true in my spirit, so I asked him to tell me something about himself. I learned that he was married, had two children, had quit his job to be available to minister, and that he was thousands of dollars in debt.

"What about your support if you go to Mexico as a missionary?" I asked him.

"God will supply," he answered rapidly.

"Will you take your family with you?"

"No," he said. "I'll leave them here."

"What about their support?" I asked.

"God will take care of them."

"What about these outstanding bills?" I pursued.

"That's God's problem," he assured me.

For the next fifteen minutes, he squirmed uncomfortably as I talked to him. I did not deny that God may have called him to be a missionary, but I assured him that since God did not incur his debts, He was not responsible to pay them off. I further told him that if he abandoned his family to pursue work as a missionary, he was worse than the rankest sinner he sought to convert to Christ, for the Bible states clearly: "But if any provide not for his own, and specially for those of his own house, he hath denied the faith, and is worse than an infidel" (1 Timothy 5:8).

I called this man's pastor over to join the conversation. The two of us urged him to get a job — maybe even two of them — and pay off his credit cards and other outstanding obligations. We said that once he was out of debt, he could secure the financial backing of friends and churches so his needs would be provided for while he was in Mexico. We then urged him to allow the local church leadership to send him from that church with their blessing extended to him and his family. Missions ministry is a team ministry; not a solo act.

I have never heard from this man since then. I hope he took our advice, for God does not want anyone to use ministry as a cop-out for meeting financial obligations and home responsibilities. We must first prove ourselves trustworthy in the smaller unit of the home before God is going to extend wider responsibilities in His Church.

If you desire to enter full time ministry, learn to rule your home lovingly, then you may be trusted to rule in the church. We don't start outside and then come back to the home.

Learning to rule in your home gives you a warm loving environment where learning to minister is less painful. It also gives you automatic checks and balances, and quick feedback from the family members. It is God's order and it makes good sense.

We Minister to One Another

After we learn to successfully minister in our own homes, which are the smallest units in the Church, we are allowed to minister to one another in the larger family — the Church. This is a major theme of the New Testament.

We read, "All that believed were together, and had all things common; and sold their possessions and goods, and parted them to all [men], as every man had need" (Acts 2:45). This early church in the book of Acts united together as one large family and lived in a community. As the church continued to grow, this proved to be impractical, but the sense of supplying the needs of others in the Church continued. They viewed it as a ministry.

After the Gentiles began to share in the gospel, "There stood up one of them named Agabus, and signified by the Spirit that there should be great dearth throughout all the world: which came to pass in the days of Claudius Caesar. Then the disciples, every man according to his ability, determined to send relief unto the brethren which dwelt in Judaea: Which also they did, and sent it to the elders by the hands of Barnabas and Saul" (Acts 11:28- 30).

Ministry by the saints to one another was a strong theme of the apostle Paul. He wrote: "Bear ye one another's burdens, and so fulfil the law of Christ" (Galatians 6:2). He never urged the saints to refer needy members of the church to the pastor or overseer. He felt that other members could pray them through, pay them through, or find someone who could do so.

In a large family the older children help the younger children face the problems of growing up. It should be this way in the church. Everyone can teach what he or she has learned. You need not have mastered the subject to be a teacher. You need be but one lesson ahead of the students.

When John the Baptist, incarcerated in prison, sent his disciples to ask Jesus if He was the expected Messiah, "Jesus answering said unto them, Go your way, and tell John what things ye have seen and heard; how that the blind see, the lame walk, the lepers are cleansed, the deaf hear, the dead are raised, to the poor the gospel is preached" (Luke 7:22). This was the best ministry they could give to their leader who was having some jail-house doubts. They had more than words to share; they had been personal witnesses to the power of God, and sharing this witness ministered to John.

Usually not everyone in the church is in spiritual victory simultaneously. Life being what it is, there are always some who are experiencing a spiritual low at the time when the saints are gathering together. Paul said that Spirit-filled believers should, "Speak(ing) to yourselves (literally, "one another") in psalms and hymns and spiritual songs, singing and making melody in your heart to the Lord" (Ephesians 5:19). Why? This becomes a spiritual ministry to those whose faith is being challenged. It is ministry to one another.

James said that when in public gatherings: "Is any sick among you? let him call for the elders of the church; and let them pray over him, anointing him with oil in the name of the Lord: And the prayer of faith shall save the sick, and the Lord shall raise him up; and if he have committed sins, they shall be forgiven him" (James 5:14-15)

All this is ministry, one to another, whether it be in testimony, faith, melody, giving, or compassionate prayer. No one should have to carry his or her burdens alone. We are a family. We can share with one another. After all, we have been instructed: "We then that are strong ought to bear the infirmities of the weak, and not to please ourselves" (Romans 15:1).

Sometimes the burden of sorrow is crushing to someone in the church. We cannot bring back the deceased loved one, and we usually don't have great words of wisdom to share with the grieving saint. We can, however, share their heartache and our love. Sometimes the greatest gift we can give to one another is merely being there for them. Isn't this the message of Romans 12:15? — "Rejoice with them that do rejoice, and weep with them that weep."

We can minister to another person by laughing with him or her in the good times and weeping with him or her in the bad times. Ministering one to another is seldom a big action, but it is a great blessing, and God takes note of it, "For God is not unrighteous to forget your work and labour of love, which ye have shewed toward his name, in that ye have ministered to the saints, and do minister" (Hebrews 6:10).

It should be obvious to all of us that if we cannot learn to minister one to another in our local congregations, we will be unable to minister to people in other congregations. We learn compassion in small ways. Ministry starts on the home turf with those with whom we have learned to share the love of God.

We Minister with One Another

The Western world is so star-struck that even our churches love its super-saints. We almost eulogize persons with a special faith for healing, or make heroes of those gifted teachers God has given to us. This may fit the mood of our generation, but it is far beneath the Bible position of plural ministries.

Although God does give us strong leaders, He has provided a support team to undergird, strengthen, and expand his or her ministries. Jesus, better than we, knows how dangerous it is for a person to stand alone in ministry. Most human egos cannot safely handle the adulation this may bring. Furthermore, any sheep standing apart from the flock is an easy prey to the wolves.

Jesus, quite early in His ministry, "Called unto him the twelve, and began to send them forth by two and two; and gave them power over unclean spirits" (Mark 6:7). "After these things the Lord appointed other seventy also, and sent them two and two before his face into every city and place, whither he himself would come" (Luke 10:1). From the very beginning, Jesus put His stamp of approval on plural ministries.

Even the great apostle Paul traveled and ministered with Barnabas or Silas as his companion. Perhaps Paul took seriously the words of the great man of wisdom, Solomon: "Two are better than one; because they have a good reward for their labour. For if they fall, the one will lift up his fellow: but woe to him that is alone when he falleth; for he hath not another to help him up" (Ecclesiastes 4:9-10).

When Jesus compassionately looked at the needs of humanity, He told His disciples: "Pray ye therefore the Lord of the harvest, that he will send forth labourers into his harvest" (Matthew 9:38). He did not instruct them to pray for a laborer, but for laborers. He wanted persons who would be "Labourers together with God" (1 Corinthians 3:9). God understands the strength of plural ministries.

God has even equipped the saints for plural, not solo, ministries. In teaching about the empowering gifts of the Holy Spirit that give unction to the function of ministry, Paul insisted that the Holy Spirit divided the distribution of gifts among the members of the body of Christ (see 1 Corinthians 12). Whether we see the gifts of the Spirit resident in believers or resident in the Spirit who lives in believers, the truth is unchanged. In God's economy, no one Christian has all the tools of ministry. They are distributed so that we are dependent upon one another.

Paul likened the Church, or the body of Christ, to the human body with its many different parts. He then asks if we could exist if all were hands or all were eyes. He argues: "But now hath God set the members every one of them in the body, as it hath pleased him. And if they were all one member, where were the body? But now are they many members, yet but one body" (1 Corinthians 12:18-20).

Ministry must remain interdependent. Just as I can contribute ministry to another member of the body, that member contributes ministry to me. Also, for that body to function in ministering outside itself all functioning members of the body must work together.

Pastoring cannot be a solo act. The entire church must function as a unit to support, strengthen, and give expression to the vision and ministry God has given to their leader. Deacons, elders, teachers, ushers, musicians, and secretaries contribute their particular ministries in harmony with the pastor in order to complete the ministry God has entrusted to them. They work as a team with a good leader.

Some years ago I was flown to a developing church with a mission to teach their elders how to function in plural ministry. Their concept was equality of ministry more than plurality of ministry. To their horror, I took them to a circus instead of meeting with them in a formal session. I insisted that they not watch the performers, but fix their attention on the many support persons in blue coveralls. Repeatedly I called their attention to the number of behind-the-scene activities going on to make it possible for the solo performer to function well and safely.

After the circus I told them to choose who would be in the spotlight, and for the rest of them to learn to support that person. Perhaps, as in the circus, different persons get the spotlight. Then those who have just stepped out of visible ministries should be willing to become a support person to whomever the Spirit has chosen to present ministry.

Everything must be done, but no one person can do it all. Peter understood this, for he wrote: "As every man hath received the gift, even so minister the same one to another, as good stewards of the manifold grace of God" (1 Peter 4:10). Perhaps Peter here remembers his experience at Gate Beautiful when the lame man asked alms from him. His response was, "Silver and gold have I none; but such as I have give I thee: In the name of Jesus Christ of Nazareth rise up and walk" (Acts 3:6). Peter knew that he could give only what he had received. We cannot minister beyond our giftings, but we must share what we have.

We Minister by God's Choice

Every member of the Body of Christ has a ministry, whether it be large or small. We have all received grace and faith, and many have also received gifts of the Spirit. We are ministers who share what we have received, whether we function in gifts of administration, giving, governments, or aid.

Beyond this "every member a minister" concept, God has also chosen to place some in the body who minister out of office, giftings, and callings on a full time basis. Some call this the professional ministry or the career ministry. These are persons God has selected to step aside from the world of commerce to give themselves exclusively to the ministry of the Word.

God purposes to place persons in the Church who can train and equip believers to fulfill their giftings and ministries. The Bible says: "(Jesus) gave some, apostles; and some, prophets; and some, evangelists; and some, pastors and teachers; For the perfecting of the saints, for the work of the ministry, for the edifying of the body of Christ: Till we all come in the unity of the faith, and of the knowledge of the Son of God, unto a perfect man, unto the measure of the stature of the fulness of Christ" (Ephesians 4:11). These persons are not replacements for the ministry of the saints. They are assistants, helpers, and instructors for the broader ministry in the Church.

Contrary to much popular teaching in today's Church, God does not do His work by volunteers. He chooses His own workers. Often, however, He conscripts His persons from among the volunteer pool, but He is not restricted to this. Most of the men and women whom God used in Bible times were not volunteers. They were arrested in their everyday activities and given a commission to minister.

Although we read of the schools of the prophets, we do not read of God using any of these graduates in divine service. Instead, God chose shepherds, as Moses and David, orchardists, as Amos, and religious zealots like Saul of Tarsus.

Jesus chose tax collectors, fishermen, and very common persons to be His twelve apostles. Not one of them had ecclesiastical training. Why Jesus selected such common persons we will never know, but He did. And look what He did through them!

Christ said, "Ye have not chosen me, but I have chosen you, and ordained you, that ye should go and bring forth fruit, and that your fruit should remain: that whatsoever ye shall ask of the Father in my name, he may give it you" (John 15:16).

I do not negate the need for education. How desperately we needed the scholarship of Paul to balance the fiery enthusiasm of Peter in the early Church. I simply point out that no matter how much education and training a person may have, it does not automatically make him or her a parson, pastor, preacher, or priest. God selects whom He wills, for what He wills, where He wills, for as long as He wills.

Unfortunately our religious systems have set up a structure of schools that train young men and appoint them to offices and positions that belong to God. What a blessing it would be to the body of Christ if God would remove from office every person He has not put into office and replace them with persons of His choosing. True ministry is not a career for which we train, it is a calling we receive from God.

This calling from God needs to be far more than a prophetic utterance given over an individual. Throughout the world, I have met persons living in complete frustration who have sold everything and traveled to another country because a prophetic word directed them to do this. After months or years of struggling to fulfill this prophecy, they face the fact that nothing that was declared has happened, and they confront the frustration of failure.

I do not despise prophesy, for I have been greatly blessed by the ministry of the prophets. I do believe, however, that such major guidance as entering full time ministry needs the inner direction of the Holy Spirit. The outer direction of prophecy may confirm the inner voice of God, but it should never replace it. I further believe that leaders in the local church should confirm the call of God upon a member of the congregation, for missions is a team ministry. The missionary is a "sent one", and those sending him need to be as convinced of the call of God as the person going out.

Much heartache could be averted by following Bible principles. The Word teaches that we learn ministry in the local church, and then God may extend that ministry out to the world. Even in speaking of officers for the local church, Paul insisted that the person be: "Not a novice, lest being lifted up with pride he fall into the condemnation of the devil. Moreover he must have a good report of them which are without; lest he fall into reproach and the snare of the devil" (1 Timothy 3:6-7).

We Minister by God's Anointing

When Moses complained to the Lord that the burden of leadership was too great for him, God instructed him to call seventy of the elders of Israel to the tabernacle: "And Moses went out, and told the people the words of the LORD, and gathered the seventy men of the elders of the people, and set them round about the tabernacle. And the LORD came down in a cloud, and spake unto him, and took of the spirit that was upon him, and gave it unto the seventy elders: and it came to pass, that, when the spirit rested upon them, they prophesied, and did not cease" (Numbers 11:24-25). These men had held the office of elder for many years, but it was not until the anointing that had rested upon Moses was shared with them that they came into a spiritual ministry. This was a perpetual anointing that qualified them for a lifetime ministry; it "did not cease".

Training, office, position, or placement in the Church does not produce ministry. We do not merely minister out of our heads. True ministry flows from the Holy Spirit who resides in the human spirit of the redeemed. God has chosen to work through people, but too many persons have chosen to work without His presence. They put His name on their work, but it always lacks His nature.

We do not only minister by the gifts of the Spirit; we minister best through the Spirit who gave the gifts. Looking forward to the coming of Jesus the prophet declared, "The spirit of the LORD shall rest upon him, the spirit of wisdom and understanding, the spirit of counsel and might, the spirit of knowledge and of the fear of the LORD; And shall make him of quick understanding in the fear of the LORD: and he shall not judge after the sight of his eyes, neither reprove after the hearing of his ears" (Isaiah 11:2-3).

Jesus said just before His ascension: "Peace be unto you: as my Father hath sent me, even so send I you. And when he had said this, he breathed on them, and saith unto them, Receive ye the Holy Ghost" (John 20:21-22). When Jesus said "As my Father ... so send I you" He assured us not only of the same call, but of the same anointing. The Father sent Jesus endued with the Spirit of wisdom, understanding, counsel, might, knowledge, and fear of the LORD, and He takes us out to minister; filled with the same Spirit. God equips those persons He calls into ministry. He does not send us to minister for Him, but *with* Him. We are not His replacements; we are His assistants. We give expression to His thoughts and the release of His power under His direction.

The world charges today's church with impotence. For the most part, the Church stands guilty as charged. Since God does not violate His chain of command, isn't it likely that the problem is lack of spiritual power in the leaders of the Church? When there is fire in the pulpit, there is warmth in the pew.

It is an irrevocable principle that "A good man out of the good treasure of his heart bringeth forth that which is good; and an evil man out of the evil treasure of his heart bringeth forth that which is evil: for of the abundance of the heart his mouth speaketh" (Luke 6:45). If our hearts are cold our ministries will be cold. If the heart is warm, vibrant, and full of the Holy Spirit, the ministry that flows from us also will be warm, vibrant and full of the Spirit's nature.

Jesus insisted that "The words that I speak unto you I speak not of myself: but the Father that dwelleth in me, he doeth the works" (John 14:10). He also declared that the works that He did were the works He saw His Father do (see John 5:6), and then He affirmed, "Verily, verily, I say unto you, He that believeth on me, the works that I do shall he do also; and greater works than these shall he do; because I go unto my Father" (John 14:12). If Jesus spoke the words of His Father and did only what He saw the Father doing, do we dare speak of ourselves and do whatever we choose in ministry?

We Minister by God's Direction

We are not independent contractors in ministry. We have been chosen by God, anointed by Christ, and should be directed by the Holy Spirit. It is not our ministry, but His ministry through us. We, therefore, are not the directors, but the directed ones in this ministry.

The nature of the ministry God flows through us may vary from circumstance to circumstance. We should be sensitive to what the Holy Spirit is doing and saying and work with Him.

To a people oppressed not only by the Roman government, but by their own legalistic religion, Jesus said, "Come unto me, all ye that labour and are heavy laden, and I will give you rest. Take my yoke upon you, and learn of me; for I am meek and lowly in heart: and ye shall find rest unto your souls" (Matthew 11:28-29). Jesus did not see inactivity as rest, but He proclaimed directed activity to be restful. When we work yoked with Him, all the responsibility for the work, the place of work, the length of work, and the energy to be exerted into that work is His. We merely go along for the walk and to hold our end of the yoke off the ground.

There is another benefit of working with our neck in His yoke. We will always be pulling the correct implement. It is sad to see persons become so specialized in their ministry that they do the same thing everywhere they go. The specialist with the plow often plows under a great harvest, while the harvester sometimes tries to harvest clods and rocks. Jesus knows what needs to be done, and He is always attached to the correct spiritual tool for the job. When we are yoked with Him, we will consistently contribute to productivity.

I have heard much teaching on the theme: "The need is a call". I have also met deeply frustrated persons who responded to a projected need as though it was the call of God for their lives. Their ministry was fruitless and their lives were misfits.

The need may alert our hearts to an inner call of God, but we should not respond to the need alone or we will find our lives being need-controlled instead of God-controlled. There will always be needs. We will exhaust ourselves if we interpret them as needs God expects us to meet.

We must learn to minister by God's direction, not only in how to minister, but also where to minister. I don't think I have yet met anyone whose ministry was accepted everywhere. God knows our personalities, dispositions, and abilities. When we let Him be "Lord of the Harvest" (Luke 10:2), we will find ourselves placed where our ministry will have value and acceptance.

It has never ceased to amaze me that more persons feel God has called them to Florida or California than to less pleasant climates. Do we actually have the right to choose where we will minister? We are God's fellow-worker, and it is God's harvest field. Years of experience have convinced me that the center of God's will for my life is a pleasant place to be. I can find beauty and contentment in any geographical location if I am there by God's direction and with His presence.

Paul urged the Corinthian believers: "We then, as workers together with him, beseech you also that ye receive not the grace of God in vain ... Giving no offence in any thing, that the ministry be not blamed: But in all things approving ourselves as the ministers of God" (2 Corinthians 6:1,3-4). Every area of our lives needs to be under God's direction, lest our lives and our lips disagree in the message they give. The God-called minister will allow God's direction in behavior, location, ministry, and duration of ministry.

If this seems unduly severe, remember that we work and await the day we can hear the Lord say to us, "Well done, good and faithful servant; thou hast been faithful over a few things, I will make thee ruler over many things: enter thou into the joy of thy lord" (Matthew 25:23). The beginnings of "the joy of thy lord" is God's welcome into His home city, the New Jerusalem, that He has prepared for His faithful saints and workers.

Chapter 16

The Basics of Heaven

Death is inevitable. Burial is desirable. Pastors comfort the bereaved during the initial shock after the death of a loved one. While ministering at the funeral, pastors can anticipate being asked: "What is Heaven like?" It is unfortunate that the church of the twentieth century has shied away from the concept of a literal heaven and substituted "spiritual ideas" in its place. How often people dismiss the whole subject of heaven with, "Where Jesus is, 'tis Heaven there."

There was a day when the church believed, preached, and looked for a literal heaven where man could share God's abode. During the nineteenth century, the idea of heaven became increasingly vague, and the twentieth century has prostituted what vestige of heaven may have remained. Today's society uses the word "heaven", but usually concerning dreams, loves, lyrics, and fiction, until it has been divested of any true concept.

But just because the world has plagiarized, polluted, and profaned the word "heaven", this does not take away from its reality; it merely distracts our attention from it. No amount of labeling lust as "heaven in my arms" can destroy the eternal abode God has prepared for His redeemed ones.

Heaven — Misconceptions

I am a preacher's son, raised in a parsonage, and I have been actively engaged in Christian work all my life. During these years, I have become aware of at least seven popular misconceptions of heaven that seem firmly fixed in the minds of Christians.

One of these is the simple statement that heaven or hell is what you make of life right here on earth. This asserts that you make your own heaven; you make your own hell. What a dynamic display of human ego to think that we are big enough to create our own heaven or hell. Heaven is not created by persons, but for them. Heaven is not the apex of our present existence; it is the residence for our eternal existence. We do not earn it; we merely enter it.

A second misconception some Christians have about heaven is that it is merely an extension of this life that goes on somewhere else. In their understanding, nothing changes but the locale. If this is true, who needs a heaven? Let's simply regain access to the tree of life and live forever right here.

The third misconception is that heaven is a place of inactivity. The inhabitants sit on fleecy clouds, strum harps, and sing hymns. It is a time of "eternal rest", a perpetual vacation. However, men and women were created for activity; not inactivity. Perpetual leisure has always been destructive for us.

A fourth misunderstanding is that heaven is a place of perpetual praise and worship — one continuous camp meeting for billions times billions of eons. I'll admit that heaven is filled with praise, but I also know from the Scriptures that it is filled with activity besides this worship.

A fifth misapprehension about heaven is that it is a place of sensual pleasure. These lecherous ones see inexhaustible sexual appetites being gratified continuously. They see heaven as a place where every pleasant physical sensation of men and women is gratified to its ultimate.

A sixth misinterpretation of heaven that I have heard Christians express is that heaven is a place of complete knowledge. "When I get to heaven," they say, "I'll know everything. All the wisdom of the ages is going to be imparted to me by osmosis; I'll merely absorb it from the presence of God." If this is so, why does God put such a premium on our learning while we are still in this life?

And, seventh, there are others whose idea of heaven is simply having an association with great persons who have gone on. They do not know who they are or just where they have gone, but they are convinced they will join them.

If these views and others that are equally weak and un-Scriptural are so common among today's Christians, then we can better understand why there is so little excitement about going to heaven. We can grasp why every time one of our brothers or sisters gets close to crossing from this life to the next, we form special prayer chains to try to talk God out of taking our friend or relative to heaven.

Since the Bible speaks so much about heaven, it must mean far more than these views have expressed. Heaven is heralded throughout the Scriptures, for the Bible starts with God creating the heavens and ends with a display of the new heaven — the New Jerusalem. In the sixty-six books of the Bible, there are only thirteen books that do not mention heaven.

Heaven — A Literal Place

Of the hundreds of times the word heaven appears in our Bibles, practically all of them are translations of the Hebrew word *shamaim* or the Greek word *ouranos*. Literally they mean "the heights", and "that which is raised up". The Bible uses these words to delineate three separate areas:

1. The aerial heavens or atmospheric space [the air].
2. The sidereal or the celestial heavens [the stars].
3. The eternal dwelling place of God [the New Jerusalem].

The first heaven (the atmosphere) is the present abode of persons. The second heaven (the sidereal heavens) seems to be the headquarters of satan, but the third heaven is the residency of God Himself. This is what Paul means when he speaks of being caught up into "the third heaven" (2 Corinthians 12:2).

It was from this third heaven that the Son of God descended to the earth to take on the form of a man, and it was into this heaven that He ascended after His resurrection. The Holy Spirit descended on the day of Pentecost from this third heaven, and it is into this third heaven that the saints will ascend at the appearing of the Lord Jesus Christ.

We, of course, realize that the Bible teaches us that "the heaven of heavens cannot contain Thee" [God] (1 Kings 8:27). We also know that one of the essential attributes of God is His omnipresence, that is, He is everywhere present. Nevertheless, the Scriptures also positively declare that heaven is, in a particular way, the habitation of God. The prophet pled with God, "Look down from heaven, and behold from the habitation of thy holiness and of thy glory" (Isaiah 63:15).

To further enlarge and strengthen our concept of God having a specific place that He considers "home", the Bible in general, and the New Testament in particular, uses at least seven different words that refer to heaven, and all of them contain the idea of a dwelling or habitation. The Bible calls heaven: (1) the tabernacle of God, (2) the house of God, (3) the temple of God, (4) the sanctuary of God, (5) the throne of God, (6) the glory of God, and (7) God's heaven.

The Bible declares that heaven exists now, not sometime in the distant future. It is now God's eternal home. It is presently the home of God's angels, who are mentioned at least 157 times in the New Testament alone. Heaven is also the resting place and sphere of activity of those victorious saints who have preceded us in death (see Hebrews 12:22). Furthermore, heaven is the command post, so to speak, of all God's activities throughout His wide realm of creation.

Among the basic instincts that God has built into our lives is a belief in and a yearning for heaven. These very yearnings argue favorable for the existence of a literal, real heaven that will satisfy these God-given cravings, for, in satisfying every other propensity with which we were born, we have found substance and reality. Surely there is something real to meet this craving as well. It is significant that an inner awareness of a real heaven has been implanted so strongly in the hearts of men and women that there is not a single religion on the face of the earth that does not accommodate a provision for a heaven.

God would never cause us to desire a heaven if there were no heaven to satisfy that desire. We've all heard preachers excitedly proclaim that "God has given us a little bit of heaven to go to heaven in." I believe that. We now have a taste for and even a foretaste of heaven, but what is yet to come will satisfy our every need and longing.

Too many Christians insist on spiritualizing heaven. Their heaven is an ambiguous, nebulous nothing that is reputed to follow the death of the believer. It lacks as much substance as the world's concept that heaven is little more than a void of shadows, mists, and dim visions of blessedness — but without reality.

Many devout believers have so spiritualized God's teachings about heaven that they have nothing left for the hereafter. They have no city, for they say that is the corporeal church on earth. They have no throne; they equate that to their hearts. They have no dwelling places, no gardens, no animals, or food supplies for the future. They somehow make figures out of the facts and then apply these things to something in the present, leaving them no substance for the future. It is no wonder that professed believers are anxious to put off getting into heaven as long as the doctor's skill can keep them out. Their heaven lacks reality; there is nothing that the soul can really reach out and grasp.

Fortunately, God has "given unto us exceeding great and precious promises: that by these ye might be partakers of the divine nature, having escaped the corruption that is in the world through lust" (2 Peter 1:4). This makes it totally unnecessary for us to make a type out of an antitype, or to chase shadows while turning our backs on the substance. If we will remember that the Hebrew word for *heaven* is neither singular nor plural, but dual, we can realize that there are glorious spiritual aspects of heaven available to us here and now without in any way violating the clear statements of the Scriptures about a concrete, solid, real, substantive heaven.

Paul clearly declares that, "there is a natural body, and there is a spiritual body" (1 Corinthians 15:46, Living Bible). Jesus, Who came in a human body, ascended into heaven in a glorified body of the same type we shall have throughout all eternity.

Since this is so, a purely spiritual heaven could never accommodate people who will always have bodies. If we're always going to be substance, we will need a heaven that has substance. God's Word teaches us that there is a literal, honest-to-goodness, solid, substantial heaven that is just as real as, although different from, this literal solid-substance earth we live on.

Why is there food in heaven if we are not expected to satisfy our sense of hunger by eating? Why is rest provided in heaven if there will never be a sense of weariness? Why are there trees, rivers, parks, animals, seas, streets, and rainbows in heaven if we are supposed to become all spirit and be absorbed into God? I am convinced that heaven is as real as its inhabitants. It is as real as earth is real and is prepared for people who are spirit, soul, and body as surely as the earth was prepared for people who are spirit, soul, and body.

Heaven — A Paradise

A native of Brazil who had never been outside the boundaries of his own small barrio might ask the Americans in a tour group: "What is the United States like?" The answers he would receive would be as different as the persons speaking, for a resident of New York City would describe America very differently than a citizen from Colorado. A resident from Alaska would have different views from a Texan. Who is right? All of them! The United States is too large and varied to be accurately described from just one perspective.

Similarly, it takes more than one perspective to get a balanced concept of heaven. The New Testament gives us at least four different characterizations of heaven. This does not mean that there are four separate heavens; merely that no one description could adequately picture the place God has prepared for them that love Him.

Heaven is spoken of as Paradise, as the Father's House, as the New Jerusalem, and as Zion. These are the same place, but various provisions and diverse functions are described. Fundamentally, Paradise is heaven's garden, the Father's House is heaven's housing, the New Jerusalem is heaven's city, and Zion is heaven's governmental monarchy. These concepts are not competitive, they are completive. Until we have seen them all, we will not understand the whole picture.

Both the Old and the New Testaments speak of Paradise. In the King James version of the Old Testament, the Hebrew word for paradise is translated as an *orchard* (Song of Solomon 4:13; Ecclesiastes 2:5), and a *forest* (Nehemiah 2:8), probably because it is actually a Persian word that was coined to describe the magnificent parks and gardens that were designed for the Persian kings. Later the Latin scholars who produced the Septuagint version of the Old Testament (a translation from Hebrew into Greek) adopted this word as a name for the Garden of Eden. Whereas our English Bible calls the first habitation of God's special creation *Eden*, the Greek translation calls Adam's home *paradise*.

Since Greek is the original language of the New Testament, it is quite normal that this word *paradise* would be used freely. When Jesus spoke forgiveness to the thief on the cross, He said, "Today thou shalt be with me in paradise" (Luke 23:43). Here Jesus obviously named the abode of His Father as *paradise*; placing this word for *heaven*. Similarly, when Paul wrote about being caught up into heaven, he declared that "he was caught up into paradise" (2 Corinthians 12:4), and yet in verse two, he had described this experience as being "caught up to the third heaven". The same placing of *paradise* for heaven occurs in Christ's promise to the church in Ephesus when He told them, "To him that overcometh will I give to eat of the tree of life, which is in the midst of the paradise of God" (Revelation 2:7).

291

So *paradise*, first seen in Eden, was on the lips of a dying Savior, was visited by Paul, and became part of the introduction of the book of the consummation of all things — the book of Revelation. Wherever we meet this word, it has one common denominator: it is a place that God has prepared for His people who are awaiting the return of the Lord Jesus Christ after their earthly life has expired.

Paradise's initial description is in the book of beginnings, Genesis, where we are told about the beauties, comforts, and perpetual supply of the Garden of Eden — Paradise. But in spite of all the luxurious comforts that the garden offered, the two most outstanding features were the "tree of life" and the presence of God.

Adam entered into eternal life by regularly eating the fruit of this tree. So powerful was the effect of this tree that although Adam was thrust out of Paradise because of his sin, he lived to be nine hundred and thirty years of age, and probably not more than one hundred of these years were spent in Paradise. While Adam lived in Paradise, the Lord came to him in the cool of the evening to walk and talk with him. What intimate communion; what fellowship! How Adam must have missed it during the last eight hundred or so years of his life.

When Jesus spoke of Paradise, He re-emphasized the availability of these two paramount features: the tree of life and fellowship with God. In the story about Lazarus the beggar, Jesus made it clear that this righteous man "was carried by the angels" to Abraham's bosom (see Luke 16:22). How comforting it is to know that the angels never take us to the grave; they take us to Paradise. Some people talk incessantly about "the death angel", but the Bible speaks of the *life* angel. None of us needs an angel to cause us to die; the sin that is warring in our lives will eventually produce death. However, there is a living angel who God has commissioned to pick us up and carry us directly to Paradise the very moment our heart stops beating and our lungs cease breathing air.

When Jesus told the story about the rich man and Lazarus, He revealed that Paradise means animation, not annihilation.

He reveals that there is memory, communication, feeling, conscience, and recognition in Paradise. The loss of a functioning body does not mean the loss of dynamic life for the Christian.

By tracing Paradise back to Eden, we may think that Paradise had its beginnings on the earth, but that is not true. In telling the story of the construction of Eden, the Genesis account speaks of "every plant of the field *before* it was in the earth, and every herb of the field *before* it grew ...", and then tells us that "the Lord God *planted* a garden ... in Eden" (Genesis 2:5,6, emphasis added).

Hebrew scholars have told us that the word we have translated here as *planted* literally means *transplanted*. God had all the plants and herbs before He formed the garden; He merely transplanted a portion of heaven's paradise into man's world to share the beauties of His home with Adam and Eve.

In the days of Christ, the Jews mentally placed Paradise within the earth and called it "Abraham's bosom". At the resurrection of Christ there was a mass transfer of these inhabitants from the depths of the earth to the heights of heaven. Paul assures us that "when He (Christ) ascended up on high, he led captivity captive" (Ephesians 4:8; quoted from Psalm 68:18). When Christ came from the grave, He walked out victorious over death, and He led all the inhabitants of Paradise out of the captivity of separation from God's presence right into the heavens.

As proof of this, Matthew records that, "The graves were opened and many bodies of the saints which slept arose, and came out of the graves after his resurrection, and went into the holy city, and appeared unto many" (Matthew 27:52-53). Jesus Christ moved Paradise back into the heavenlies with Himself. These Old Testament saints had been packed and ready for "moving day" from the moment Christ preached to them after the crucifixion and they shared His ascension.

This completed the cycle. God moved the paradise He had planted on the earth back to the heavens where it had originated. Now, for the believer, when we say *goodnight* here, we say *good morning* up there.

Paul said, "Now we look forward with confidence to our heavenly bodies, realizing that every moment we spend in these earthy bodies is time spent away from our eternal home in heaven with Jesus ... And we are not afraid, but are quite content to die, for then we will be at home with the Lord" (2 Corinthians 5:6,8, Living Bible). Since Paradise has been returned to the presence of God, the Christian dead are not merely called, "the righteous dead", but, "the dead in Christ" (1 Thessalonians 4:16). God has a memorial park in heaven that is waiting for the "spirits of just men made perfect" (Hebrews 12:23), but it is not a memorial to the dead; it is a memorial to the living. It is not sold in plots five by ten feet, nor do they put people in it; they lead them to it. No one brings them flowers, they pick their own from the living plants in the garden. The gold-paved streets are not for the mourners or the funeral procession, they are for the comfort and convenience of the residents of this magnificent park. Paradise is a living place for living people.

These citizens of Paradise have access to something that has been denied men since the fall of Adam: the tree of life. There will be no more dying in heaven, no sickness, pain, or suffering, for the curse of sin will have been forever removed from these people.

Just as the overcomer was promised access to the tree of life (Revelation 2:7), he or she is also promised, "Him that overcometh will I grant to sit with me in my throne, even as I also overcame, and am set down with my Father in his throne" (Revelation 3:21). The victorious believer has access not only to life, but to God.

As Adam had fellowship with God, so will the heavenly residents enjoy a personal association with Jesus, for all that Adam lost for mankind through his sin, Jesus has restored to persons through His sacrificial death.

One thing that runs consistently through the teaching of Jesus, and the testimonies of those who have had glimpses into Paradise, is that Paradise is a real place, inhabited by real people, who are not disembodied spirits wandering around waiting to be reunited with their bodies.

Those who have died in Christ have not been cheated out of life; they have been metamorphosed into the real life. They are forever removed from temptation and satanic pressure. They enjoy the company of the angels and fellowship with God. They enjoy seminars that Isaiah, Paul, and others will teach. They revel in the artistry of the greatest musicians, poets, and painters. They may be restricted to heaven's garden, for they have not come into the complete fullness of heaven, but what they have is so superior to anything we have here that it is most certainly heaven to them.

Heaven — Father's House

Just before His arrest, Jesus told His disciples: "Let not your heart be troubled: ye believe in God, believe also in me. In my Father's house are many mansions: if it were not so, I would have told you. I go to prepare a place for you" (John 14:1-2). Because Jesus knew He was going to come from the grave with His glorified body, He did not speak of going to Paradise; He was going directly to Father's house as the first fruits of the resurrection.

Jesus was the only one who ever spoke of heaven as the Father's house, and He did so on three separate occasions. Of the Temple in Jerusalem He said, "Make not my Father's house an house of merchandise" (John 2:16). Although in the Old Testament the Temple had been called the "house of God", only Jesus could call it "My Father's house".

Jesus dared to refer to the earthly structure of the Temple as His Father's house because the symbol of God's presence rested there. Furthermore, it was at the Temple that God was worshiped, and it was there that His people communed with Him. It was the Father's house on earth by design, dedication, and function. But when the religious leaders rejected Christ as God's son, Jesus disowned the Temple, saying, "Behold, *your house* is left unto you desolate" (Matthew 23:38, emphasis added).

Ever since Jesus introduced this term, it has been a favorite concept of heaven for most Christians. It is so very comfortable. Home! Believers are now in a strange country, in an enemy's land, and, like soldiers serving on a lonely post, we dream of going home. Home is where we are loved for our own sake; a place where we are always welcome; a place where we can retire from the strife of the world and enjoy rest and peace.

Home, to the child, is a place of safety and security. It is a place of unlimited provision and a place of intimate love that binds the family unit together. To adults home is often viewed as a place of reunion, where the scattered family gathers again around father's table for renewed fellowship. To those who have enjoyed a good home, it is a fitting symbol of heaven and for those who were cheated out of a good home life, heaven will make it up to them.

But this is more than just home — it is the Father's house, the abode of God. It is even more than the Father's house; it is "my Father's house". After His resurrection, Jesus told Mary, "Go to my brethren, and say unto them, I ascend unto my Father, and your Father; and to my God, and your God" (John 20:17). He is our God, our Father, and it is to our Father's house where Jesus has gone to prepare a place for us.

Since it is the Father's house, there is no possibility of shortages. He who created the entire universe with the word of His mouth will never lack anything that His children need. As the prodigal son discovered, there is a fatted calf, an extra robe, a reserved ring, a choir, an orchestra, and dancers all awaiting our arrival. "No good thing will he withhold from them that walk uprightly" (Psalm 84:11), and "Fear not, little flock; for it is your Father's good pleasure to give you the kingdom" (Luke 12:32).

Sometimes my ministry exhausts me. On those occasions I want to go home. Home is a place of rest and peace for me. It is a place of escape from the pressures of life, and it is a place of tranquility that allows the inner tempest to be stilled. If an earthly home can offer this, how much more will our Father's heavenly home bring us rest, peace, well being, and restoration?

There will be no arguments in our Father's house, no competition, no drive to excel over another, and no desire to belittle another. All responsibilities will be equally shared among its inhabitants, so none will feel that he or she is overworked. The emotional tenor of the place will be pleasant, and the atmosphere of the home will be relaxing. It is the Father's house; a place of rest and peace.

When we get to the Father's house, we will be surrounded by a family love that breaks down prejudices, melts hardness of heart, blends what is divergent into a united whole, and generally makes a family out of many children. We will no longer be brothers and sisters in name only, but we will be merged into a family whose filial responses are joyful, responsible, considerate, and consistent. When we get home to the Father's house, it will be not only a family reunion, but a genuine uniting of that family. His love for us will become our love for one another; we'll truly love with His love.

When Jesus told His disciples that He was preceding them to "my Father's house", He added that there were "many mansions" (John 14:2). The Greek word we have translated *mansion* is used only twice in the New Testament; both times in this chapter. In verse 23, "Jesus answered and said unto him, If a man love me, he will keep my words: and my Father will love him, and we will come unto him, and make our *abode* with him" (emphasis added). Because this second use of the word seems to have a more spiritual application than a literal one, some preachers spiritualize away the "mansions" Jesus spoke of by translating it *placements*, and then they point out the differing levels of Christian service and relationships that are available while we are still here on earth.

But this does not stand up to good scholarship. Jesus was speaking to bewildered, confused, despondent disciples who couldn't fully grasp that Christ was going to leave them. In answer to their question about where He was going, Jesus told them, "Let not your heart be troubled: ye believe in God, believe also in me" (John 14:1). To give them a basis for faith instead of fear, He told them that He was going to the Father's house where there were many mansions to prepare a place for them to come and be with Him. They were concerned with a literal separation from Christ and His actual ascension into heaven. They wanted to go with Him; they feared separation from Him. Would it have comforted them to be told that there were many spiritual levels here on earth where God could place them? No! They wanted to go with Jesus, and He was going to a very real heaven that He called "Father's house".

Men who have devoted their entire lives to the study of New Testament Greek and have translated the New Testament into English always translate this verse consistent with the King James translator's use of the word *mansions*. In checking 20 different translations of the New Testament, I found that all of them translate this word as a definite place. None of them spiritualize it as levels of appreciation of God.

Jesus taught His disciples that there are distinct dwelling places in His Father's house — durable dwellings. Our living here may be nomadic and our house may be rented, but we will have a permanent residence in heaven. Our estate won't last us just a few years, but for all eternity.

We are assured that there are dwellings or rooms in the Father's house, thereby assuring us that although we will be one large family, we will not lose our individuality. We are assured that there are *many* of them, for there are many sons to be brought to glory. The book of Revelation reveals that there are many citizens in the city, many subjects in the kingdom, many children in the household, many worshipers in the temple, and many angels, principalities, and powers in heaven. It will take "many homes" to house them all.

Jesus does not say a *great* mansion, but *many* mansions. He promised that these dwelling places are where God the Father, God the Son, and God the Spirit live. It is the home of the angels, and God is preparing it to house the redeemed sons of God who shall ascend with Christ in the rapture.

Jesus has ascended to prepare this place for us. He knew better than any of us just what this preparation would entail, but by retrospect, we realize that He had to go to the cross to obtain the right for believers to enter heaven, and then in His ascension, He established that right. Christ has done everything necessary to secure a welcome and a permanent place in heaven for His people. As our advocate, He preceded us to take possession for us and to secure our title.

Jesus suggested that a new thing was about to take place: people brought into heaven! Men and women were not made for heaven, but for earth, so Christ had to remake them. Equally true, heaven was not made for people; so heaven's citizens are being prepared for our arrival.

There will be no strangeness when we enter the Father's house, for all its inhabitants will have been prepared for us by Christ Jesus. Heaven is being prepared not to tolerate us, but to receive us. We will be more than special guests; we will be citizens of that heavenly land. We will not be dependent upon heaven's graciousness to us; we will rest upon our rights.

We will not have to exert those rights, for the Lord Himself is going to usher us into heaven. He assured His disciples and us that, "I will come again, and receive you unto myself; that where I am, there ye may be also" (John 14:3). Although the angels are commissioned to carry the dying believer to Paradise, our triumphant entrance into the Father's house will be led by Jesus Christ our Lord. At the coming of Christ, all believers, including those who have been awaiting His return in Paradise, will receive their glorified bodies, which qualifies them to enjoy a more intimate relationship with God.

Paul wrote: "For if we believe that Jesus died and rose again, even so them also which sleep in Jesus will God bring with him ... For the Lord himself shall descend from heaven with a shout, with the voice of the archangel, and with the trump of God: and the dead in Christ shall rise first: then we which are alive and remain shall be caught up together with them in the clouds, to meet the Lord in the air: and so shall we ever be with the Lord. Wherefore comfort one another with these words" (1 Thessalonians 4:14,16-18).

Jesus will not send for us; He will come for us! That coming is to bring us to the same Father's house that Jesus lives in. The place that was due the Son of God is the place grace has given to the sons of God. We shall live with Him forever and ever.

Heaven — The New Jerusalem

Consistently, men of faith have been made to anticipate heaven as a divinely-built city. Notable among them is Abraham, of whom the Bible declares, "He looked for a city which hath foundations, whose builder and maker is God" (Hebrews 11:10).

Many generations after Abraham's time, a vast number of faith-filled men and women, called "strangers and pilgrims on the earth" (Hebrews 11:13), also looked for this city. The Bible records, "They desire a better country, that is, an heavenly: wherefore God is not ashamed to be called their God: *for he hath prepared for them a city*" (Hebrews 11:16, emphasis added).

Even the New Testament saints looked forward to a permanent and eternal home in the form of a city. We read: "[We] are come ... unto the city of the living God, the heavenly Jerusalem" (Hebrews 12:22). So the place Jesus promised to prepare for us is described by the inspired writer as "the city of the living God". As if to emphasize this idea, the writer further says, "Here we have no continuing city, but we seek one to come" (Hebrews 13:14).

So the saints of all ages have anticipated heaven as a city — except the people of this generation, whose application of most of the Scriptures concerning heaven is very materialistic and humanistic, until they begin to think of heaven. Then they try to make exclusive spiritual application of what seems to be so clearly stated as a literal place — a city for heaven's residents to dwell in.

Jesus didn't spiritualize heaven; He consistently spoke of it as a literal, real, and glorious place. He left this earthly abode to enter heaven as a pioneer intent upon blazing a trail and preparing a place for us. He does not ask us to search for that trail; He has promised to backtrack and personally conduct us into heaven.

Through Moses, God promised Israel a land, but Israel did not have to pioneer the way or build cities or homes. The Israelites merely had to follow God's leader into Canaan and possess and enjoy the cities, houses, vineyards, and grain fields. So it is with us. We need only follow God's forerunner — Jesus — into a totally prepared place that already has everything we will ever need to sustain and fulfill our lives.

Heaven is the home of the saints and God has prepared dwelling places for them; houses that are incorporated into a city. These houses of heaven are God-built, and are as enduring and incorruptible as their builder. We will have bodies after the resurrection; transfigured after the model of Christ's glorious body. Although these bodies will be refined and made spiritual, they will require houses to dwell in. What houses they will be! Fitted essentially for every use, employment, and enjoyment of the heavenly citizens, worthy of God their builder, reflecting honor on and bringing glory to Him by the untold beauty, magnificence, and grandeur of these God-built houses.

In his Gospel, John always uses the Greek word for Jerusalem, for it signified the political city, but in the book of Revelation, he consistently uses the Hebrew name; the original and holier name. Paul makes this same distinction in his writing. This New Jerusalem is the fulfillment of everything for which the old Jerusalem was merely a figure.

During the Millennium, Jerusalem will again be the headquarters city for Christ's reign. It will be the central seat of government for the whole world. But with the passing of the old world and the coming of the new heavens and earth, the New Jerusalem will become the world's capital and will be the headquarters and residence of God.

301

Just as David's presence gave Jerusalem a distinction above any other city in Israel, so the peculiar splendor of the New Jerusalem is the localized presence of God. His throne will be there, His home is there, and His glory and His presence will be there, too.

David's Jerusalem became the center of Jewish hopes. Their hearts were there, their songs eulogized the city, and their prayers were directed toward it several times daily. When they were in captivity away from it, they had no songs or prayers. "If I forget thee, O Jerusalem," the psalmist wrote, "let my right hand forget her cunning. If I do not remember thee, let my tongue cleave to the roof of my mouth; if I prefer not Jerusalem above my chief joy" (Psalm 137:5-6).

Similarly, heaven has become the hope, the joy, and the excitement of the saints down through the ages, for the New Jerusalem will be the complete expression of everything the old Jerusalem exemplified: location, habitation, family, government, social joys, prosperity, security, continuity, and so on.

From the days of Christ through the pages of church history, this New Jerusalem has been the center of all Christians' hopes. It has calmed the fears of the persecuted, strengthened the courage of the martyrs, and impelled the missionaries to greater zeal. It really didn't matter what their circumstances were, because they had been promised residence in God's capital, the New Jerusalem. Temporal joys or hardships cannot be compared with the eternal provisions God has promised to the overcomer. Heaven will be worth it all.

When the Millennium has been completed, and the last judgments have been executed, and the new heavens and the new earth have superseded the old, then, and not until then, will the New Jerusalem descend from God to make its orbit over the earth, and then it will be said, "The tabernacle of God is with men, and He will dwell with them, and they shall be His people, and God himself shall be with them, and be their God" (Revelation 21:3).

God's revelation of this city through John should help us to crystallize our rather nebulous ideas of heaven as we recognize that it really is a literal city designed by God, built by God, and inhabited by God and His people. The city that John describes in Revelation 21 has all the elements of a city. It has specific dimensions, it has foundations, it has walls, it has gates, it has guards on the outside, and inhabitants on the inside. John called it a city, the "Holy City" or "the New Jerusalem". It is also called "the Lamb's wife" — not because of those factors that make it a city, but because of the glorified, sanctified inhabitants who dwell in it. They are the bride, and the city is their home. Christ will not be married to a city, but the bride of Christ will enjoy living in this city. John sees the city and the bride as an integrated whole, just as when we speak of a city, we mean far more than concrete, buildings, lighting, and transportation. It takes people to make a city, and it takes buildings to house those people. Together they create a metropolis with a distinct personality and individuality.

God, Who flung the countless stars into endless space, Who spoke our world into existence, and Who formed man with His own fingers, has built a city out of celestial materials, and has kept it in His heavenly abode, far from the eyes of carnal persons, just waiting to reveal it to the saints of the ages who will be its inhabitants.

Furthermore, this city of celestial design, origin, and materials has a unique location. It will not be situated on the earth, but above the earth. Very much as the cloud of fire rested above Israel's camp in her wilderness wanderings, this New Jerusalem will be above the earth in such perfect orbit as to become the source of light for the inhabitants of the earth below.

From this orbital position, the saints will have access to both the city above and the earth below, and the earth will have a constant awareness of the presence of God and His people. No activity on the earth will go undetected by the inhabitants of the New Jerusalem. It will function very much as our

303

spy satellites do now. This will greatly simplify our role as administrators of God's authority and rule on the new earth.

We would expect that any city God built would be colossal. And it is! John says that the city is a cube twelve thousand furlongs in each dimension (Revelation 21:16). Since a furlong is 582 1/2 feet (or approximately one-eighth of a mile), this translates to fifteen hundred miles in all directions.

If this city were set on the earth on United States territory, it would extend from the northernmost tip of Maine to the southernmost point of Florida, and would reach from the Atlantic Ocean to the Colorado River. If it were placed over the European countries, it would cover all England, France, Germany, Italy, the Balkan countries, and half of Russia.

But that is only the measurement of the first level, for John declared that the city was as high as it was wide. It is a cube. Imagine a high-rise apartment building or a skyscraper that was fifteen hundred miles tall — but this is an entire city built layer upon layer, mile after mile, to this total height.

I must admit that these dimensions for a city stagger the imagination, but everything God has ever done has been beyond our belief until some man was able to see it either by faith or by fact. John did not write from a position of faith, but from participation in fact. He was there. He watched it being measured and recorded the figures for the rest of us.

Heaven is not a solitary fleecy cloud where a saint will play harp solos. It is a city filled with happy people busily engaged in the activities of God and enjoying social fellowship with other members of the family.

No chamber of commerce on earth has ever written a brochure that comes close to describing how livable heaven will be. It is tailor-made by God for His special redeemed people who have become the peculiar object of the divine love. It is inconceivable to imagine any lack in this city. It will not be an inadequate or a lonely place. It is a very lovely place.

It is not, none-the-less, the final abode for all people. Only the redeemed will walk the golden streets of this heavenly Jerusalem. Those who have rejected God's redemptive plan have an entirely different place to spend eternity. Jesus called it hell.

Heaven — A Beautiful Place

We have learned in life that taking time to look intently at a flower can flush the mind of much tension, and viewing a snowcapped mountain or gazing into the depths of the Grand Canyon can bring a sense of deep inner tranquility and peace. A glimpse of the beautiful does for the human spirit what a recharge does for a storage battery; it becomes a renewing of life, a regeneration of energies.

What it must have done to John when the Spirit took him to that giant mountain and gave him a view into the New Jerusalem! What exquisite beauty, what entrancing symmetry, what magnificent magnitude he saw. Nothing on earth could adequately compare with it. It was the "heavenly Jerusalem" (Hebrews 12:22); designed and built by God of heavenly materials so superior and beautiful that the earth has only rare deposits of any of them. No explorer or mountain climber has viewed such a breathtaking scene as John did, and since God commanded him to write and describe what he saw to the best of his anointed abilities, we have been given a vicarious view into the beauties that God has prepared for us.

After poetically describing Jesus as superior to anything known on this earth, the Song of Solomon summed it up by saying, "He is altogether lovely" (Song of Solomon 5:16). If He is lovely or beautiful, then surely His home must be exquisite beyond comprehension. And it is! Gold is used more lavishly than we use concrete or bricks. Valuable gemstones form the foundations of the city, and its gates are elegant pearls. It is, as we have already seen, immense, but it is equally elegant. There is nothing that is beautiful in the eyes of God that will not be part of His great city, and He has promised to share this city as the home of His bride. Look at it.

John writes, "In the spirit he took me to the top of an enormous high mountain and showed me Jerusalem, the holy city, coming down from God out of heaven. It had all the radiant glory of God and glittered like some precious jewel of crystal-clear diamond. The walls of it were of a great height, and had twelve gates; at each of the twelve gates there was an angel, and over the gates were written the names of the twelve tribes of Israel ... The city walls stood on twelve foundation stones, each one of which bore the name of one of the twelve apostles of the Lamb" (Revelation 21:10-14, Jerusalem Bible).

John's first impression was that the city actually glowed with the glory of God. Knox translates it that the city was "clothed in God's glory" (Revelation 21:11). In trying to describe this glory, John says, "Her brilliance sparkled like a very precious jewel with the clear light of crystal" (Revelation 21:11, Living Bible), and while the King James translators call the stone jasper, the Jerusalem Bible calls it a diamond.

No one has accurately described the glory of God, for earth has few things with which to compare it. The Old Testament refers to this glory as a cloud, as an incense, as a fire, and as a radiant light, but John says the entire city had the fire, sparkle, depth of beauty, and flashing spectrum of a giant diamond in brilliant light.

The New Jerusalem sparkles like a gemstone and produces a display of light that reveals every color of the rainbow. Man has attempted to create this effect with his strobe lights and colored gas-filled tubes, but the very material out of which this city is built catches the radiant glory of God and reflects it in continually changing hues of pure color that sparkle like a diamond.

Any who have observed the fascination that a young lady displays as she plays with her first diamond under a bright light will have a miniature picture of the delight God's radiant glory will give to its inhabitants. It will be expanding, enveloping, ever-changing, enchanting, and endless. The visual joy of this displayed glory of God will make heaven an enviable place to spend eternity. To whatever extent our visual senses can stand this stimulation, heaven will excite us completely. There will be no need for psychedelic substitutes; God's glory will more than suffice.

From his vantage point, John saw six thousand miles of walls of such clear jasper as to be like crystal. Some translators call it diamond. Imagine a city whose very walls were of polished diamond! John saw twelve massive, costly gemstones forming the foundation for these walls. If it takes only twelve of these stones to form the foundation for these walls, each stone must be five hundred miles long. There is no place on earth where such stones could be found, for these same gem stones, merely the size of hen's eggs, would cost a man's life savings here on earth. But this city was not constructed on earth or of earthly materials. It was built in God's heaven by the hand of the Creator of the earth, to Whom securing materials is no problem.

Still, walls, however beautiful, would cease to be protective and would become prohibitive if there were no openings in them — just ask any penitentiary inmate. The walls of God's great city have twelve costly gates in them made of solid pearls — the gemstone that held the highest rank among precious stones in John's day. What pearls they must have been. Twelve giant pearls large enough to control the flow of traffic for a city of 3,375,000,000 cubic miles. This could provide more than nine quadrillion rooms thirty feet long, thirty feet wide, and thirty feet high, even if we allowed half the area for streets.

My brother Jim and I wrote a book titled: *The Pearlmaker* (published by Creation House). Its theme is these twelve gates of massive pearls. These twelve gates lead into the main streets of the city that are made of gold so pure as to seem to be crystal clear. Try to imagine the excitement of walking on the lower level of heaven and looking straight up through fifteen hundred levels of pure gold streets all sparkling as crystal strong and glorious. Incalculable tons of gold worth more than three hundred dollars an ounce by American monetary standards form these streets. Then look around you and observe majestic mansions and magnificent houses as far as the eye

307

can see, all made of this same highly purified gold. It is, indeed, a crystal city with nothing to hinder the flow of light and color. Everything is constructed of durable materials. Nothing is used that could decay, rot, mold, or rust, for this city will endure eternally.

Earth has nothing with which to compare this city. Our vocabulary is too limited, our experience too shallow, our spiritual vision is too dim to really grasp "the things that God hath prepared for them that love him" (1 Corinthians 2:9). But whether or not we can comprehend its glories, Jesus said, "When the Son of man shall come in his glory, and all the holy angels with him, then shall he sit upon the throne of his glory ... Then shall the King say unto them on his right hand, Come, ye blessed of my Father, inherit the kingdom prepared for you from the foundation of the world" (Matthew 25:31,34). Our entrance into heaven is not dependent upon our ability to comprehend its glories, but upon our willingness to love its King while we are still residents of the earth.

This splendid city is the eternal home of the redeemed, but only of the redeemed. All who have rejected God's salvation will have a separate residence that Jesus calls hell. It is as real a place as heaven, but it is opposite as day and night.

Chapter 17

The Basics of Hell

As I was sitting in a booth in the restaurant of a small midwestern farm community, my mind was on this chapter as I ate my sandwich. The voices of two men and a woman seated at the counter pierced my meditation as one of the men described their fishing trip of the day.

"It's one hell of a lake," he said loudly.

"We had a hell of a time," the other man chimed in, "and Joe there, caught a hell of a fish — almost twenty pounds!" he added.

If persons with limited vocabularies did not punctuate their conversation with the word hell, we might not hear the word at all. It certainly is not in the language of most Christians, nor do we hear it spoken across the pulpits of America.

In the month before I wrote this chapter, I traveled widely and attended several gatherings for ministers. I asked every preacher I talked with, "Have you preached on hell in the past ten years?" Not one had, but many said, "I have never preached on hell."

Perhaps this contributes to the results of a recent CNN poll that reported that 77% of Americans believe in heaven while only 18% believe in hell. Maybe this underscores that we get what we preach for. Or, as David Alsobrook wrote in *Sure Word*:

> *[It is] probably because we do not want to face the unpleasant reality that we know, in our heart of hearts, that we deserve hell, not heaven. Plus, the enemy has*

been successful in our day in diverting our attention
from this matter. [Another reason is] the new-age her-
esy that the next stopping place for every soul at death
is heaven.

(Volume 8, Issue 6)

Hell is Unpopular

God's inspired Word which teaches us about heaven also
teaches us about hell. Consistency demands that we believe in
both or in neither. There are some persons who have chosen to
completely reject all belief in a life after death. They say that
men and women are only enlightened animals with a body and
soul, and death is the cessation of both.

This proves to be a difficult belief to maintain, for there is a
spirit in everyone that makes its presence known from time to
time. There is an inherent knowing in all of us that there is
something awaiting us beyond the grave. God made us eternal
creatures, and no mind-set can change that.

The Scriptures clearly teach that every person born on this
earth will go to an eternal place where he or she will be
assigned an eternal position. God, Who founded eternity and
created all creatures of time, tells us in His Word that there
are only two places where persons will dwell eternally. The
first is heaven and the second is hell.

Heaven, as we saw in the preceding chapter, is God's home
enlarged to accommodate all the redeemed and the elect
angels. In contrast, hell is to be the home of the devil and his
fallen angels plus all persons who have rejected God's plan of
salvation — the Lord Jesus Christ. If heaven is a place of bliss,
blessing, and benefit, then hell is the exact opposite.

To say that the subject of hell is unpopular is the under-
statement of the year. Still for all its unpopularity, "To hell
with you," is still the favorite curse of angry people. In spite of
what they tell the pollsters, people do believe in hell or they
wouldn't be trying to assign their enemies to its flames.

Why *wouldn't* it be unpopular to believe in hell? To believe breeds an enormous responsibility to avoid going there. Since there is only one alternative, "go to heaven" persons are confronted with the cross of Jesus and the ransom of His blood. A person need do nothing to go to hell, but he or she must consciously allow God to do something marvelous and miraculous to avoid going to hell. This mystery of redemption demands a radical change in lifestyle, and most persons see this as a penalty instead of a progression.

Like the inebriated driver who ignores red flags and flashing lights while racing his car up to the approach of a collapsed bridge, persons ignore God's warnings and plunge their lives into a hell that He never intended for them to enter. Their unbelief in the warnings did not prevent their destruction.

One wonders whether some persons have misapplied Christ's promise, "According to your faith be it unto you" (Matthew 9:29). This does not teach that we can create or delete by use of faith. Jesus spoke these words to two blind men who had pled with Him to heal them. To twist this verse to mean that if we choose to have faith in the non-existence of hell then there will be no hell, is not only foolish, it is fatal.

Taxes are also unpopular, but they are a reality that we must face. Persons who declare that they do not believe in the income tax and will not pay it, usually end up in prison. Our faith or feelings do not change the nation's laws. After all our arguments, the law must be obeyed.

Whatever God says is true and real, and it never depends upon what we believe. Our personal faith is not creative; it is merely the way we participate in God's promises. To refuse to believe in a life after the grave will not exempt a person from participating in eternal existence. It will merely prevent that person from preparing for a future life. God says that there is a heaven to enter and a hell to shun. That should settle the issue no matter how unpopular it may be.

It is unfortunate that religion has helped to undermine God's warning about hell. For many years religious leaders, most of whom have shown serious doubts about the divine inspiration of the Scriptures, have offered us alternatives to the Bible's teaching of an eternal hell. These teachings fall into four categories.

First, is the teaching of universalism that declares that everybody will finally be saved. They argue that God is too loving to exclude anyone from heaven. In reality, letting a sinner enter into heaven would be just as miserable for him as placing a saint in hell.

A second teaching that diminished the awfulness of hell is the teaching of restorationism that says the punishment in hell is not eternal. This teaching projects hell as a temporary experience that will purify the sinner to fit him for heaven. If this were the case, the fires of hell would have more power than the blood of Jesus.

A third teaching that countermands the Word of God about hell is second probationism. This doctrine says that all persons who die without Christ will have a second chance or opportunity to accept salvation between death and the resurrection. This is based upon hope, not on the clear teaching of the Word of God that says, "It is appointed unto men once to die, but after this the judgment" (Hebrews 9:27).

The fourth false doctrine that seeks to take the fear of hell out the heart of persons is called annihilationism. They point to passages in the word, such as "Who shall be punished with everlasting destruction from the presence of the Lord, and from the glory of his power" (2 Thessalonians 1:9). Similar passages say the wicked shall be destroyed, and God will annihilate the wicked. However, in scriptural usage, the word destruction does not mean annihilation, but ruin. If the word destruction in this verse really means annihilation, then the word eternal would be superfluous, for annihilation would be forever.

Of course concepts of hell are unpopular, but they are undeniable. Because of its terrible nature, hell is a subject from which a person naturally shrinks; yet it is one that must be faced, because it is a positive truth of the divine revelation. We cannot manufacture any doctrine that will successfully refute what God has said about hell in the Bible.

Hell Is Undeniable

The King James Version of the Bible uses the word *hell* thirty-one times in the Old Testament, and in each case it is a translation of the Hebrew word *Sheol*; a place where both the ungodly and the godly went at the time of death.

Hades, a comparable Greek word in the New Testament, is translated 11 times as hell. It, too, refers to the place where all the dead dwelt until the resurrection of Jesus. Jesus associated judgment and suffering with the condition of some inhabitants of hades (see Matthew 11:23; Luke 16:23).

Both sheol and hades mean "place of departed spirits", both good and bad. From the story of the rich man and Lazarus, some Bible scholars say that hades has two compartments where the dead are kept: "the bosom of Abraham", or Paradise, where Lazarus resided, and the place of torment where the rich man suffered.

At His resurrection, Christ transferred the inhabitants of "Abraham's bosom" to *paradise* which Paul calls "the third heaven" (2 Corinthians 12:1-4). Perhaps this is what the prophet meant when he wrote: "Therefore hell hath enlarged herself, and opened her mouth without measure: and their glory, and their multitude, and their pomp, and he that rejoiceth, shall descend into it" (Isaiah 5:14). It also gives understanding to Paul's affirmation: "Wherefore he saith, When he ascended up on high, he led captivity captive, and gave gifts unto men" (Ephesians 4:8). All the righteous who had been held captive by the grave were released to enjoy the presence of the Lord forever. From Christ's resurrection to the end of time, the dead in Christ are absent from the body and present with the Lord (2 Corinthians 5:8).

Contrastingly, the wicked dead are in hades not in hell. In the final judgment, hades will be cast into the lake of fire which is hell. Still, hades is consistently translated *hell*. It is stage one in the downward passage to hell.

Bible scholars view the story of the rich man and Lazarus a bit differently. Rather than seeing hades in two compartments, they say that the contrast Christ pictured in this story is more a distinction between "the bosom of Abraham" and an altogether different place; opposite and different from the place the rich man was. It does not seem to be speaking about two separated divisions both included in hades, but about two altogether different locales and conditions separated by an impassable and fixed gulf. The intent of Christ's story is not to give topographical information about the realm of the dead, but to give a warning to those who are not prepared for life after death. Whatever else this story may tell us, it is a very clear illustration of what men and women can expect in hell. This man was alive, conscious, and in full possession of his faculties. His memory was alert, he could talk, and he had lasting regrets gnawing on him. This doesn't sound like "soul death" to me.

No matter which view prevails, the Bible clearly teaches that death does not bring the wicked directly to hell, nor the Christian directly to heaven. The wicked go to hades where torment and punishment happen immediately, but much less so than hell itself will dispense. The righteous go to "be with the Lord", probably in heaven's outer garden called Eden.

On eleven other occasions in the New Testament, the word hell is used to translate the Greek word *Gehenna*. The word is actually a transliteration from the Hebrew of the Old Testament, "valley of Hinnom", a ravine on the south side of Jerusalem. This valley was the center of idolatrous worship where parents sacrificed their children by fire as an offering to the heathen god Molech (2 Chronicles 28:3; 33:6). Josiah, in his reforms, made this valley a place of abomination, and he polluted it by filling it with dead men's bones and the filth of Jerusalem (2 Kings 23:10-14). A fire burned continuously in this valley, so it became a symbol of judgment to be imposed on the idolatrous and the disobedient (Jeremiah 7:31-34; 32:35).

Once Peter used the Greek word *Tartarus* and the King James Version translates it as hell. Peter wrote: "For if God spared not the angels that sinned, but cast them down to hell (Tartarus), and delivered them into chains of darkness, to be reserved unto judgment" (2 Peter 2:4). Some see this word as referring to "the lake of fire" that God has specifically prepared for the fallen angels.

The Bible consistently teaches that an insufferable and indescribable doom waits for the sinner who dies without the saving grace of Jesus. The most graphic descriptions of the torments the lost will suffer came from the lips of the loving Savior Himself. He knew too much to be mistaken. He was too righteous to deceive us, and He was too kindhearted to conceal the truth and not warn us of the impending doom the lost will encounter.

The doctrine of hell cannot be settled by appealing to Jewish theology and the popular thought of Jesus' day. Nor can we build the doctrine on the meaning of Hebrew and Greek words. Our strongest evidence is the teaching of Christ and His apostles, and even here it is better not to depend on single texts, but rather on the whole trend of thought written in the words of the Bible.

Jesus was not dependent upon a study of the meaning of Hebrew words in the Bible when He wanted to declare His mind, nor did He ever show the slightest trace of rabbinical teaching. Jesus did not hide Himself behind the ambiguity of an adjective, nor did it matter to Him what the Rabbis thought. He taught with divine authority. Throughout His teaching, He leaves the profound impression that He regarded the fate of the sinner with extreme horror. He compared the sinner's awful estate to the Valley of Hinnom with its foul, thick, unceasing smoke, and its festering, writhing, unspeakable corruption. With tears in His voice, He pled with men and women to make any necessary sacrifice in this life to avoid going to hades and, eventually, hell.

The simple use of a Bible concordance will show that Jesus taught more about hell than He taught about heaven. He said:

"Whosoever shall say to his brother, Raca, shall be in danger of the council: but whosoever shall say, Thou fool, shall be in danger of hell fire" (Matthew 5:22).

He also taught that the punishment of hell is so severe that it would be better for a person to lose an eye or a hand rather than let these be instruments of sin that would lead to hell (Matthew 5:29-30). Twice Jesus spoke of the whole body being thrown into hell.

Jesus was obviously speaking of the punishment of hell when He said that the tree that does not bear good fruit will be cut down and "thrown into the fire" (Matthew 7:19). Both teachings come from the beautiful Sermon on the Mount. In this sermon, Jesus also said, "Then will I profess unto them, I never knew you: depart from me, ye that work iniquity" (Matthew 7:23). Part of the punishment pronounced upon the ungodly will be their separation from the presence of Christ.

Jesus said that part of the punishment of hell will include "the outer darkness" which will cause persons to "weep and gnash their teeth" (Matthew 8:12). Hell, according to Jesus, is not mere separation from God. It is a place of torment.

Jesus said that God has the power to "destroy both soul and body in hell" (Matthew 10:28). Furthermore, Jesus taught at the conclusion of the Parable of the Tares, that sinners will be: "Cast them into a furnace of fire: there shall be wailing and gnashing of teeth" (Matthew 13:42).

In other parables, Jesus underscores the horror of being cast into "outer darkness" or into "flames of fire". In the parable of the Sheep and the Goats, Jesus says to those whom He condemns, "Depart from me, ye cursed, into everlasting fire, prepared for the devil and his angels" (Matthew 25:41). Later, in this same parable, Jesus says, "And these shall go away into everlasting punishment: but the righteous into life eternal" (Matthew 25:46).

Only a person who deliberately chooses not to believe could fail to see that Christ repeatedly warned of the dangers of hell and described some miseries to be found in that place of the damned. It is popular with those who want to disbelieve in hell to charge that besides the synoptic Gospels, we have no mention of hell. They claim that Paul did not use this word, nor did Peter or John. While it is true that Paul did not use the word hell, he speaks of the impending judgment of God that will result in eternal life for those who do good, and "wrath and fury" for those who do wickedness. He said that for the evildoer "there will be tribulation and distress" (Romans 2:3-9).

Paul also taught that our appearance before the judgment seat of Christ will result in receiving "good or evil" — depending on the actions during this life (2 Corinthians 5:10). He told the Thessalonians that persons dwelling in complacency will experience "sudden destruction ... and there will be no escape" (1 Thessalonians 5:3). He also told them: "Seeing it is a righteous thing with God to recompense tribulation to them that trouble you; and to you who are troubled rest with us, when the Lord Jesus shall be revealed from heaven with his mighty angels, in flaming fire taking vengeance on them that know not God, and that obey not the gospel of our Lord Jesus Christ: who shall be punished with everlasting destruction from the presence of the Lord, and from the glory of his power" (2 Thessalonians 1:6-9). Paul may not have used the word *hell*, but he described it, affirmed it, and warned about it.

Other New Testament writers speak of hell in their own way. The author of Hebrews says that "eternal judgment" is a fundamental of the Christian faith (Hebrews 6:1,2), and tells of the threat of punishment as: "A certain fearful looking for of judgment and fiery indignation, which shall devour the adversaries" (Hebrews 10:27).

James speaks of the tongue as "set on fire by hell" [Gehenna] (James 3:6), and Peter tells us, "The Lord knoweth how to ... reserve the unjust unto the day of judgment to be punished" (2 Peter 2:9). He says that for them, "The mist of darkness is reserved for ever" (2 Peter 2:17).

We read in the book of Jude: "The angels which kept not their first estate, but left their own habitation, he hath reserved in everlasting chains under darkness unto the judgment of the great day. Even as Sodom and Gomorrah, and the cities about them in like manner, giving themselves over to fornication, and going after strange flesh, are set forth for an example, suffering the vengeance of eternal fire" (Jude 1:6-7).

John may have sidestepped hell in his gospel and epistles, but when he wrote the book of Revelation he reported: "The smoke of their torment ascendeth up for ever and ever: and they have no rest day nor night, who worship the beast and his image, and whosoever receiveth the mark of his name" (Revelation 14:11). He also told us, "The fearful, and unbelieving, and the abominable, and murderers, and whoremongers, and sorcerers, and idolaters, and all liars, shall have their part in the lake which burneth with fire and brimstone: which is the second death" (Revelation 21:8).

Jesus may have been the only New Testament person to use the word *hell*, but the rest of the writers of the New Testament spoke of the reality, severity, and inevitability of hell for those who have refused to embrace the covenant God has offered in Jesus Christ. Based on the Bible record, hell is undeniable.

Hell Is Unbearable

Perhaps one reason Jesus spoke so much about hell was His knowledge that the tortures of hell would be unbearable for men and women who were made for heaven. The Bible's doctrine of hell uses many synonyms that describe the tortures of hell. We read of "unquenchable fire" (Matthew 3:12), "outer darkness" (Matthew 22:13), "the blackness of darkness" (Jude 1:13), "furnace of fire" (Matthew 13:42), torment "in fire and brimstone" (Revelation 21:8), "the smoke of their torment" (Revelation 14:11), the "place prepared for the devil and his angels" (Matthew 25:41), and "where their worm dieth not, and the fire is not quenched" (Mark 9:44,46,48).

More than fifty years ago in my Bible college days, Clauda, a young lady in the school, interrupted a chapel session with screams and sobs. She yelled that she was descending into hell. The pain and suffering she experienced even in the vision was more than she could bear. When the vision ended, she cried out to God for mercy and gave her life to Him unreservedly.

It does not matter that God has told us so little about the future of the unredeemed, or that we do not know the location of God's hell. What God has told us is enough to defy the imagination of the most vivid thinker. The Bible tells us that hell is an actual place of physical torment and literal fire. That there will be emotional torment, deep regrets, and spiritual separation from God is true, but these do not replace the Bible's teaching of actual physical torment.

Just as the Scriptures teach of varying degrees of reward for the faithful, it also speaks of different degrees of punishment for the wicked. Jesus said: "That servant, which knew his lord's will, and prepared not himself, neither did according to his will, shall be beaten with many stripes. But he that knew not, and did commit things worthy of stripes, shall be beaten with few stripes" (Luke 12:47-48). God is just in all His ways. He will not punish the good religious person who never accepted the grace of God with the same degree of punishment He punishes the rankest of sinners. Still, hell is hell, no matter what degree one is assigned to.

John Bunyan, author of Pilgrim's Progress, had a very vivid vision of hell. He tells of seeing devils of hades deliberately tormenting fallen men and women. He saw them pour liquid brimstone down the neck of a miser. He saw the demons throw a man into a pit of fire. As he crawled out, they picked him up only to throw him back. Bunyan tells of such screams of torment and pain as to be unbearable.

The testimony of the rich man in hades was that his pain was unbearable. He wanted his brothers to be warned by the return of Lazarus and his testimony to them. This suggests that the affliction of hell is not limited to the physical. This rich man's full memory assaulted him for his failure to live differently.

Hell will be made even more miserable by the tormenting memories of missed opportunities. Just as a good parent will not punish his or her children without making them aware of the reason for the punishment, so God, Who is a perfect Father, will not punish persons without making them know the reason for their grief.

Even if there were no fire, no brimstone, no tormenting demons, and no everlasting darkness, these recalled memories would give an eternity of painful regrets. Hell is a place of torture; physical, mental, emotional, and spiritual. Whether these tortures are consecutive or concurrent, they are continuous.

In the three page article by David Alsobrook that I quoted from earlier in this chapter, he also writes:

> *No one who has not died can fully understand the glories of heaven nor the pains of hell and that both realities will be forever settled ... Hell will be worse than anything anyone can see or experience on earth — worse than the slums of Calcutta, the agonizing death of cancer, public shame, or private guilt.*

He offers a striking contrast between heaven and hell by writing:

> *There will be no pain in heaven, no joy in hell. There will be no aloneness in heaven, no companionship in hell; no sickness in heaven, no health in hell; no remorse in heaven, no satisfaction in hell; no memory of former things in heaven, no lapse of memory in hell; no thirst in heaven, no water in hell; no torment in heaven, no comfort in hell; no devil in heaven, no God in hell; no sin in heaven, no righteousness in hell; no darkness in heaven, no light in hell; no filthiness in heaven, no holiness in hell.*

> *(The Sure Word, Volume 8, Issue 6)*

What a contrast! Heaven is all bliss; hell is all curse. God attends heaven with His angels, while hell has the devil and his demons as prisoners, and they satiate their misery by inflicting an ever increasing suffering on lesser inhabitants of hell.

Over sixty years ago, Lorne F. Fox, an evangelist I knew as a boy, had a vision of hell. What he saw and experienced was written in a tract that was published by The Gospel Publishing House. I have kept it in my files all these years. He tells of being strengthened by an angel of God to go through the great pillar of fire that marks the entrance to hell. He wrote:

> *Not only will the souls of lost men and women be tormented eternally by literal fire, but they also will be tormented by the sins and vices that caused them to be lost. For I discovered, as my angelic conductor led me through the various caverns and corridors, that hell was divided into sections.*
>
> *(I Have Seen Hell, Lorne F. Fox)*

He saw persons from earth being forced to continue doing the things they did on earth that sent them to hell. He describes vast gambling rooms where men and women are forced to gamble day and night. Their money and chips are burning hot, but they must play the gaming devices endlessly.

He saw a beautiful dance floor crowded with persons who were forced to dance eternally. He described them as tired, haggard, and begging for a chance to sit out even one dance, but they were forced to continue dancing.

He viewed adulterers forced to continue sexual activity long after they were so dissipated they could barely function. Similarly, drinkers stood at a tremendous bar to continually drink the poison they once craved.

Rev. Fox also said:

> *In another place in hell I saw the rankest, rawest form of fear that ever existed. Every time there was a cry, a shriek, a groan, or any other sound — any time the crackling of the flames of hell could be heard — these poor, abjectly fearful people darted back into the shadows, trembling, horrified. These, the messenger who was with me said, were the millions of people who were*

> *too fearful to publicly and openly confess Jesus Christ.*
> *Their fears had taken them to hell.*
>
> *You may be shocked when I tell you that I also wit-*
> *nessed a form of religion in hell. The music that went*
> *with it was enough to make a man tear his hair. You*
> *talk about minor music, but you never heard anything*
> *like this. It was the worst kind of funeral dirge that*
> *grinds into the very bones, and into the very marrow*
> *inside the bones. Religion! No worship of God, but a*
> *form of religion. And as I looked at these multitudes I*
> *was told by my messenger that these were they who*
> *once had a form of religion but who denied the power*
> *of the gospel and of the blood of Jesus as their way of*
> *salvation.*
>
> *(I Have Seen Hell, Lorne F. Fox)*

These inhabitants of hell, as Lorne Fox saw them, were forced to continue to do the things that once drew them away from submitting to God. They wanted their way, and they got it eternally. I would assume that some will be forced to play sports in hell continually, since an inordinate love for sports replaced a love for God on earth. What once was thought of as pleasure will become extreme punishment in hell just because it will be forced upon a person continuously. Certainly hell is torment; unbearable, unending torment.

Hell Is Unending

Just as the blessings of the righteous are eternal, so the punishment of the wicked is forever and ever. Not only does Jesus speak of everlasting fire and unending torment, the book of Revelation records:

> *And her smoke rose up for ever and ever (19:3).*
> *[They] shall be tormented day and night for ever and*
> *ever (20:10). The smoke of their torment ascendeth up*
> *for ever and ever: and they have no rest day nor night*
>
> *(Revelation 14:11).*

Arguments for the endlessness of hell are drawn from many directions. The words and pictures in the New Testament imply finality. Offers of pardon from the Bible are restricted to the present world. Also, the judgment occurs at the close of the redemptive era and becomes final. Furthermore, every unrepented sin deserves endless retribution. Even the human conscience expects and demands unending retribution in another life.

There is a long history of this belief in an endless hell. There have been eminent supporters of it in every age. Not only did the early church believe the doctrine of hell, the period immediately after the New Testament days clearly taught the reality of hell. Many martyrs of that period considered hell to be the fate of those who denied the faith. They took courage to face martyrdom by the inner conviction that this was the easier of the two alternatives — heaven or hell.

Hell is a place in eternity; not in time. Nothing God does to purify this earth will affect His hell. Like heaven, it just keeps on as an entity. It does not depreciate, decay, or know destruction. It just keeps on being.

Hell is not a temporary purgatory. It is a permanent place. It is not a place of rehabilitation; it is a place of retribution. There is no indication anywhere in Scripture of lost sinners in hell being capable of repentance and faith. If in this life they did not turn from sin and receive Christ as Savior with the favorable circumstances and opportunities afforded them on earth, it is unreasonable to think that they will do so in the life to come with none of these encouragements to believe and forsake sin available to them.

Punishment cannot cease until guilt and sin come to an end. When the sinner ultimately resists and rejects the work of the Holy Spirit when he is convicted of sin, there remains no more possibility of repentance or salvation. He or she has submitted to an eternal sin (Mark 3:29) that deserves eternal punishment.

Although there are different degrees of punishment, everyone gets the same term — eternity. Men and women in our western courts who have been given a lifetime jail sentence can usually hope for a parole within twenty years, but "life in prison" in God's court means eternity. There is no parole from hell. What abject hopelessness this produces. There can be no escape. No merciful judge or officer of the court can give a pardon. When the gates of hell close behind a prisoner, those gates will never open to him or her again. They will never be told that they have paid their debt to society and may now go free.

Hell Is Unnecessary

In declaring hell as unnecessary, I do not mean that the place called hell is superfluous. That is not true. Just as society cannot exist without prisons to lock away dangerous rebels from society, so heaven needs the protective exclusion from wicked, rebellious persons that hell provides. Heaven wouldn't be bliss for women who have been severely abused by their husbands if these women had to spend eternity with those men. No one would enjoy heaven if they had to share it with thieves, thugs, and rapists.

When the devil and his angels rebelled against God in the highest heaven, it became necessary to prepare a place for them once their usefulness to God ended. The lake of fire, into which hades (the temporary abode of the unrighteous dead) shall be cast, has been prepared for the devil and his angels, but it is also available to any who prefer not to go to heaven.

Even a casual observation of persons in this life will establish that our individual characters which begin to form in our youth become inflexible as we age. To see a person in his or her fifties submit to the character changing work of Christ is rare enough to be classified as a miracle. As a response to the character an individual has developed, persons of like nature tend to want to be with others of similar natures. Drinkers fellowship with other drinkers in the bars. Homosexuals prefer the company of other homosexuals, while gamblers enjoy the company of other gamblers.

What reason have we to believe that this will change because of death? The Bible ends by saying: "He that is unjust, let him be unjust still: and he which is filthy, let him be filthy still: and he that is righteous, let him be righteous still: and he that is holy, let him be holy still" (Revelation 22:11). What we become in life, we take into eternity with us.

Heaven would be a miserable place for unregenerate persons. They found the company of Christians to be intolerable on earth; surely they would not want to spend eternity with them. There is mercy in God's provision of hell. It allows "the birds of a feather to flock together" no matter how miserable their lot may become.

Also, heaven gains value because of those who are excluded from it. There will be no form of unrighteousness, defilement, or rebellion in heaven. These will be consigned to hell where they originated. Hell is necessary in order for heaven to be pleasant.

In saying that "hell is unnecessary" I simply mean that it is totally unnecessary for any individual to go to hell. Hell was never prepared for people. It was prepared for the devil and his angels. Men and women do not go to hell because they are sinners, but because they do not want to be saved. Jesus said: "He that believeth on the Son hath everlasting life: and he that believeth not the Son shall not see life; but the wrath of God abideth on him" (John 3:36).

The issue of punishment is actually the issue of sin. Even in this life, punishment follows sin as effect follows cause. Would life here be worth living or could human society stand if wrong doing had no penalties, and the man who did evil was treated the same as the man who lived righteously? No!

It is, of course, a slander against God to suggest that the punishment of the ungodly is an act of personal revenge on His part. God takes no satisfaction or delight in seeing souls agonizing in hell. Furthermore, the sovereignty of God does not demand, as was once widely taught, that some persons will automatically go to heaven while others will, by divine choice, go to hell. The Bible states very clearly, "The Lord is not slack concerning his promise, as some men count slackness; but is longsuffering to us-ward, not willing that any should perish, but that all should come to repentance" (2 Peter 3:9).

It is equally true that persons do not go to hell because of creed. It is not correct doctrine, but the embracing of the Christian life or rejecting it that determines whether we'll spend eternity in heaven or in hell. The issue has always been the acceptance or rejection of Jesus as Savior. John assures us: "This is the record, that God hath given to us eternal life, and this life is in his Son. He that hath the Son hath life; and he that hath not the Son of God hath not life" (1 John 5:11-12).

Some raise the question: "How can God send men and women to an everlasting Hell?" The answer is that God does not choose this destiny for persons; they freely choose it for themselves. God simply concurs in their selection. I say again, hell was not made for persons. It was created for the arch rebel, satan, and his angels. All who decide to join him in his cause will also join him in his consignment to the lake of fire.

In his theological treatise sent to the Christians in Rome, Paul said:

> *Because that, when they knew God, they glorified him not as God, neither were thankful; but became vain in their imaginations, and their foolish heart was darkened. Professing themselves to be wise, they became fools, And changed the glory of the uncorruptible God into an image made like to corruptible man, and to birds, and fourfooted beasts, and creeping things. Wherefore God also gave them up to uncleanness through the lusts of their own hearts, to dishonour their own bodies between themselves: Who changed the truth of God into a lie, and worshiped and served the creature more than the Creator, who is blessed for ever. Amen.*
>
> *(Romans 1:21-25)*

God does not "send" persons to hell, He merely gives them up to their delusions, idolatry, and sinfulness.

We must constantly remind ourselves that God is not only loving; He is also holy and righteous, and there must be some adequate reckoning with justice in the universe where a revolt against God has brought evil consequences of enormous proportions.

Because of the severity of hell and its eternal duration, many persons raise arguments against the doctrine of hell. It must always be remembered that the Bible is our rule of faith for the doctrine of hell, however difficult the doctrine may seem for natural reason or for human sentiment. The Scriptures leave no doubt about the terrible nature and the eternal duration of hell. This doctrine of hell is a thoroughly Biblical doctrine that needs to be preached with a passion.

Amongst other titles by Judson Cornwall available from Sharon Publications are :-

Whose Love is it Anyway? *
Whose War is it Anyway? *
Whose Mind is it Anyway? *
Jesus is Better than ...
Let God Arise
Maintaining the Miracle
Mrs Judson Cornwall
Samson
The Sprinkled Blood
What is there about *No* you don't understand?

Written jointly with Dr MSB Reid

Sharon Publications stocks an extensive range of popular Christian books, videos, audio cassette tapes (music and spoken word) and compact discs in English and Dutch.

For our current catalogue, write to :-

Dept BB
Sharon Publications Ltd
49 Coxtie Green Rd
Pilgrims Hatch
Brentwood
Essex
England
CM14 5PS

Tel (01277) 373436
Fax (01277) 375046